Anthony Salvin

Northallerton Vicarage, watercolor perspective.

ANTHONY SALVIN

Pioneer of Gothic Revival Architecture, 1799–1881

Jill Allibone

University of Missouri Press
Columbia, 1987

Library of Congress Cataloging-in-Publication Data

Allibone, Jill.

    Anthony Salvin, 1799–1881.

    Bibliography: p.
    Includes index.
    1. Salvin, Anthony, 1799–1881.   2. Architects—
England—Biography.   I. Title.
NA997.S25A87   1987   720'.92'4 [B]   86-16477
ISBN 0-8262-0629-8 (alk. paper)

For art permissions, see p. 208.

For David, Shirin, Finch, and Jessamy
with love and in memory of Starky,
a most sagacious dog, who came too.

Foreword

By Mark Girouard

The great men of Victorian architecture are steadily receiving the monographs that they deserve. Peak after peak has been climbed by enterprising biographers, but many have remained unscaled: among the giants Barry, Pugin, Street, Webb, Waterhouse, and, until the publication of this book, Salvin. It is all the more of a pleasure to have his life and work finally made accessible by Dr. Allibone.

The invaluable catalogue of his work which closes the book makes clear the range and the richness of the practice that sent him traveling all over England and Wales, kept him from family and holidays, and imposed on him an overpowering physical strain only gradually lessened by the spread of the railways: too late, in Salvin's case, if the rigors of his early life are to be held responsible for the stroke that crippled him in 1856. But a large practice is not in itself enough to make an architect interesting. What distinguished Salvin from his contemporary rivals in the country-house field, Blore and Burn, was his creative power— perhaps not the power of genius, but certainly that of talent of a very high order.

It is for his country houses that Salvin will be remembered. His work as a restorer of castles, notably Windsor and the Tower of London, is impressive, based on formidable scholarship, but not especially congenial. His churches are seldom interesting, his university buildings are relatively minor. His designs for the Houses of Parliament and the Carlton Club, resurrected for us by Dr. Allibone, are intriguing discoveries but it is hard to regret that neither was built. His country houses are a different matter.

Salvin's achievement was to fuse together three elements: the domestic or castellated architecture of the Middle Ages and the Tudors; the design techniques of the Picturesque; and the needs of the early Victorian upper classes. His clients may have thought that they were getting a re-creation of a gothic castle or a Tudor manor house, but although his detail derived from past centuries his complex plans, boldly asymmetric compositions, and skillful use of changing levels did not. All three were skillfully employed to make visual capital out of the complicated requirements of large early Victorian households. His starting-off point was the existing Picturesque tradition, but at his best his free compositions were more daring and original than those of any earlier practitioners of the Picturesque and exerted perhaps rather more influence on his contemporaries and successors than Dr. Allibone allows for. At the same time they projected just the image of traditional values and "Old English" hospitality that his clients welcomed. In short, he used the past as a basis for creation, not copyism, an approach that still has lessons for architecture today.

Thanks to Dr. Allibone's researches we can see how relevant his background was to his achievements. As the eldest son of an ancient family (if only of a junior line), but one that had had to sell its land, the desire to re-establish the Salvins of Sunderland Bridge among the landed gentry at once fueled his professional ambition and made "Old English" images come naturally to him. As soon as he could afford to, he played with being a landed gentleman on a few acres on Muswell Hill; in later life he acquired his own modest country estate in Sussex, and built a country house to go with it. In the end, perhaps, being a gentleman became more important to him than being an architect, and this may have contributed as much as his stroke to the decay of inventiveness in his later buildings. But the ensuing pages make clear how much he had given to English architecture before decline set in.

Preface

No one can write a book like this without a great deal of help from family and friends. My family, to whom it is dedicated, have suffered a disrupted home life and endured holidays in places that were dictated by the presence of works by Salvin rather than the facilities that they might have expected, such as the sea. Their complaints were few, and for this I am grateful. My friends have contributed much in the way of information and advice, and I must particularly mention Maija Bismanis, who found I had a half-written book on Salvin and made me finish it, Margaret Richardson, Mark Girouard, and Jill Franklin, who all read it in draft and made helpful suggestions. Two whom I cannot now thank, but whose encouragement in the early stages I must record, are Nikolaus Pevsner, who supervised my thesis on Salvin, and Christopher Hussey, who lived at Scotney Castle and gave me the run of the house and his archives. The owners of houses and the incumbents of churches who unlocked their doors, showed me around, and lent me their drawings and records are too numerous to mention individually, but my thanks are due to every one. I must also thank the staff of the Drawings Collection of the British Architectural Library and the many librarians, curators, and archivists who have searched for Salvin material for me.

Most of Salvin's works still survive; an inspection of the catalogue will show that few of importance have been demolished. The chief casualties are the country houses, which as a class were ruthlessly pulled down in the thirty years following the Second World War. This trend has eased, but there is no cause for complacency, and it now seems that the churches are to be the next victims as they are declared redundant and demolished for the value of their sites. The continuous threat to Victorian buildings through greed and ignorance is a fact that cannot for an instant be ignored if we are to have anything of merit to hand down to our grandchildren.

Jill Allibone

Hemsted Toll, Benenden
April 1986

Contents

Introduction

On December 21, 1825, the central tower of Fonthill Abbey fell into the Fountain Court. Only one man saw it go, as it sank silently and very slowly, still upright, and then burst and spread out over the adjoining wings of the house. An enormous cloud of dust darkened the air around for several minutes, alerting the villagers, who rushed to the scene of the disaster. Inside the house, the elderly owner, who had bought the place only three years before, was waiting for his dinner; his servants were in the kitchen preparing it. No one was aware that anything untoward had occurred until they saw the agitated crowd through the windows. Indeed, Mr. Farquhar could scarcely be persuaded that anything had happened; once he had seen the ruins he remarked that he was glad, because the house would no longer be too big for him to live in.

There had never been anything like William Beckford's great house, more theatrical scenery than architecture and something of a sham in the matter of building techniques, and there was never to be anything like it again. Within six months of the falling of the tower, a young architect named Anthony Salvin had been given the commission to build his first large country house. He was born in 1799 and was to be in practice for approximately sixty years, from about 1820 to 1880. Over this considerable period, which began during the reign of George IV, seventeen years before Queen Victoria came to the throne, his buildings and the circumstances in which they were built reflected the artistic, political, economic, and religious developments in nineteenth-century England. His preferred style was the Gothic Revival, and his career demonstrates two distinct and important changes in contemporary attitudes in this manner of building: its general recognition as a national style, and a rejection of Gothick in favor of a painstaking search for authentic medieval examples as models for new buildings.

It is at least possible that the Revival has been given undue emphasis by architectural historians. The reason for this is that those who promoted it, and we need only name A. W. N. Pugin and the Cambridge Camden Society as examples of the vehemence with which this was done, created a considerable disturbance in both government and vicarage. But there was by no means a "Road to Damascus" conversion of a generation of architects; it is clear from any study of the architecture of the seventeenth and eighteenth centuries that all the great men, from Sir Christopher Wren to Robert Adam and Sir John Soane, designed buildings in the Gothic style when they were required to do so. This state of affairs usually occurred when they had to make additions to an existing Gothic building, such as Wren's adding Tom Tower to the gateway of Christ Church, Oxford. "I resolved it ought to be Gothick to agree with the Founder's Worke, Yet I have not continued soe busy as he began."[1] Besides such alterations and additions, a certain category of antiquarian-minded gentlemen adopted Gothic for their houses because of its romantic associations. Horace Walpole is a typical example, buying Strawberry Hill in 1847 and putting in fireplaces that derived their design from engravings of medieval tombs, among other extravagances. Fonthill, begun in 1796 for another great collector, was the most prodigious example of a building in a wildly eclectic Gothic style. This sort of thing had the visitors agog, but it could not have been regarded as serious, and it did not disturb the general commitment to an architecture based upon the work of Palladio, which had become almost universal since it had been introduced by Inigo Jones.

In the early nineteenth century, however, some members of the public and the profession began to maintain that a classical architecture that had its origins in pagan Greece and Rome and that had dominated all types of building, domestic, ecclesiastical, and official, for a couple of centuries, was less appropriate than a native style derived from medieval buildings. Sir Gilbert Scott tried to rationalize this, denying that the change was occasioned by "mere fashion" or "popular caprice." It was, he claimed, "a craving after the resumption of a natural architecture, the only genuine exponent of the modern as distinguished from the ancient world, of the Northern as distinguished from the Southern races, and in some degree, of Christian as distinguished from Pagan art."[2]

Scott was twelve years younger than Salvin, and he had begun his four-year period of articles two years after the collapse of Fonthill with an obscure practitioner chosen by his parents for his religious convictions rather than his architectural worth. He was converted to Gothic, or "morally awakened," as he put it, by reading an article by Pugin in the *Dublin Review*, which was reprinted as *The Present State of Christian Architecture*. Later he was to be a leading protagonist in, and the victim of, the Public Offices Competition for buildings to house the War Office and the Foreign Office in Whitehall. The rumpus this caused dragged on from 1856 to 1862 and effectively divided the nation into Classicists and Goths. Lord Palmerston summed up the high feeling that had been aroused: "Sir, the battle of the books, the battle of the Big and Little Endeans, and the battle of the Green Ribbands and the Blue Ribbands at Constantinople were all as nothing compared with this battle of the Gothic and Palladian styles. If I were called upon to give an impartial opinion as to the issue of the conflict, I should say that the Gothic has been entirely defeated."[3] But Palmerston was not impartial, and he was wrong, misled by Scott, who, unable to resist a plum commission, had given in and substituted an Italian variant for his original Gothic design.

By this time the terms of the conflict were becoming an increasingly academic matter. The younger and more progressive men, such as R. N. Shaw, had already begun to investigate vernacular models, initiating a process that led to the Queen Anne Revival and then to the Arts and Crafts movement. Despite these alternatives, Gothic remained acceptable for public buildings, such as Scott's own Midland Grand Hotel and Alfred Waterhouse's Manchester Town Hall; for coun-

1. Sir Christopher Wren to Bishop Fell, May 26, 1681. In *The Wren Society*, vol. 5, ed. A. T. Bolton and H. D. Hendry (Oxford: Oxford University Press, 1924–1943).

2. G. G. Scott, *Remarks on Secular and Domestic Architecture* (London: John Murray, 1857), p. 11.

3. *Hansard* 3: 164, cols. 507–40.

try houses, such as E. W. Pugin's Carlton Towers and William Burges's Castell Coch; for the Law Courts in the Strand; for university buildings, city offices, and warehouses; and for churches and schools. It had become the national style.

Throughout its history, Gothic has constantly evolved, and this process continued with the advent of the nineteenth century. Fonthill's original inspiration was the sixteenth-century Portuguese monastery of Batalha, which Beckford had visited in 1794. It was adapted and anglicized by his architect, James Wyatt, who was one of the first to combine accurate medieval details, usually of ecclesiastical origins, with picturesque and asymmetrical massing. This combination anticipated what may be termed the "archaeological" phase of the Gothic Revival; the next generation, men like Edward Blore and Salvin himself, made old buildings the subject of earnest study, and this was paralleled by the work of the antiquarians, who at the same time were publishing the big, illustrated county histories; by Thomas Rickman's researches into church architecture, during which he invented a system of nomenclature that is still in use; and by the successive publications by John Britton and others on cathedrals and other ancient buildings. Increasing scholarship made the architectural solecisms of untutored eighteenth-century builders intolerable.

Salvin led the way in this return to real Gothic architecture. His designs are securely based upon his own researches, and his models were often quite humble buildings. As a result, his style is reticent, as suited a man who was to be chiefly concerned with the restoration and improvement of medieval buildings. His work does not obtrude itself upon the notice of the observer; when he designed a new house or church, what he built was an unemphatic recasting of earlier styles that blend happily with genuinely old buildings nearby without disguising their own actual date. On the occasions when he broke with this self-effacing manner, he was building for very grand people indeed, of great wealth and frequently of great eccentricity. Yet Harlaxton is an Elizabethan house that would have instantly appealed to the Elizabethans, and the armies of Edward I would have recognized Peckforton Castle as a useful defense against Welsh incursions. This was as far as Salvin was prepared to go.

Younger architects were less inhibited, as Scott quite blatantly describes: "I do not advocate any extreme carefulness in ascertaining whether the features thus arrived at were actually ever used in the fourteenth century: this really does not in the least concern us; our business being simply to cull from works of any date, or from our own conceptions, such ideas as are practically suited to meet our requirements, and to express them consistently with the feeling of the style in which we are working; and if the result should differ from anything before done, so much the better, if it only be good."[4] What came out of this was the adoption of Continental models, constructional polychromy, and everything that led to what has been called the High Victorian movement.[5] Salvin was quite unaffected by such developments. His houses, with very few exceptions, are Tudor or Jacobean; his churches are Norman, Early English, or Decorated, and this remained the case until he died.

4. Ibid. p. 19.
5. Stefan Muthesius, *The High Victorian Movement in Architecture, 1850–1870* (London: Routledge & Kegan Paul, 1972).

2

The Salvins and the Nesfields

Of the architects who dominated their profession during the first half of the nineteenth century, Edward Blore, born in 1787, was the son of a solicitor who had become a topographer and local historian; Charles Robert Cockerell, born in 1788, was the son of a surveyor; William Burn, 1789, was the son of an Edinburgh builder; Charles Barry, 1795, was the son of a stationer; George Webster, 1797, was the son of a marble mason who had improved himself and practiced as an architect and surveyor; and Decimus Burton, born in 1800, was the son of a successful speculative builder. In no instance could the father boast of inherited wealth and a distinguished or even recorded lineage.

In this respect Anthony Salvin stands apart from his contemporaries, for his family appears in the first edition of Burke, where they are traced back to an Osbert Silvan, who was High Sheriff of Nottingham in the reign of King Stephen.[1] The Salvins held land in Yorkshire, but early in the fifteenth century one of their sons acquired an estate in County Durham by marrying Agnes, Lady of Croxdale, where the family have continued in possession despite their attachment to the Royalist cause during the Civil War and their adherence to Roman Catholicism. However, one branch of the Durham family, who are called the Salvins of Sunderland Bridge, and thus distinguished from the Catholic Salvins of Croxdale and Burn Hall, were members of the established Church, as an Anthony Salvin who died in 1707 married his second wife Mary Belasyse at St. Oswald's in the city of Durham. His grandson, another Anthony, married Anne Smith of Burn Hall; there were five sons and five daughters of this marriage.

There is no record of the occupations pursued by the successive members of the Sunderland Bridge family, although it is known that they were mill owners; but in this generation four of the five sons went into the army and one into the church. The eldest, Anthony, joined the 33d Regiment of Foot as a cornet in February 1776. The regiment sailed the same month for Charleston, South Carolina, and Salvin had been promoted to captain and had seen a good deal of fighting before Cornwallis surrendered at Yorktown. By 1784 the 33d was home and stationed at Taunton, reduced to 162 rank and file, and Captain Salvin had been put on English half-pay at five shillings a day. He was twenty-six years old and remained on half-pay for the next twenty-five years. His brothers, George, Henry, and Jeffrey, were respectively in the 15th, 18th, and 4th Regiments of Foot. The first two became their regiments' paymasters, while Jeffrey fought at Corunna, Walcheren, in the Peninsular Campaign and in the southern states of America during the War of 1812.[2] Hugh was a naval chaplain before he was preferred to the Vicarage of

1. John Burke and Sir John Bernard Burke, *The Genealogical and Heraldic History of the Landed Gentry* (London: Henry Colburn, 1846).
2. *The Salvin Pedigree*. Salvin MSS. Croxdale Hall, Co. Durham. *The Army List*. London 1776–1840.

Alston in Cumberland. Of the Salvin sisters, the two eldest married and led uneventful lives, and the youngest died as a child. Mary and Matilda, however, shared with their eldest brother a most unpleasant adventure in France. The family woollen mill at Castle Eden had supplied the government of Louis XVI with over £20,000 worth of cloth. The Revolution had prevented payment of this account, and Captain Salvin and his sisters, clearly with very little idea of what was going on in France, journeyed to Paris to attempt to collect the money owed. They received payment in Assignats but were immediately afterward imprisoned in the Luxembourg. Matilda attracted the attention of one of their jailers and promised to marry him; thereupon he secured their release. On arriving home, the Assignats proved worthless and the mill had to be closed. This sort of thing occurred repeatedly after the declaration of war by France, precipitating a financial crisis that caused the bankruptcy of the Salvins' relative Rowland Burdon, among many others.[3]

Captain Salvin married twice, first in 1785 to Catherine Wharton of Old Park, Durham. There were two children: Thomas, who joined the East India Company's service, became a Cornet of Cavalry, and died in Madras in 1804; and Anne, who was born in 1788. Their mother died the following year. Nine years later, on September 11, 1798, Captain Salvin married Eliza, one of the four daughters of Colonel Henry Mills of Willington, at St. Brandon's Brancepeth. The only child of this marriage was Anthony, born at Worthing in Sussex on October 17, 1799, baptized at Patching on November 9, and christened at St. Brandon's on February 20, 1800.

In the autumn of 1803, when it appeared most probable that Buonapart would hazard the Channel crossing and attempt the invasion of England, Captain Salvin was taken off half-pay and placed in a reserve battalion, then promoted to lieutenant-colonel; by 1811 he had been appointed the Inspecting Officer of a recruiting district. This post obliged him and his wife to move about the country, and his small son spent much of his time at Willington with his grandfather, until he was old enough to go to Durham School, then in its original buildings on Palace Green. This school was no doubt chosen because the headmaster, the Reverend James Britton, had married another of the Mills sisters, with whom Anthony probably lodged during the school term. His holidays were spent partly with his grandfather and partly with another aunt, Marianne Mills, who was to become the second wife of the Reverend William Nesfield.

Now Nesfield was a considerable personality. He was Rector of Brancepeth, Perpetual Curate of Chester-le-Street, Volunteer Chaplain to the 68th Foot, Justice of the Peace, and he had on one occasion at least negotiated the settlement of a major strike over colliers' "binding time" when the jails were full and three hundred men were imprisoned in the stables of the Bishop of Durham. He had nine children by his first marriage, of whom seven survived. Until the birth of the last, and the death three days later of Mrs. Nesfield, he had lived in the city of Durham under a License for Non-Residence. This was about to expire, and he resolved to move his family to Brancepeth, where, just a year later, he married Marianne. She took over the running of a household that consisted of the six

3. Elizabeth Burdon, *Reminiscences* (Privately printed, n.d.).

youngest children (the eldest, William, having begun his military training at Woolwich three months after the wedding); two nephews of the rector, whose education he was supervising; Anthony Salvin on his holiday visits; and a Miss Caldecleugh, who had been engaged as a governess.[4]

William Andrews Nesfield was sixteen years older than Anthony, yet despite the difference in their ages they became great friends, business associates, and brothers-in-law. William had been educated at Winchester and at Trinity College, Cambridge, which he left without taking a degree to become a cadet. He was commissioned in the 95th Foot and fought in the latter part of the Peninsular Campaign, but while attending Woolwich he had discovered that he had a talent for painting in watercolor. Officers were required to learn how to draw maps and make topographical sketches by way of reconnaissance; the *Rules and Orders of the Royal Military Academy at Woolwich* specify that "the Drawing Master shall teach the method of sketching ground, the taking of views, the drawing of civil architecture and the practise of perspective." The Drawing Master was often an artist of real merit; David Cox taught at Farnham and Sandhurst, and Paul Sandby at Woolwich until 1796, when he was succeeded by his son Thomas Paul Sandby, who would therefore have taught Nesfield. In 1813 Nesfield exchanged into the 89th Foot, which was about to go to Canada under the command of Lieutenant Colonel Sir Gordon Drummond. Drummond had married the eldest daughter of William Russell of Brancepeth Castle, who would have known the rector and his family well. He appointed William his aide-de-camp with the intention that he should have every opportunity of painting the wild Canadian scenery, but it is doubtful if the bitter fighting with the Americans in which Drummond became engaged upon his arrival permitted his young officer to do much in this line. On his return to England, Nesfield exchanged again but was put on half-pay in 1819. With all chance of promotion then gone, he determined to make his living as a landscape painter.

Colonel Salvin had intended his son to follow him and his uncles into the army, after he had completed his studies at Durham School. However, Brancepeth Rectory and the Church of St. Brandon are within a few hundred yards of the walls of Brancepeth Castle, which had been sold in 1796 by Sir Henry Vane Tempest to William Russell for the sum of £70,000 (Fig. 1). Russell had sold his family estate at Rowenlands in Cumberland, which had passed to him after the deaths of his father and elder brother; he had already inherited half of a considerable fortune from an uncle who had been a general merchant in Sunderland, succeeded to the uncle's business, and gone into banking with his brothers-in-law. He began to speculate in collieries when he took a half-share in a small enterprise in settlement of a debt. He then founded the banking firm of Russell and Wade and acquired the Wallsend Pit Company, which made profits in excess of £20,000 per annum over a period of twenty years.[5] During the Napoleonic Wars he raised two companies of

4. *Notes on Family Events from the Memorandum Book of the Revd. William Nesfield.* London Borough of Barnet Library Services. MSS. Acc. 6787/6

5. The shaft of the Wallsend Pit Company was sunk by Messrs. W. Chapman & Bros., who ran out of money before they came to the coal. They turned over their rights to Russell & Wade, who were their bankers, in return for the discharge of their overdraft. Russell & Wade reached coal in 1771, and the High Main Seam was wrought out in 1818. Their profits averaged out at £20,000 a year for twenty years, and one year it was £60,000. Revd. Collingwood Bruce, *Roman Wall* (n.p., 1863).

1. Brancepeth Castle, the Rectory, and St. Brandon's Church from the air.

volunteer infantry and a troop of yeomanry cavalry at his own expense and later founded a hospital for old people at Cornsay. For all this, and although he was regarded when he died as one of the richest commoners in England, he is said to have written with an illiterate hand, was always known as "Billy" Russell, and retained his Sunderland accent and manners until the end of his life. He acquired a number of pocket boroughs, among them Saltash and Bletchingly, which he managed in the Whig interest, and he had some political connections in Lincolnshire; it was probably through these that he came into contact with the Tennysons.

George Tennyson had begun in life as a solicitor but was by this time involved in politics and was a considerable landowner, in the process of building up the Bayons Manor estate, which he had purchased in the uncharacteristically romantic belief that he was, through his mother's family, descended from the holders of the Barony of d'Eyncourt, formerly Lords of this Manor. Tennyson had four children: George, the eldest and the father of Alfred, whom he was later to disinherit; and Charles, Elizabeth, and Mary. In 1797 Elizabeth married William Russell's only son Matthew, a large, amiable, pleasure-loving major in the Durham Militia, who after their marriage became the Member for his father's borough of Saltash and Vice-Lieutenant of County Durham. In 1817 the elder Russell died, and Matthew and Elizabeth began the restoration of Brancepeth Castle.[6]

6. Charles Tennyson, *Alfred Tennyson* (London: Macmillan & Co., 1968).

It would be interesting to know what had induced Billy Russell to buy the castle in the first place. It may have been the vanity of a self-made man, or a desire to match the estate of the Tennysons; it certainly seems, from the date of purchase, that the castle was bought in anticipation of the marriage between Matthew and Elizabeth. But it seems doubtful if either Matthew or his father had any anti-quarian interests, and the latter had restricted his outlay after purchase to a minimum of necessary repairs. So it seems probable that the Tennysons, who may have urged Billy to buy the castle at the outset, then inspired the project for its restoration. As a family they had a strong romantic streak and a passionate interest in the Middle Ages. Alfred was eleven at this time and already under the spell of Walter Scott's *Border Minstrelsy,* and he had composed an epic of six thou-sand lines in the style of *Marmion.* His father, the temperamental Rector of Somersby, had built a Gothic addition onto his dining room. It was a time when rich men like Sir Samuel Rush Meyrick were spending a fortune collecting medi-eval arms and armor, and when, somewhat later, a much richer man, the thirteenth Earl of Eglinton, spent a sum in the region of £40,000 staging a tourna-ment on his Scottish estate in which the participants wore such armor. Elizabeth's brother Charles was as ardent a medievalist as either Meyrick or Eglinton, as he was to prove when his father died ten years later and he was able to embark upon an extensive rebuilding of Bayons Manor in the castle style. He had already persuaded old George to provide in his will that their Usselby lands should only pass to him on the condition that he should adopt by royal license the additional name and the arms of d'Eyncourt. Now he indulged his medieval fancies vicariously. As the Member of Parliament for Grimsby, he was obliged to spend much time in London. There he threw himself heart and soul into the role of adviser to the rehabilitation of Brancepeth. He engaged domestic staff, assembled a collection of ancient armor, and chose wallpapers, carpets, and stained glass, for which he placed orders and gave instructions that from time to time conflicted with those of the architect to whom the work of restoration had been entrusted.

This was John Paterson of Edinburgh, who had been Robert Adam's Clerk of Works in Scotland and who had begun in practice on his own account after Adam's death in 1792. His first commission seems to have been the building of stables at Castle Fraser, Aberdeenshire, in 1794, and Monzie Castle, Perthshire, the follow-ing year. He had rebuilt Eglinton Castle, Ayrshire, in 1797, Barmoor in Northumberland in 1801, and had enlarged Fetteresso, Kincardineshire, in 1808. Monzie, Eglinton, and Barmoor were all essays in the Adam castle style, but Paterson uses it without the decorative lug-turrets, crosslets, and crenellations. Indeed, his work is distinguished by stout round towers with splayed bases and uncompromising areas of stone wall pierced by large sash windows. It seems likely, judging by those of his houses that survive, such as Chillingham Castle in North-umberland and Barmoor, that his castles had neoclassical interiors, suites of oval and polygonal reception rooms with Adamesque decorations. His knowledge of medieval architecture was minimal, and he had little interest in the picturesque, but he had established a reputation both north and south of the border, and as an ex–Clerk of Works he must have had a sound grasp of building techniques.[7]

7. James Macaulay, *The Gothic Revival, 1745–1845* (Glasgow and London: Blackie & Son, 1975), pp. 181–89.

Work on Brancepeth was put in hand very soon after Billy Russell's death. The estimate for plumbers' work is dated April 22, and that for plastering July 2, 1818.[8] In February 1819 Rowland Burdon wrote from Castle Eden to John Soane: "I am here in the midst of Masons etc. collected to build a huge addition to this antient Baronial Castle. My friend Mr. Russell has set out very boldly, and as his powers are great he will not be easily stop'd. It is to bear the name of its founder 'the Russell Tower,' and he seems to be executing it well according to the pattern of other parts of the Castle. . . . Besides the Tower in question he makes extensive alterations and additions to the habitable part of the Castle so as to render it one of the largest and probably most magnificent dwellings in the island."[9] Letters from Paterson show that the chimneypieces were being chosen in May 1819, and by October 1821 estimates for the carpets were being sought. Paterson was paid £500 a year for his supervision, which seems to have been most conscientious, as Salvin's daughter Eliza Anne, writing nearly fifty years later, comments: "He was thought a great deal of in those parts, I believe. Sure it is he devoted himself to the work before him and spent most of his time on the spot. Alas, he wanted that most necessary of things—good taste."[10]

Employing as it did a work force of more than three hundred men, the restoration of Brancepeth was plainly a very large undertaking; and quite apart from problems with London tradesmen, such as the glass manufacturer William Collins caused by contradictory orders from Charles Tennyson, Paterson had other troubles on site. At one stage all fourteen masons employed had to be discharged for demanding higher wages and trying to involve the rector in their dispute. At another time he reported to the Russells: "There is an execution this morning in Durham which has taken off one half of the masons and three fourths of the carpenters." But work went on steadily, and, it was popularly believed, at a cost of £80,000 a year, quite apart from decorative items such as a set of stained glass windows for the great hall, designed by Thomas Stothard and costing £600 each.[11]

Any large building project exercises its own fascination, and the restoration of a great medieval castle on the doorstep of the rectory, along with the rector's inevitable concern with his new temporary parishioners, the workmen employed, his friendship with Paterson (who dined regularly at the rectory and who could report on progress), to all of which must be added the popular enthusiasm for the Middle Ages then prevailing, aroused young Anthony's interest in architecture as a career. This met with immediate parental disapproval, which was not easily overcome. Eliza Anne wrote: "At that time it was not considered to be a profession for a gentleman, but his bent was so marked that Colonel Salvin resolved to throw no obstacle in his way." Colonel Salvin may also have reflected that with the termination of the wars with France and half the Army on half-pay, opportunities for soldiering were much reduced and largely confined to service in India. After the death of his first son there, he cannot have been anxious that Anthony should face such a hazardous climate, so, as "the large works going on at Brancepeth seemed

8. Boyne MSS. Burwarton House.

9. Rowland Burdon to John Soane, February 2, 1819. Div. III Cor. Col. I 14. This and other quotations from the Soane correspondence are published by permission of the Trustees of Sir John Soane's Museum.

10. Eliza Anne Salvin, *Reminiscences and notes of Bye-gone Years*. London Borough of Barnet Library Services. MSS. Acc. 6787/7.

11. Sir H. Maxwell, ed., *The Creevey Papers* (London: John Murray, 1904).

to offer a good school," he was placed with Paterson as a pupil.

The problems that faced Paterson at Brancepeth were a foretaste of those that Salvin was to meet with only too frequently in the course of his long career as a country house architect specializing in the restoration and modernization of ancient buildings. When Paterson began, the Constable and Neville Towers were in a semiruinous condition, and only the west range was habitable, though neither comfortable nor convenient. Eighteenth-century engravings show the old fabric picturesquely overgrown with ivy, and it had been much pulled about and added to as required by successive occupants, who had inserted, among other things, casements and sash windows of various sizes. A number of lean-to buildings had been put along the curtain wall, and the range between the Westmoreland and the Constable Towers and the ground floor of the Constable Tower itself had been turned into stables. However Billy Russell and his wife were prepared to live, if indeed they ever moved into the castle, the younger Russells could not tolerate such accommodation in what must have been a rather overpowering ruin.

Paterson provided a series of immense reception rooms: a drawing room, a salon, a baron's hall, a chapel, and a state bedroom occupied the whole of the principal floors of the six great towers, and in new ranges built on the south and west sides of the curtain wall he put a billiard room, an armor gallery, and a quantity of smaller rooms, some of his favorite oval plan, for the use of the family on informal occasions (Fig. 2). An entrance hall with a porte cochère and a Gothic "timber" roof constructed of plaster was placed diagonally across the corner of the courtyard opposite the entrance to the inner ward. This entrance had been little more than a gate in the wall until Paterson replaced it with an imposing barbican, the outer gate of which is flanked by a massive pair of round towers, battlemented and machicolated, with spurs, and relying in design not on any English model, but upon Robert Adam's studies of Italian fortresses.[12] After the restoration, and despite an increase in size, the castle lost a good deal of its original impact. Paterson's ignorance of medieval architecture and insensitivity to his materials meant that he built using repetitive and frequently inaccurate detail, such as Norman windows with ogee tracery, and put up vast ranges of well-dressed masonry that did not marry well with the old fabric. The antiquity of the building clearly meant little to him, and he would probably have preferred to abandon it and its irregular courtyard and to build in its place a symmetrically planned, many-windowed castelleted mansion like Eglinton. That he did not was probably due to the Tennysons, and despite all, the castle still appears massively and genuinely defensible, despite the flat skyline, punctuated by identical small square turrets and the long dull runs of machicolated ramparts.

However mediocre Paterson's talent as a designer and an antiquarian, he must have had a good deal to offer when it came to teaching the principles of construction; it cannot have been easy to build an open timber roof in plaster. And his presence at Brancepeth and acquaintance with the rector were providential at that time, when Salvin came to choose his career. Indeed, failing Paterson, it is hard to see where Colonel Salvin could have placed him as a pupil in the north of England. By 1817 Joseph Bonomi was dead, and his son Ignatius was barely established in practice; James Gillespie Graham was approaching his most active period, but

12. Macaulay, *The Gothic Revival*, p. 187.

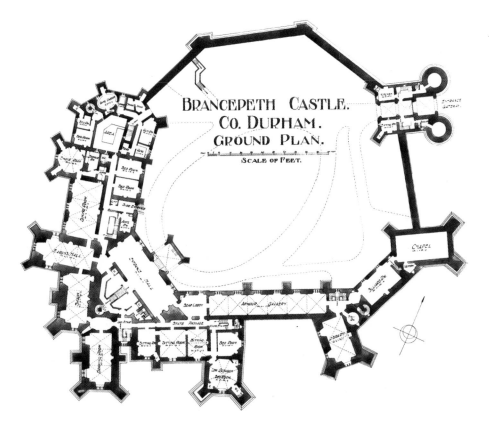

2. Brancepeth Castle, ground plan.

his office was in Edinburgh and his buildings often in the remoter parts of
Scotland, and so not widely known. Robert Smirke had built Lowther Castle in
Westmoreland between 1806 and 1811, but his practice was based in London, and
his pupil William Burn was only just beginning to make his way. Another London
architect, John Nash, had rebuilt Ravensworth Castle in County Durham around
two thirteenth-century towers and added a salon and conservatory in 1808 and
1822. The later work was in a Perpendicular Gothic no doubt designed by Auguste
Pugin, but here again the direction came from London. John Dobson had begun
to work in Newcastle, but between 1813 and 1817 he had obtained only twenty or so
commissions and had discovered that "although he was (with the exception of
Ignatius Bonomi) the only professional architect between Edinburgh and York
. . . the demand for his services had to be created."[13] So the alternative to studying
with Paterson would have been that Colonel Salvin should send his son to either
London or Edinburgh, to be taught by men who were not known to him, and
whom he did not regard as gentlemen.

By November 1821 work on the castle was nearing completion. The rector noted
in his *Memorandum Book* on the twenty-eighth: "On this evening Mr. and Mrs.
Russell and family slept for the first time in the Castle in the Russell Tower."
Salvin did not continue with Paterson in his Edinburgh office but went instead to
London wilh William Andrews Nesfield, where they took lodgings at 52 Newman

13. M. J. Dobson, *A Memoir of the Late John Dobson* (Newcastle-upon-Tyne: Hamilton, Adams & Co., 1885).

Street, which runs between Oxford and Goodge Streets. Both young men were starting new careers. Salvin had been given a letter of introduction to John Soane by Rowland Burdon. Dated at Castle Eden March 24, 1821, it reads: "My Dear Sir, I am requested by my relation Col. Salvin to give his son Mr. Anthony Salvin, a letter of introduction to you, he having determined to make choice of architecture as a profession. Allow me therefore the privilege of an antient friend on the occasion, and say that any attention you may favour him with will oblige your old ally."[14]

Salvin did not go into Soane's office; conditions for assistants at No. 13 Lincoln's Inn Fields were so cramped that there may well have been no room for him, and according to his nephew William Eden Nesfield, he went to work with John Nash.[15] Eliza Anne, on the other hand, makes no mention of Nash in her account of the family's activities at this date. Still, the younger Nesfield had worked in the Salvin office and was more likely to have taken an interest in his uncle's training, and indeed goes further in saying that he was with Nash when Auguste Charles Pugin was working for him. Pugin's book *Specimens of Gothic Architecture* was published between 1821 and 1823, and it is quite possible that Salvin went to Nash for the sake of an opportunity to work with Pugin, rather than on the designs for the Regent's Park Terraces and All Souls Langham Place, which Nash then had in hand; they would have seemed a sad substitute for Brancepeth Castle to any young enthusiast for Gothic. But even with Pugin there, Nash's office seems an odd choice, and William Wilkins or Robert Smirke, both of whom had built large country houses in the Gothic or Tudor style, would have seemed more attractive. And Nash seems an even stranger option when one considers the opinion that Rowland Burdon had of him; Burdon, as the prime mover in the project for building Sunderland Bridge and the patron of John Soane, must have been regarded by the Salvins as their family authority on architects: "I see that fellow Nash's name coupled every now and then, with Sir B. Blomfield's, & others, to whose names I am used to attach some respect. Tis passing strange!" On another occasion: "I hear miserable accounts of that ------ Nash's proceedings—Has nobody the boldness, I had almost said honesty to inform his Master of his real character."[16] Still, there is in Salvin's early works a good deal that is reminiscent of those of George Stanley Repton, who had recently left Nash after fifteen years or so and whose place there Salvin might possibly have filled.

Salvin makes no mention of working in Nash's office or any other in the only surviving letter of this period. He wrote this to William's sister, Anne Andrews Nesfield, to whom he was unofficially engaged. It is dated December 1, 1824, and as it is both delightful and informative, it is worth quoting in full:

> My dear Anne,
>   May I trouble you with a message for Wm. viz that being quite sick of house hunting, as well as the loss of time, I have thrown the concern into the hands of a house agent of Mr Robson's recommending who I find is a north country man intimately acquainted with all my kin, a shrewd fellow quite up to the business and much more likely to make a good bargain than I should. Therefore at this conjuncture I do not see much likelyhood of my being fixed in a new residence till near Xmas—he can form his plans accordingly. Harding has returned a travelled man! Thales Fielding has also return [*and*]

14. Burdon to Soane, March 24, 1821. Div. III Cor. Col. I 18.
15. *The Builder* (December 31, 1881): 809–10.
16. Burdon to Soane, December 5, 1818, November 5, 1822, Div. III Cor. Col. I 13 and 20.

dances, fences, and plays the LUTE!!! Oh ye Gods. The box has at length arrived, I had begun to fear it was lost and open'd it in hopes that is to say, to see all was right. I found no damage done. My Mother informs me that your Father is much better for his visit to Harrowgate and has I trust many years before him. She talks of going over to see him as soon as A leaves her. No dazzling the old woman from that quarter either. I have got you the literary souvenir wh. I shall send as soon as Miss Rs hair is finished also a sketch of myself by Paris to tell you the truth I cannot bear those pritty miniatures they are by no means suitable, though beautiful for the likeness of a female. This is a masterly looking thing and as like as such things generally are indeed I think much more so than the highly finished concerns, as from being done rapidly they catch the expression better. Having laboured hard to make you satisfied I shall leave you to judge for yourself. I only wish I had something of you though when I shut my eyes I can recall each feature but patience, I will wear the original next my heart. I have now got into my old habits and get on as comfy as can be for the present spending a great deal of my time in the antiquaries library where I find some very useful books there is a musty smell that is quite delightful tho I confess I do not think it would be agreable anywhere else I have just received the publications due to me from the society In short my library grows some of them quite fit for any ant—library and of the genuine smell. I know not what you will say to it but they must turn out rather than deprive me of the company of a certain [illegible]. In years only! I have had two or three walks in the Regents park and think it looks very dreary in the winter the fogs are more perceptible than in the sr. I often speculate on the respective qualities of the streets as I pass through them and fancy that the merit of the house must entirely depend on the furniture, a good prospect within doors is the main thing. Remember me kindly to Miss Ca and all others. you [illegible] Remember also that I am living in hopes. ever your Anthy Salvin

P.S. they call the servant of this house Anne a plague on her could she find no other name I always call her Betty. Good enough[17]

Salvin had been elected a Fellow of the Society of Antiquaries on March 4, 1824, and was remarkably young for such a distinction.[18] He had acquired a reputation even then as an authority on medieval military architecture, and it is possible to see how this knowledge was acquired. Throughout his working career he made innumerable drawings of houses, churches, castles, and of architectural details, which vary in quality from careful perspectives to brief scribbles on scraps of paper. Every one was painstakingly trimmed and mounted in albums, from which they are now often removed. The largest collection of such sketches is in the British Architectural Library Drawings Collection, and others remain with his descendants in Canada; but by far the greater number must have perished when Salvin's youngest son Osbert inherited the family home in Sussex in 1881, when he cleared out a lifetime's collection of drawings and papers and had them taken by wheelbarrow to the bonfire.

It might have been expected that Salvin would at this time have spent a while traveling on the Continent, as did his contemporaries Charles Barry, who set out for France and Italy in 1817, and C. R. Cockerell, who a year or so earlier was obliged by the wars with France to go further afield, to Greece and Turkey. But there is no evidence that Salvin went abroad until ten years later, and there are

17. University Library, Durham. Salvin MSS. The painter of Salvin's portrait was probably Edmund Thomas Parris, 1793-1873. This letter is quoted with the permission of Durham University Library.

18. "22 January 1824. A Testimonial was presented, and read, recommending Anthony Salvin, Esq. of Durham, a Gentleman very conversant in the History and Antiquities of this Kingdom, for Election into this Society; He being desirous of that Honour, and certified on the personal knowledge of the Subscribers to be highly deserving thereof, and likely to prove a useful and valuable Member. Signed, T. L. Parker, A. B. Lambert, John Gage, I. Weston, Mr. Bentham, W. H. Hammer." Society of Antiquaries: S.A.L. Minute Book. From November 20, 1823, to February 25, 1830, XXXV.

only a handful of sketches made in Europe to set against a few hundred of medieval buildings made almost entirely in England and Wales. Salvin's interest was in the archaeology of British medieval buildings, which is where his future work was to lie, and he seems to have had no sympathy for the classical styles. His sketching tours, and we know he made a lengthy one in the summer of 1824, took him to the castles at Belsay, Langley, Dilston, and Prudhoe. This was in August, and the following month he visited Beverley, Bolton Abbey, Fountains Abbey, Malham, Markenfield Hall, and Skipton Castle; in October he went to Dallam Tower and Levens Hall. Some of this material was worked up into rather dark-toned finished watercolors and exhibited, a useful form of self-advertisement. One, titled "Cloister Door, Cathedral of Durham," was his first work to be shown at the Royal Academy, where it was hung in 1823. The catalogue of this exhibition shows that he by this time moved to 70, Quadrant, St. James.[19]

In addition to assembling collections of his own drawings, Salvin made scrapbooks of tracings of prints and engravings of buildings, armor, costume, furniture, and monumental effigies of the Middle Ages. Two of these survive, and the paper of which they are made is watermarked 1824. The prints in these include a series of sheets illustrating various antiquarian objects issued by J. Nichols & Sons in 1823–1824, views of old buildings cut from *The European Magazine, The Gentleman's Magazine,* and J. P. Neale's *Westminster Abbey,* which was published in 1818. This laborious extracting and self-instruction was a necessary exercise at this time, as little had been published on the subject. It must be remembered that Thomas Rickman had only made the first practical trial of a system for defining the development of Gothic architecture in 1815, and that this had not been generally noticed until it was republished in book form two years later as *An attempt to discriminate the Styles of Architecture in England.* Earlier efforts at this had been made by antiquarians rather than practicing architects, one of the most eccentric of which must be Sir James Hall's thesis that Gothic was derived from large-scale basket-work. Of more help, and more satisfactory, were the series of publications covering the cathedrals and other major ecclesiastical buildings, such as that by James Bentham on Ely Cathedral, James Milner on Winchester, and John Britton's systematic coverage of Great Britain, which came out over a period of thirty years.[20] A small part of Salvin's own library has been kept together, but it is not possible now to say whether any of these books were acquired by him at a particularly early date, apart from *An Encyclopaedia of Antiquities* by Thomas Dudley Fosbroke, to which Salvin subscribed while still living in Newman Street, and *Rudiments of Ancient Architecture* by J. Taylor, which had been published in 1804. It bears the inscription: "With the best wishes of Thos. Lister Parker to Anthony Salvin, London. Feb. 19, 1823."

Thomas Lister Parker, F.S.A., F.R.S., of Browsholme Hall in the West Riding, was Hereditary Bowbearer of the Forest of Bowland, Trumpeter to the King, and

---

19. Algernon Graves, *The Royal Academy of Arts* (London: Henry Graves & Co. and George Bell & Sons, 1905–1906).

20. Sir James Hall, "Essay on the Origins and Principles of Gothic Architecture," *Transactions of the Royal Society* (London: Royal Society, 1797); James Bentham, *The History and Antiquities of the Conventual and Cathedral Church of Ely* (Cambridge: At the University Press, 1771; John Milner, *Historical Account of Winchester Cathedral* (Winchester 1798). John Britton published monographs on Bath Abbey, St. Mary Redcliffe, Salisbury, Norwich, Winchester, Lichfield, Oxford, Canterbury, Wells, Peterborough, Bristol, and Worcester Cathedrals, York Minster, and more general works such as *The Architectural Antiquities of Great Britain.*

Member of Parliament for Clitheroe. He was a man of antiquarian interests, which had led to a wide acquaintance in the north of England, where he had first come across young Salvin. He never married and had by this time sold his Yorkshire estate to a cousin and had come to live in London. He had employed both Jeffrey Wyatt and John Buckler to make additions to Browsholme Hall and was a patron of J. M. W. Turner, Benjamin West, George Romney, and James Northcote. He had promised to introduce Salvin "in the right circles" when he came to London.[21] Who or what the "right circles" were we cannot now say, although, as has been noted earlier, Parker had been responsible for his election to the Society of Antiquaries. One of the most curious aspects of Salvin's beginnings in architecture is that it is impossible to discover how he obtained his early major commissions. The first of these was for Mamhead Park in Devon, built for Robert William Newman, and of sufficient importance to enable him to marry Anne Nesfield, the rector being satisfied that his prospects were now improving. This was begun in 1826, and it must be presumed, although there is no record of any contact between the clients concerned, that this led to the next two big commissions, for Moreby Hall near York, begun in 1828, and for Harlaxton in Lincolnshire, a truly remarkable house that was begun in 1831. How Newman came to discharge an experienced architect and to choose in his place a young man of twenty-six with only the most minor works to his credit to design a house the size of Mamhead remains a mystery. Although he had a house in London, and was, like Parker, a Member of Parliament, his business was based on Plymouth and Oporto, and he seems to have had no interest in antiquities or to have moved in the sort of artistic circles that Salvin and Nesfield joined when they came south. The whole circumstances of the placing of this commission remain obscure.[22]

Indeed, very little is known of Salvin's early years in practice. All that can be said is that he exhibited the drawing of Durham already referred to in 1823 and a "Design for an Exchange, North of England" at the Academy in 1825. The latter has not survived but may be connected with the Competition for an Exchange at Leeds, which the young Charles Barry entered unsuccessfully.[23] Then, quite unexpectedly, there comes the Mamhead commission, and another, for a new vicarage at Northallerton. Northallerton is in the Diocese of Durham, and this employment was almost certainly obtained through his family connections. One job then began to lead to another. Before beginning on the vicarage, Salvin had to swear an affidavit exhibiting plans, a specification, and a valuation in support of an Application to the Governors of Queen Anne's Bounty. He did this before a Justice of the Peace, the Reverend W. N. Darnell. Within a year Darnell was to recommend Salvin for the restoration work at Norwich Cathedral and, as a trustee of Lord Crewe's Charity, had him work on some outbuildings of Bamburgh Castle, which was owned by the charity, and on the new church at North Sunderland.

Salvin produced two alternative sets of designs for the vicarage. One shows a

21. Eliza Anne Salvin, *Reminiscences.* Parker would have been able to help Salvin by giving him access to his library where he kept "a large collection of our ancient castles and manor-houses, forming a series to illustrate the style of each different reign, by Mr. Buckler, who has so well executed the drawings in this work, and whose other productions do credit and honour to the British school." T. L. Parker, *Description of Browesholme Hall* (London: S. Gosnell, 1815). This material would have been of great assistance to a young architect.
22. Dr. Mark Girouard has suggested that the Salvin family's involvement in the wool business might have been a source of commissions. The Prestons and the Traffords had interests in woollen mills.
23. Alfred Barry, *Life and Works of Sir Charles Barry* (London: John Murray, 1867).

3. Northallerton Vicarage, north elevation.

fairly nondescript building of brick, with sash windows and a hipped roof; the other is in the Tudor style. Built of brick with stone dressings, it was more expensive but was the one preferred and was built in 1826–1827 (Fig. 3). The entrance front demonstrates Salvin's virtues and deficiencies during this period. It is nearly as high as it is broad and is dominated by two vertical elements, the battlemented staircase tower and a chimney breast topped by three diagonally placed stacks, which is of equal importance and makes the tower look mean. These break the otherwise horizontal skyline, and the whole is given further interest by details such as the stepped hoodmold and tablet above the door, and the rainwater head and downpipe. The authenticity of the parts is unexceptional, but Salvin has yet to organize them as a coherent whole.

A similar repertoire of Tudor details appears in a perspective that Salvin prepared three years later for the competition for the new Harpur School buildings in Bedford (Fig. 4). This shows a rambling set of buildings to which are applied mullioned and transomed windows, battlemented parapets, pinnacles, polygonal chimney stacks, and a variety of towers. It is not a very convincing effort, and as a drawing it has certain infelicities. It is not clear, for instance, whether the octagonal turret above the main entrance springs from the tower or from the roof of the hall behind. Salvin did not win this competition and was to be disappointed in another project, namely the proposed new gallery for the Old Watercolour Society in Trafalgar Square. Nesfield had been elected an associate of the society, and a member in 1823, and no doubt tried to use his influence to get Salvin the job. In any event, the society decided that the lease of its existing gallery in Pall Mall should be renewed, so nothing came of this opportunity. Salvin's domestic work in the 1820s, apart from the big houses already mentioned, was confined to minor estate buildings or alterations and additions of which details are generally irrecoverable. On the other hand, there are two ecclesiastical designs that are of considerable interest and are well documented. These are for the restoration of the chapel of Magdalen College, Oxford, and for the Trafford Mausoleum.

In June 1828, a college meeting resolved that an advertisement should be inserted in the London papers offering a premium of a hundred guineas for the best plan for the refitting of the interior of the chapel. This had become an

4. The Harpur School, watercolor perspective.

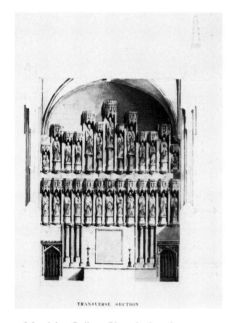

5. Magdalen College Chapel, elevation
of reredos.

6. Magdalen College Chapel, elevation
of organ and stalls.

inharmonious mixture of classical and Gothick items dominated by an oil painting
of Christ carrying the Cross framed by six Corinthian columns by way of an
altarpiece, with a fresco of the Last Judgment above. It was intended that such
inappropriate furnishings be eliminated, with an attempt made to impose some
unity on the whole. Salvin was not successful with his entry, the designs of Lewis
Cottingham being preferred by the president and fellows. Four of his drawings
survive; two are alternative versions of a reredos, one for the organ screen and
stalls at the west end, and one a longitudinal section. So far as the reredos is
concerned, Salvin's model would seem to be that at All Souls, although his design
does not display the *horror vacui* of that fifteenth-century work (Fig. 5). The rules of
the competition have not been preserved, but it is possible that something of this
sort was stipulated, as Cottingham's design is not dissimilar. The stalls at the west
end were to have elaborate tabernacle work, but Salvin does not attempt as complex a roof as that put in by Cottingham (Fig. 6). Possibly he lacked the confidence

7. The Trafford Mausoleum.

to try anything more complicated than a simple quadripartite vault with flat bosses resting on corbels, or perhaps this is an early example of the attitude toward restoration that he expressed later in life, when he had no objection to combining in one design features of different periods, apparently demonstrating a historical sequence of building and additions.

His first executed ecclesiastical work, the Trafford Mausoleum, was a simpler problem and a more satisfactory effort than one suspects the Magdalen Chapel proposals would have turned out to be (Fig. 7). It is naturally rather small, about twenty feet long and twenty feet high, and stands on a slight mound in Wroxham Churchyard. It was designed between August 1827, when Sigismund Trafford Southwell died, and March the following year, when his wife obtained a faculty for sinking a family vault and erecting the mausoleum above. A model was shown at the Royal Academy in 1830, when it was praised by *The Gentleman's Magazine* as "a pleasing and exquisite miniature chapel, the architecture the style of Westminster Abbey."[24] There is a gabled roof, with gabled chamfered angle turrets, three bays of blind tracery lengthwise, consisting of pairs of cusped arches with a quatrefoils above, and at the east end four bays with a sexfoil in the gable. Inside there is a fine coat of arms carved above the door, a blind arcade running round, cusped arches of two rows of dog-tooth, with a paneled wagon roof above. The intersections of the molding framing the panels are decorated with red cinquefoils from the Southwell arms and the gold leopard masks of Crowe used alternately. They are cast in lead and painted, and just the sort of thing that A. W. N. Pugin might have done ten years later. The success of the mausoleum no doubt became a factor in Salvin's appointment as architect for the restoration of the south transept of Norwich Cathedral the next year.

Indeed, his life, both professional and personal, was beginning to take shape.

24. *The Gentleman's Magazine* 1 (1830): 541.

He had married Anne and brought her down to London, to rather cramped lodgings in a dark street. She did not take to her new way of life at first, clearly missing the busy country rectory, full of family and friends. She was intimidated by her cook, found her page impertinent, and housekeeping difficult and sometimes frightening. Salvin, who had till then eaten chiefly in chop houses, was unable to help her in her dealings with tradespeople of doubtful honesty. He was, anyway, often away from home, visiting works that he had in hand in counties so far apart as Durham and Devon, and fully occupied with seeing clients and preparing drawings when he was in town. He had at least one assistant by this time, Frederick Caldecleugh, who one assumes was a relative of the Nesfields' governess. He made the working drawings and conducted the routine correspondence of the office. James Deason had come into the office by 1833 and was employed not only on the preparation of survey drawings, but also on the large perspectives that were sent for exhibition in the Academy; yet the greater part of the work of what rapidly became a busy practice fell largely on Salvin's shoulders.

The arrival of children soon reconciled Anne to separation from her family. The Salvins' first son, Anthony, was born in 1827, when the family moved to 32 Somerset Street near Portman Square, where Salvin was to keep his office for the next fifteen years. A second son, William Parker, was born in 1829, but died within a year, chiefly, it seems, from the medical treatment of the time, teething problems being dealt with by bleeding and cupping. A daughter, whose birth took place a few months after this tragedy, died of scarlet fever at the age of two. It was then decided that Somerset Street was unhealthy for children, and new lodgings were found in Porchester Terrace, a quiet street in Bayswater, close to Kensington Gardens. Emmeline was born here. Shortly thereafter, Salvin decided to move his family right out of London and took a lease on a large house in Finchley, which remained their home until after Anne's death and Salvin's ill health obliged him to move nearer to his office in central London. Here two more children were born, Osbert and Eliza Anne; and Miss Caldecleugh, now that the rector's children at Brancepeth had all grown up, came down from the north and took over the task of bringing up the next generation.

3

The Country Houses: Mamhead, Scotney Castle, and the Tudor Model

Mamhead and Moreby Hall were not only highly regarded in their own day; their significance in the general development of the English country house was also handsomely recognized by Charles Lock Eastlake forty years later, when the achievements of High Victorian Gothic might well have obscured the humble beginnings of the Revival. In the table of important buildings that Eastlake appended to his *A History of the Gothic Revival,* Moreby Hall and Mamhead are listed in the wrong order, as numbers 7 and 8, and both are dated 1828. Only one country house precedes them in this list, and that is J. C. Buckler's Costessy Hall, which is dated 1823.[1] It is plain that Eastlake admired Moreby Hall a good deal more than Mamhead, and indeed he uses this house to illustrate the freedom of planning that the Gothic style gave to those who employed it. But Eastlake by no means gives us the full story. The use of the Tudor style had begun nearly ten years before, and George Gilbert Scott has left an amusing account of the rejection of classicism in favor of the native model.

When he published his *Remarks on Secular & Domestic Architecture* in 1857, he was writing not only as an apologist for his own personal interpretation of Gothic, but also for the style in general, which he maintained was that most suitable for the climate and best harmonized with the English countryside. But he was almost as disparaging about the adoption of what he felt to be the wrong models for the new Gothic as he was about their classical predecessors. The latter he castigates for their "uncongenial character" and "their cold and proud Palladianism, [which] so far from inviting seems to forbid approach; one feels under a painful restraint so long as they are in view; and the only rural thoughts they suggest are of game-keepers and park-rangers."[2] Gothic, on the other hand, even the "confectionery Gothic" of the early Revival, was not forbidding: it fitted cosily into the scenery and inspired in visitors thoughts of hearty old-time welcomes and hospitality. But its early practitioners took some time to hit upon the right version: "The first attempts were in the form known as 'abbeys'; could anything be expected from an idea so absurd? The next form adopted was the 'castle'; a type equally obsolete, yet even now not wholly set aside. The manifest absurdity of two such types led to the adoption of the Elizabethan mansion as a guide. This approved itself to common sense, and success has generally attended it. It produces neither castles nor abbeys, but houses."

There was, however, another factor to which Scott does not refer, but that was of

1. Charles Lock Eastlake, *A History of the Gothic Revival* (London: Longmans, 1872).
2. George Gilbert Scott, *Remarks on Secular and Domestic Architecture Present and Future* (London: John Murray, 1858).

equal importance. The wars with France, and the resulting turmoil on the continent of Europe, had put a stop to the grand tour. The young heir to a country
estate had only the books and engravings in his library, rather than the personal,
vivid recollection of the villas of the Veneto and Tuscany, or the palazzi of Florence
and Rome, to refer to when he set about modernizing or rebuilding his father's or
grandfather's old, inconvenient, and shockingly unfashionable house. This political prohibition of European travel, which extended from 1793 to 1815, with only a
slight interlude at the time of the Peace of Amiens, began a year before Uvedale
Price published his *Essays on the Picturesque* and coincided with a growth of interest
in native ruins and scenery of the more mountainous kind. Since the middle of the
eighteenth century a few hardy souls had been making their way to the wilder
parts of Yorkshire and the Lakes, and later, when the novels of Scott came to be
widely read, to lowland Scotland and the Highland Fringe. These travelers were
often competent botanists, ornithologists, or geologists and were interested in
ancient remains. Nearly all could sketch with a great deal of competence, and an
initial banditti-cum-ruin type of subject matter, with antecedents traceable to
Salvator Rosa, was superseded by an antiquarian approach that began with drawings of the more imposing and derelict castles and monastic buildings but had
transferred itself by the first decade of the nineteenth century to the curious
features of fortified manor houses and farms.[3] This process of looking at old
houses, their romantic settings, and an idealization of life during the great days of
Queen Elizabeth I began to manifest itself in the buildings put up for the upper
classes over the next ten years or so, and it steadily increased in popularity.
William Wilkins seems to have been one of the first to use elements of the Tudor
style in the new wing at Pentillie Castle, Cornwall, in about 1810, where he mixed
it with Gothic, and subsequently at Dalmeny in West Lothian, an important
house built in 1814–1819 in an East Anglian Tudor of the type he would have seen at
East Barsham when he was a boy. Tregothnan, near Truro, was remodeled and
added to a year or so later in a similar style. Wilkins, however, did not have an
extensive country house practice, and Dunmore Park in Stirlingshire was his only
other attempt in this manner; thereafter he was almost entirely occupied with
large classical public buildings, until his death in 1839.

It is clear from his designs for Blairquhan, Ayrshire, and Carstairs in Lan-
arkshire, in 1820 and 1821, that William Burn or his clients had been impressed by
Dalmeny; and it was Burn, Edward Blore, and George Webster of Kendal who
were, with Salvin, among the first habitually to employ the Tudor and Jacobean
styles with increasing accuracy and conviction. Burn and Blore were Salvin's
principal rivals in the country house field when he was establishing himself in
practice. Webster was a lesser figure who suffered from poor health and gave up
architecture in 1846. He died in 1864 and was in any event the least formidable
competitor for commissions, as his practice was almost completely confined to
north Lancashire and the Lake District. Blore retired three years after Webster
and died an exceedingly wealthy man thirty years later. Burn died in 1870 and
seems to have practiced to some extent to the end of his life, leaving a thriving
office headed by Macvicar Anderson and William Colling, which continued into

3. Edmund W. Hodge, *Enjoying the Lakes* (Edinburgh: Oliver & Boyd, 1957).

the beginning of the twentieth century. Salvin completed his last commissions ten years after Burn died.

Edward Blore was the oldest of this group and had received no formal training in architecture. He had inherited his father's interest in medieval buildings, and he became a skilled draftsman and engraver, contributing illustrations to some twenty-two topographical works, including no less than six of Britton's publications. He himself produced *Monumental Remains of Noble and Eminent Persons.* This was in 1826, and the following year he was appointed Surveyor of Westminster Abbey. He was a Fellow of the Royal Society and, like Salvin, a Fellow of the Society of Antiquaries and a friend of Thomas Rickman. When he died he left forty-eight volumes of drawings of "almost every example of ancient castellated and domestic architecture remaining in England."[4] His earliest work in the Gothic style seems to have been advice and unexecuted designs for Abbotsford, Sir Walter Scott's house in Roxburghshire, and a library at Althorpe, Northamptonshire, in 1816 and 1820. At the time Salvin was instructed to build Mamhead, he was working on four country houses in the Tudor or Jacobean style, of which Canford Manor in Dorset, 1826–1836, was the most significant. Two years later Meyrick commissioned him to build Goodrich Court to house his armor collection, which had finally grown beyond the capacity of his house in Upper Cadogan Place. This last demonstrates Blore's commitment to the Picturesque castle style of the late eighteenth and early nineteenth centuries, of which Charles Augustus Busby's Gwrych Castle is a fair example; it also illustrates his inability to apply his immense knowledge with accuracy. Triple lancets lighting the ground floor of a massive spurred round tower immediately destroy any illusion that Goodrich is a real defensible castle. Blore's houses combine a smoothness of masonry surfaces with an attenuated spiky design, and he never makes the attempt at the authentic proportions that characterize Salvin's buildings.[5]

There is no evidence of any intense archaeological research on the part of either Burn or Webster. Burn was a pupil of Robert Smirke at the time of the building of Lowther Castle, and Webster's father was the Clerk of Works on this job. Like Gwrych, Lowther is very much the product of the previous century, and it was completed in 1811. Burn began to practice on his own account the following year and by the mid 1820s had in hand about ten houses designed in a composite style made up of Tudor, Jacobean, and Scottish Baronial. This last, with an unequaled skill at arranging the suites of rooms and independent routes of circulation in which the occupants of country houses lived and moved as relationships between the classes and the different categories of residents became more sharply divided, was to be his chief contribution to nineteenth-century architecture. At first his work was almost confined to Scotland and the borders; apart from the rebuilding of the fire-gutted Cliveden in 1827, and some projects for Knowsley dated 1836, he did not work in England until he was called in to replace Salvin at Harlaxton in 1838. This led to many other English commissions, and within five years he had moved from Edinburgh to London. Webster is by comparison a minor figure but

4. They are in the British Museum Add. MSS 42000–42047.
5. For Edward Blore see Hugh Meller, "Blore's Country Houses" (Master of Arts Report, Courtauld Institute of Art, 1975), and "The Architectural History of Goodrich Court, Herefordshire," *Transactions of the Woolhope Naturalists' Field Club* 42:2 (1977).

one who produced surprisingly early essays in the Jacobean manner, although he had little or no influence on other architects, on even a parochial level. Some of his houses are, for their date, very advanced specimens of design in an archaeological style. Underley Hall, Westmoreland, was begun in 1825 and exhibited at the Royal Academy the following year. It is symmetrical, with a frontispiece based on that at Browsholme Hall and corner turrets like those at Burleigh. Its long, low facade was intended to act as a base for a Wollaton-type central prospect tower, which was never built. It was, however, still very much a classical house in Jacobean dress, which is not the case with Webster's other early attempt in this manner, Eshton Hall, Gargrave in Yorkshire of 1825–1827. Here he makes a positive break with classical symmetry, placing an octagonal tower at one end of the principal facade, and another Browsholme-type entrance porch between two very broad bays. The office ranges are large and full of Jacobean cupolas and shaped gables. At this stage Webster was in advance of his contemporaries in his free use of Jacobean motifs, but he did not continue along this path, and his later Gothic Revival buildings became rigidly symmetrical.[6]

These then were Salvin's rivals in the country house field. It is doubtful if he ever met Webster, or Burn, before he moved to London, but Blore was a friend of long standing, and Salvin consulted him on a number of matters, including the problem of the reseating of the choir of Norwich Cathedral. All four architects were moving in the same direction and had similar aims. What they were getting away from was described by *The Gentleman's Magazine* in 1830 as "the contemptible gewgaws of the Wyatt school, in the shape of abbeys, priories, and castles, of six rooms." The same review of the Royal Academy's architectural section describes a model of Mamhead that was exhibited by Salvin: "A splendid mansion of the Elizabethan character; the oriel windows, tower staircases, and numerous chimnies; the gables crowning the attics, and the total absence of ecclesiastical architecture, are the characteristic features."[7]

Robert William Newman was the senior partner of Newman & Co., a prosperous firm of general merchants that traded with Portugal and Newfoundland and owned its own small shipping fleet. He bought the Mamhead estate in 1823 and later became the Member of Parliament for Exeter and a Baronet. The original house on the estate was quite substantial and had been built on low ground near the lake in the preceding century. But Newman, financed by port and salt codfish, was advancing socially and no doubt regarded it as insufficiently grand. It also lacked the magnificent view across the Exe estuary that was obtained when the new mansion was built about half a mile up a hill to the west, where an area of rough woodland still provides a wild and picturesque background for the Tudor house and its pele tower (Fig. 8). The change in site was probably suggested by Salvin, as an early plan prepared for Newman by Charles Fowler places the stables at the rear of the main building, indicating a level building area.

Fowler would have come to Newman's notice because he was born at Cullompton and articled in Exeter. He was a local man who had made good, and

6. For information on George Webster and illustrations of his houses, see Angus Taylor and Jeffrey Haworth, *The Websters of Kendal* (Kendal: Abbot Hall Art Gallery, 1973).

7. *The Gentleman's Magazine* (1830) 1: 541.

8. Mamhead Park, watercolor perspective.

by this time had built the London Bankruptcy Courts, the New Market at Grave-
send, and a good, large Gothic church at Teffont Evias in Wiltshire. Newman had
had him prepare a set of designs for a pair of houses in Berkeley Square and a
classical design for the new mansion. This was not proceeded with, either because
Newman had become generally aware of the new fashion for houses designed in an
indigenous style, or, more probably, because he had an opportunity to see such a
house, namely George Stanley Repton's remodeling of Kitley for Edmund Bas-
tard. Kitley is a short distance to the south of the main road from Torquay to
Plymouth, where Newman's shipping business must have taken him fairly frequently. It was worked upon from around 1820 to 1825 and is one of the first houses
in England to be attempted in an authentic Elizabethan style.[8] The change in
styles at Mamhead led to a change of architect, and one must hope that Fowler's
natural disappointment was mitigated by two enviable commissions that he
received the following year, for Covent Garden Market and the Duke of Northumberland's conservatory at Sion House. Despite the change in styles from
classical to Tudor, Newman retained the ground plan of the Fowler design (Fig. 9).
No doubt it had been settled after a good deal of discussion, and he saw no reason
to change it.[9] The house is arranged around a central courtyard, with the four
main reception rooms on the garden front and the principal staircase in a tower
projecting into the court. The offices are placed in a longer, lower range to the

8. Christopher Hussey, *English Country Houses: Late Georgian, 1800–1840* (London: Country Life, 1958). The
Reptons were among the first to promote Tudor. In 1792 Humphrey deplored the destruction of Lamer before
he was consulted, and this was two years before the publication of Richard Payne Knight's poem *The
Landscape,* which has an illustration of a Wollaton-type country house in a woodland landscape. In the
Panshanger Red Book his comments anticipate those of Gilbert Scott: "The Castle Gothic consists of a large
mass of wall with very small apertures and is rather calculated for a prison. The architecture of Abbey Gothic
. . . is only applicable to halls and chapels of colleges. We are therefore driven to the date of Queen
Elizabeth." George Carter, Patrick Goode, and Kedrun Laurie, *Humphrey Repton Landscape Gardener, 1752–1818*
(Norwich: Sainsbury Centre for Visual Arts, 1982).
9. Fowler's designs for both the Berkeley Square houses and Mamhead, and Salvin's designs and working
drawings are among the Newman MSS, Blackpool House, Devon.

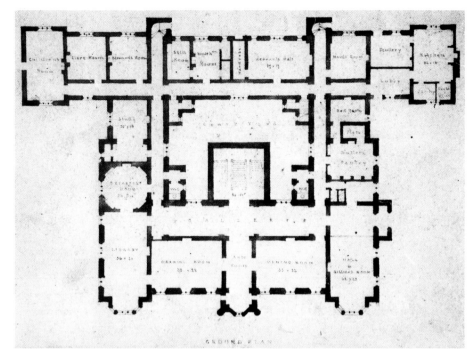

9. Mamhead Park, ground plan.

rear. The imposition of a symmetrical plan suitable for a classical house meant that
Salvin was obliged to make his elevations symmetrical, and this makes for a
certain dullness in the design of the main block, particularly on the garden front,
where gable and canted bay is balanced by gable and canted bay. There is little
attempt to give interest to the skyline, which is broken only by grouped chimney
stacks, gables that stand little higher than the ridge and are in some cases uncom-
fortably narrow, pinnacles and the octagonal shafts flanking the oriel. Even the
staircase tower, which might have formed a point of vertical emphasis, is kept to
the height of the roof.

The shell of the house was erected in 1827–1828, but work on the interiors
proceeded slowly, probably because Newman was building out of income. Drawings for the plaster ceilings of the library, breakfast room, and bedrooms were
made in 1832, and those for the ceiling, screen, and overmantel in the entrance hall
are dated 1835. This is the year that the planning of Scotney Castle was begun and
Harlaxton was half built, and these fine designs show how much Salvin had
improved both as a designer and in his grasp of archaeological detail during the
nine years the house was being built. Now he plainly found his early elevations
both unconvincing and unexciting, and he tried to overcome this by making the
house one of a group of buildings in diverse styles.

Three alternative Gothic designs for the conservatory were prepared in 1831,
along with a rather plain scheme for the stables. As mentioned earlier, the stables
and coach houses had been placed by Fowler to the rear of the service range, but a
steep rise in the ground now made this impracticable. By the following year Salvin
had hit upon the idea of building a pele tower containing the laundry and
brewhouse at one angle of a stable yard, and giving the yard a splendid barbican

entrance defended by squat towers with a portcullis and arrow slits. This was built somewhat up the hillside to the north of the house, and it removed those activities that caused the worst smells in nineteenth-century establishments from its immediate vicinity (Fig. 10). The idea of putting a tower here had occurred to him at an early date, as shown by a very early elevation, but this clearly did not contain the stables (Fig. 11). When the stables came to be built, this plain castellated tower was replaced by a replica of the pele tower at Belsay, built of the local red sandstone, which has a roughness of texture that contrasts with the smooth Bath stone of the house and is intended to suggest a building of greater antiquity. This Northumbrian fortification does look rather out of place in the lush Devon countryside; not so the conservatory, which was added to the south front, a single-story range

10. Mamhead Park, the stable block, watercolor perspective.

11. Mamhead Park, elevation of garden front.

12. Mamhead Park, the conservatory, watercolor perspective.

with four large Perpendicular windows with fancy glazing, terminating in a two-story pavilion. With its carved scrolls and verses from the *Romant de la Rose,* heraldic shields, mottoes, beautifully carved panels of flowers in the spandrels, and pinnacles at every angle, it is as gay and frivolous as the stable block is dour (Fig. 12).

The stables and conservatory certainly show an increase in knowledge of architectural detail. The detail of the house remains much the same as that which Salvin uses at Northallerton and in the Harpur School design, with the addition of the triple oriel on the garden front, which is copied from that at Hengrave Hall (Fig. 13). Sometimes Salvin's models were only twenty years old, for we know that the variously patterned chimney stacks were taken partly from examples at Hampton Court and partly from William Porden's Eaton Hall, completed in 1812.[10] What must be said about Mamhead is that the work was beautifully carried out; the main contract was taken by Philip Nowell & Son of London, whose masons were responsible for the crisply cut carving and fine masonry, and the plumbers' work was by Thomas Willement, who made, among other things, the delightful lead rainwater stacks attached to the walls by flanges decorated with a rose, or a twig impaling a crown. As had been the case with the Trafford Mausoleum, Salvin exercises a taste for decorative detail that anticipates Pugin; there are titled scrolls, heraldic achievements, and other odder items. It is understandable that a library chimneypiece should bear projecting figures of a lady reading a book and a scholar writing, both in Elizabethan dress, but it is not at all clear why angels should be similarly placed on the breakfast room chimneypiece. These were designed in 1833, the same year as the plaster ceilings of the gallery and staircase.

10. Anthony Salvin to R. W. Newman, November 27, 1829, Newman MSS.

The dining room chimneypiece was made the following year, and this bears the figures of Edward the Confessor and the Pilgrim, who do not appear to have any connection with the business of eating. Odder still are the life-sized statues carved by Charles Raymond Smith, which stood in the gallery (Fig. 14). These were of Lord and Lady Daubeny, Henry VII and Elizabeth of York, Henry VIII and Lady Jane Seymour, Queen Elizabeth and Sir Walter Raleigh, and Cardinal Wolsey and an unidentified bishop. It would be interesting to know who thought of this scheme; it had, of course, been quite usual for the owners of English houses of classical design to decorate their halls with antique statuary or its contemporary equivalent by Flaxman or Canova. Here the gods and goddesses, emperors and senators are replaced by personalities of the apparent date of the house. The only precedent for such a thing seems to be the Temple of British Worthies at Stowe, where Elizabeth and Raleigh appear in company with Shakespeare, Bacon, Milton, Hampden, Newton, Locke, William of Orange, King Alfred, the Black Prince, Sir John Barnard, Drake, Inigo Jones, and Pope. The next such gathering, which includes most of the foregoing, is on the Albert Memorial in Kensington Gardens.[11]

11. These statues remained *in situ* until July 1985, when they were scandalously removed and sold by auction, the owner arguing that they did not form part of the building and were therefore not protected by historic building legislation. A possible parallel to the statues at Mamhead are the portrait busts of Queen Elizabeth and two members of the Lucy family at Charlecote. They are copies of the Maxmilian Colt effigy and monuments in the Parish church. Their date is not known, but they could be by Thomas Willement who was working at Charlecote at the very time Mamhead was being completed.

13. Mamhead Park, the oriel, watercolor perspective.

14. Mamhead Park, the gallery, pencil and wash sketch by Anne Salvin.

Salvin designed furniture for Mamhead: the dining room and library tables, a sideboard, and a bench for the hall of which he obviously did not approve, and said so (Fig. 15). He also built a village school at Ashcombe and altered a number of estate buildings, including the two lodges, adding round and octagonal rooms to the existing box-like buildings, with verandas, half timbering, fretted boarding, rustic poles, and thatch (Fig. 16). Similar to these lodges is a design for a three-room cottage in rustic style, which is sufficiently close to the work of Nash and George Stanley Repton at Blaise Hamlet to give further credence to the story that Salvin spent some time with Nash. But all these small buildings hark back to the *cottage orné* of the eighteenth century and are generally at variance with Salvin's search for authentic medieval detail in his small buildings, and he never produced anything like this again (Fig. 17).

At Moreby Hall Salvin was free of the necessity of working to the plan of another architect and adopted for the first time an arrangement that was to appear

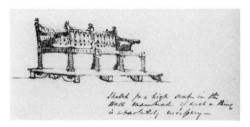
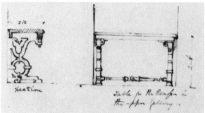

15. Mamhead Park, designs for furniture.

16. Mamhead Park, entrance lodge.

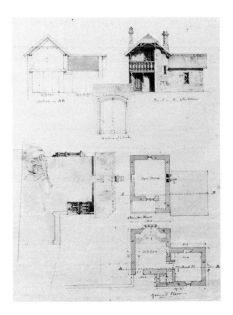

17. Mamhead Park, design for a cottage.

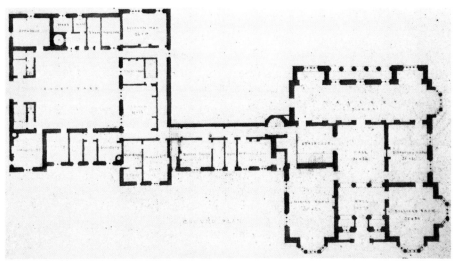

18. Moreby Hall, ground plan.

in a number of his country houses (Fig. 18). This consisted of a two-story central hall with the principal reception rooms—that is, the drawing room, dining room, billiard room, and gallery—leading off it, access to the bedrooms above being obtained from a corridor running around the hall at first floor level. One advantage, apart from the grand effect of the two-story hall, is that warm air from the ground floor can rise directly to the upper rooms, which are no longer reached by way of long corridors, freezing in winter. Where it had been used earlier, by Sir Charles Monck at Belsay in 1810, James Wyatt at Ashridge in 1813, and by Thomas Hopper at Leigh Court a year later, the hall incorporates the main staircase, and little attempt is made to conceal the passage of domestics passing to and from the bedrooms in the course of their duties. At Moreby Hall Salvin clears the floor area by placing the stairs in a tower that stands between the house and its offices and also has a separate servants' stair concealed in an octagonal turret; the bedroom corridor or landing is hidden by a screening wall pierced at intervals with arches, and thus protected from the view of the family and guests who used the hall as a sitting room.

The Prestons, for whom the house was built, were merchants and bankers and had traded in Leeds since the seventeenth century. Henry Preston had inherited the Moreby estate from an uncle. He had pulled down the original Elizabethan house, which was doubtless derelict, and set about building a new mansion in the same style, but on a much more convenient plan, with larger, grander rooms. He probably acted in anticipation of his appointment to the office of High Sheriff of the county in 1836. Moreby is smaller than Mamhead, and much more compact, but the offices are kept as a separate unit, arranged around a courtyard with the brewhouse and laundry furthest from the house, and only connected to it by a corridor along which Salvin placed Mr. Preston's business room and the butler's pantry, which act as a buffer zone between the parts of the house occupied by the family and servants, respectively (Fig. 19).

Eastlake devotes a number of paragraphs to this house and comments that it had no very remarkable characteristics but demonstrated "a gradual return to the manorial Gothic of old English Mansions" and that Salvin showed a "steady advance in his knowledge of the style which was his special study." Eastlake points out that the chief advantage of the Tudor style was that the facade could be adapted to the plan desired and not impose a possibly inconvenient arrangement on the occupants in the interests of symmetry. In addition, the offices might be removed from the back of the house or the basement and be housed in a separate, lower building that would emphasize the bulk of the main block, as well as afford increased light and air to the servants. This Salvin has certainly done, but he has not availed himself of the opportunity to break with symmetry, which prevails on each facade and is only broken by the imposing keep-like stair tower, its turret, and the service wing. It was not until he came to prepare the drawings for

19. Moreby Hall, watercolor perspective.

Derwentwater Manor in 1833 that he finally extricated himself from the tenets of eighteenth-century classicism and produced his first irregular designs. Moreby Hall is plainer than Mamhead both inside and out and has none of the decorative carving that is such a delight there. Eastlake complains that the roofs are of too low a pitch, but he approves other features, such as the double transom, which distinguishes the windows of the most important rooms. And many of the less correct details have disappeared, such as the square hood mold above every window and the continuous battlemented parapet running round the eaves. Here, only the tower and the bay windows have battlements, but the rather unconvincing triple oriel with its four tiny pinnacles and the fine rainwater stacks remain much the same.

Before he received the Scotney Castle commission, Salvin designed two other houses in the Tudor style, in which he developed the Moreby plan and improved the authenticity of his detail. These houses were much the same size, as were Cowesby Hall in the North Riding, begun in 1832 and burned down and rebuilt this century, and Derwentwater Manor, for which plans were prepared, but the house not built. Both were for gentlemen who had just bought themselves country estates, and there is a pleasant lack of pretension about these designs. By this time Salvin had had the opportunity to work on some major examples of the Tudor manor house, namely Somerhill, Methley, and Parham; and there is a decided increase in his sensitivity to the actual appearance of old houses. The Gothick decorations of Moreby, the pretty, fussy oriel and the carved chimney stacks perched on the spring of the gables have gone.

Both these houses were intended to be of stone, and rough cut blocks laid in irregular courses are shown in the drawings; gone is the smoothness of the wall surfaces in the Moreby perspective, which give the impression that it could equally well have been carried out in plaster or cement, and there is a solidity in their design more appropriate to a stone building. At Cowesby Salvin makes a rather timid advance in design (Fig. 20). Although the garden front is still perfectly symmetrical and indeed simply a smaller version of that at Moreby, the entrance front is a different matter. There are identical gables on either side, but the three-

20. Cowesby Hall, pen and wash perspective.

bay center recalls his design for Northallerton, with an entrance porch and staircase tower with a chimney stack rising from the battlements. He makes better use of the kitchen quarters in the design; instead of being removed from the house by a corridor, they are here attached, so the difference in scale is immediately obvious. They are also brought forward to form one side of the entrance courtyard. Salvin liked to enclose the approach to the main entrance to his houses, and he does the same thing at Harlaxton and in later mansions. Cowesby, as it was built, is solid and unaffected in design; but there had been an earlier scheme for a house of quite different character (Fig. 21). This had a verticality emphasized by spiky vanes and pinnacles and a tall battlemented tower, reminiscent of that at Moreby, at the junction of house and offices, which rises well above the rest of the building. Whether the client disliked this flamboyance or was alarmed at the cost of such an effort cannot be said, but it was the simpler version that was built.

There is no plan for the proposed house on Derwentwater; all that remains are alternative elevations for the entrance front and for that at the rear (Fig. 22).

21. Cowesby Hall, pencil sketch of preliminary design.

22. Derwentwater Manor, elevation of entrance front.

These very important drawings mark a stage in Salvin's progression from "confectionary" Gothic to the correct Elizabethan of Scotney Castle. The offices are again on the left and partially enclose the entrance courtyard; the porch leads into an entrance hall lit by a single-story bay window, much the same as that built later in Kent. Beyond this there is the staircase in a four-story tower. At Scotney this tower was to be a modification of the Belsay pele and placed on the other side of the porch, and there it does not actually contain stairs but a number of small rooms. In both houses the facade terminates in a more or less blank stretch of wall, hidden now at Scotney by a garden wall and shrubbery, which were added later.[12] Salvin has at last broken away from all regularity in the design of his buildings, which now spread in a sequence of architectural forms seemingly added at random as in an old building slowly enlarged by its owners over the years. Only the thin tower, the curious octagonal turret, and the rather ecclesiastical string course with grotesque sculptures at the angles remind the observer of the building's real date.

Edward Hussey's decision to build a new Scotney Castle arose from a family tragedy (Fig. 23). He had not lived at the old castle since the deaths of his sister, father, and grandfather within a year or so had convinced his mother that the moated house in its low-lying valley was a thoroughly unhealthy place, whereupon she removed to St. Leonard's with her son. When Hussey came of age and took over the management of the estate, he was confronted with the problem of finding himself somewhere to live. The old house had fallen into disrepair, and a connection was beginning to be made between bad drainage and disease. Eventually, after consulting William Sawrey Gilpin, a watercolor painter who, like Nesfield, had turned landscape gardener, he chose a site on high ground overlooking the fourteenth-century castle and its attached seventeenth century wing, which were deliberately ruined and kept as an eye-catcher. This was a brilliantly successful idea, and they are much photographed to this day.[13]

The first stone was laid in 1837, after a series of no less than thirty-two conferences between Salvin and his twenty-six-year-old client, of which numerous small-scale plans drawn by both parties form a record. This took a year and nine months, and the construction of the house took more or less the same amount of time. The decoration of the interiors, with elaborate plasterwork ceilings, paneling, and the fitting of Flemish sixteenth-century woodcarvings (acquired from Hull of Wardour Street), painting, and paperhanging took another three years. As at Mamhead, Salvin designed a few pieces of furniture: a four-poster, a wardrobe, tables and sideboards for the dining room, and a cupboard for the hall made up from old woodwork.

At some stage in the long planning process, a cardboard model of the house was made by Thomas Deighton, who described himself at a later date as "Architectural Modeller to her Majesty and Prince Albert" and who also exhibited at the Great Exhibition in 1851. Salvin appears to have used models quite frequently to explain his proposals to his clients, and those for the Trafford Mausoleum and Mamhead were shown at the Royal Academy (Fig. 24). In plan Scotney Castle is an improve-

12. To keep out the wind that howled round the exposed hilltop site. Information from Christopher Hussey.

13. William Sawrey Gilpin was an indifferent watercolorist who also taught drawing to cadets; he was appointed Drawing Master at the Royal Military College, Great Marlow, in 1806, and in 1832 published *Practical Hints for Landscape Gardening* (London: T. Cadell, 1979).

23. Scotney Castle, watercolor perspective.

24. Scotney Castle, the model.

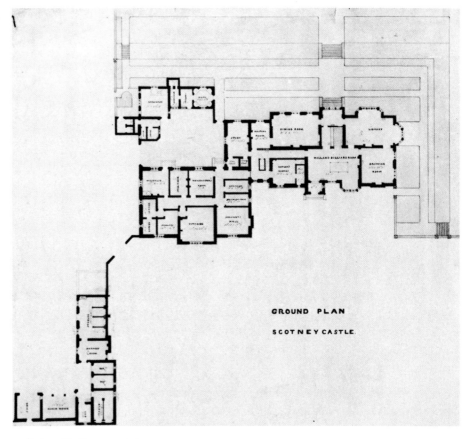

GROUND PLAN

SCOTNEY CASTLE.

25. Scotney Castle, ground plan.

ment on that of Cowesby (Fig. 25). The three main reception rooms, drawing room, library, and dining room are in much the same position, but instead of being grouped around what must have been a rather dark, straightened hall, together with a narrow porch and stairs, they are reached from a spacious room large enough to hold a billiard table if required, and well lit by a bay window. The office wing is in the same position, projecting forward from the left of the entrance front, and an L-shaped range of stables and coach houses lie further forward still, linked to the main block by an arch. A small kitchen court is closed on the garden front by a range containing the dairy, with its louvred ventilator, the bakehouse with a tall chimney, and the brewhouse; they are an attractive group when seen from the terraces. The architectural details are the same as those used at Cowesby and Derwentwater and are applied with great authenticity and freedom. It is the most successful attempt at the small Tudor manor required by the gentry, but it was in many ways the end of the line. Salvin did not get the opportunity to build this sort of house again.

His country house work at this period was not entirely restricted to buildings in his developing Tudor style. Skutterskelfe House is a rather large, plain classical building of 1832–1838 (Fig. 26). Burwarton House, an early essay in the Italian Villa mode, was to lead to a number of commissions for buildings in this style, which Salvin executed during the 1840s and which are dealt with in a later chapter.

26. Skutterskelfe House, pen and ink perspective.

But his chief preoccupation had been with the Elizabethan manor, and here he could not advance further after Scotney for the simple reason that he received no commissions for such houses after 1836, although it must be remembered that work at Scotney Castle continued until 1844, so far as decorating and furnishings were concerned. Apart from Peckforton Castle, Salvin received no commissions whatsoever to build an entirely new house during the 1840s, and indeed the next new house he was to build was the problematical Bangor Castle, begun in 1852. By that date there was a marked deterioration in his ability to look at ancient buildings and transform them into something new. He had been given no opportunity to plan a house without having to take into account the existing portions of earlier buildings that had to be incorporated in his plans, or to design his elevations without respecting what was there already.

He was also quite overwhelmed with work of other kinds. He was constantly sought after to alter and add to old houses of great merit. In the late 1830s he was occupied with, among others, Greystoke and Rockingham Castles and Rufford Hall. In the following decade he was engaged at Naworth Castle, Flixton Hall, and Warkworth Castle; the 1850s saw the commencement of his long restoration programs at the Tower of London, Windsor Castle, and Alnwick Castle, and the renovation of Thornbury Castle. To these major undertakings must be added much minor country house work, eight new churches in the 1830s, and fourteen in the 1840s, together with a series of church restorations beginning with that of Holy Sepulchre for the Cambridge Camden Society. In his country house business he was primarily concerned with making additions that married happily with the old fabric, and this he did well. His new churches range from the competent to the frankly pedestrian, and his church restorations are the same; it was chiefly a matter of money. His office staff does not seem to have been large, and the pressure on Salvin himself was unremitting. None of this sort of thing was likely to develop his talent for imaginative design, but he did acquire a merited reputation for solving the planning problems encountered when fitting new work in with the old.

27. Bayons Manor, the great hall,
pen and ink perspective.

Three other works must be mentioned before this chapter is brought to a close: first, Salvin's connection with Charles Tennyson d'Eyncourt's rebuilding of Bayons Manor. Old Mr. Tennyson had died in 1835, having bequeathed a small trust fund to his eldest son, and the balance of his not inconsiderable fortune to the youngest. How far Salvin contributed to Tennyson's later additions—the Eagle Tower, the ruined keep, and the barbican—is doubtful, but he certainly produced designs for the remodeling of the existing house, and the addition of extra rooms such as the new library and the great hall[14] (Fig. 27). At the same time Salvin was engaged in adding another Gothic hall onto Michael Field's house at Pyrgo Park in Essex.[15] The only house on the Pyrgo estate was a farmhouse, and it seems likely that Field may have had in mind a building program along the lines of that undertaken at Bayons. However, only the hall, required for entertaining neighbors and the tenantry, was built before Field died, and his brother Robert, unaffected by the fashion for Gothic, encased it in a vast mansion built by Cubitt to the designs of Thomas Allason; all is now demolished.

Finally there is Salvin's design for an episcopal palace for the newly created Bishop of Ripon. Robert Nesfield, who was later to become the Duke of Rutland's agent and able to send a little work Salvin's way, met the Bishop shortly after his appointment. Together with a friend he put forward Salvin's name for the palace,

14. Lincolnshire Archives Committee. Tennyson d'Eyncourt MSS 2TDE K/61/22. Mark Girouard, *The Victorian Country House* (New Haven and London: Yale University Press, 1979).

15. Montague Browne, *The Yearly Records of Pyrgo Park* (privately printed, 1889).

28. The Episcopal Palace, Ripon, watercolor perspective.

together with a list of his most important clients to date: Lord Falkland, Lord Mexborough, Lord Vernon, Mr. Cust, Mr. Hamilton (Lord Boyne), Mr. Preston, Mr. Tennyson, and the University of Durham. "Mr. C. gave the names to the Bishop and he said it was the second time Mr. S. had been mentioned to him— and that he had heard that Mr. S. never exceeded his first estimate of expenses wh. in his case was of the first consideration—the matter rests with the Commissioners, but his recommendation will of course do much."[16] A pencil and wash perspective records Salvin's proposal (Fig. 28). The building was to be of brick; a three-story main block has two- and single-story ranges to the rear. Designed the same year as Cowesby, it is curiously *retardataire,* with its attenuated elevation and repetitive decoration in the way of diapering, ornamental rainwater stacks, pinnacles, and vanes. It represents an earlier and less correct Gothic than that which Salvin had been advancing in the sequence of houses leading up to and culminating in Scotney Castle.

16. University Library, Durham. Salvin MSS. The clients mentioned had employed him at Skutterskelfe House, Methley Hall, Sudbury Hall, Belton, Burwarton House, Moreby Hall, Bayons Manor, and Durham Castle.

4

Harlaxton, the Houses of Parliament, and Other Competitions

"Today we went to see the house Mr. Gregory is building five miles from here. He is a gentleman of about 12,000 l. a year, who has a fancy to build a magnificent house in the Elizabethan style, and he is now in the middle of his work, all the shell being finished except one wing."[1] Charles Greville had been invited to Belvoir Castle in January 1838 to celebrate the Duke of Rutland's birthday; of a house party numbering nearly forty, the Duke and Duchess of Sutherland, Lady Salisbury, Lord Exeter, Lord Wilton, Lady Adeliza Manners, Lord Aberdeen, Lord Fitzgerald, Lord John Manners, and Greville rode or drove out to see Gregory Gregory's prodigy house and the improvements he had already completed in Harlaxton village. His activities were clearly the talk of the county, and it is curious that so little is known about the man himself (Fig. 29).

Gregory Gregory-Williams, who dropped his second surname when he inherited the Harlaxton estate, came from a family that had been established in Nottingham since the seventeenth century. He was born in 1786, and in 1814 his father died, leaving him the Rempstone and Lenton estates in Nottinghamshire and the Denton estate in Lincolnshire. Eight years later the Harlaxton estate, which had come to his grandmother from a distant cousin named Daniel de Ligne, also fell into his hands. He found himself in possession of a good deal of land; Harlaxton consisted of about 2,500 acres, Rempstone about 1,300, and Denton about 1,000; but it was the 2,000-acre Lenton estate that seems to have provided the greater part of the money for his collecting and building activities. Lenton was on the outskirts of the city of Nottingham and had become industrialized during the first quarter of the nineteenth century, when the population of the Parish of Lenton increased by 2,000, and 400 houses were built between 1821 and 1831. All this was caused by the building of factories for the manufacture of Nottingham lace and textile machinery and the establishment of bleach and starch works. The value of land sold off for such industries increased tenfold, and there was in addition a five-foot seam of coal running under it, the working of which was leased to Lord Middleton of Wollaton Hall.

One year after Gregory's father's death the final defeat of Napoleon made Continental travel possible again, and Gregory began a series of extensive foreign tours, probably from a base in Paris, where he is said to have had some sort of position with the Embassy.[2] The Napoleonic Wars had left Europe in a state of confusion, and pillage and revolution had separated many owners from their

1. Charles C. F. Greville, *A Journal of the Reigns of King George IV, King William IV & Queen Victoria* (London: Longmans & Co., 1896), 4:43.
2. Sir Bruno Welby, Bart, private communication.

29. Harlaxton Manor,
view of entrance front.

possessions. In this situation, Gregory found it was possible to form large collections of tapestries, furniture, marbles, and *objets de vertu,* provided the collector was
prepared to be undiscriminating as to quality and the actual ownership of the items
purchased. He acquired "an ample stock of vases, statues and other sculptural
ornaments, and of rich gates, and other iron work," which he proposed to set
about his gardens.3 He also bought a great number of pieces of furniture, favoring
the periods of Louis XV and Louis XVI, gilt armchairs, parquetry escritoires,
marble-topped pier tables and mirrors, and an array of *torchères,* candelabra,
chandeliers, and sconces, necessary when big houses were lit by nothing but oil
lamps and candles. What his acquisitions had in common was that they were
all rather large, and the collecting seems to have got rather out of hand; silver
plate, Beauvais tapestries, Aubusson carpets, Chinese porcelain and marble vases,
busts of Greek Gods and Roman senators tended to be the biggest available. So far
as paintings were concerned, those we know about were mostly copies of portraits
of English and European royalty, and he does not seem to have owned many
pictures of any quality, although he did have a seascape in oils by Richard Parkes
Bonnington. Bonnington was born at Arnold near Nottingham and had enjoyed
great success in France, winning a gold medal at the Salon in 1824; it could be that

3. J. C. Loudon, *The Gardener's Magazine* (July and November, 1840).

Gregory was here patronizing a local boy whom he had known for some years.[4] Gregory remained unmarried and had no interest in the normal occupations of the English country gentleman: hunting, shooting, and entertaining friends and neighbors on a grand scale. If fact, he enjoyed his privacy like William Beckford at Fonthill. Beckford and Horace Walpole, at a somewhat earlier date, afford an interesting parallel to Gregory's activities. Both were collectors on a grand scale, both expanded an initial interest in their own genealogy into a general study of medieval times and architecture, and both, when they were obliged to build to house their collections, chose to do so in the Gothic style. Walpole set about the gradual transformation of the old house at Strawberry Hill into a Gothic villa. Beckford, a much richer man and more reclusive, built a wall around his estate at Fonthill and then employed James Wyatt to design him the immensely picturesque abbey, which was developed over a period of years from a place where picnic dinners could be eaten into a vast cruciform building intended to have a spire rivaling that of Salisbury Cathedral. It was no doubt the abbey that Gilbert Scott found so absurd. All three men were bibliophiles; Walpole's and Beckford's libraries are well recorded, and Gregory's was impressive enough for Loudon to devote a page or so to listing the titles of some: "The library contains an admirable collection of books on architecture and ancient gardening, more especially foreign works on these subjects." Gregory, with no children and not caring much for the heir upon whom his estates were entailed, and probably with most of his treasures still in their crates, resolved in 1822 to build a new mansion house in the style of the period of James I. When, nine years later, he chose the architect, he found in Salvin one whose knowledge of domestic architecture of that time was equal to the task.

He already had three houses: Harlaxton Old Manor, of which two ranges had collapsed and which had not been lived in since his grandmother's death; Rempstone Hall, a house of little importance, which he let; and Hungerton Hall, which he made his home for the period when his grand new house was under construction, it being conveniently near the site he had chosen on his Harlaxton estate. Harlaxton was selected for its fine views of the Vale of Belvoir and of four neighboring churches, despite the Gregory family's longer connection with their Nottinghamshire properties and his own with that county, of which he had been High Sheriff in 1825. This duty behind him, and having accumulated sufficient funds to begin building, Gregory made more material preparations by leasing a local brickyard and kiln to a Stamford brickmaker for six years beginning June 24, 1826, during which period he was to be supplied with 400,000 bricks each season and as many other bricks and tiles as he might require. These were for the foundations, drains, and core of the building, which was to be faced with Ancaster stone.[5]

When Burke called on Gregory at Harlaxton in 1853, he was told that the owner had been his own architect and had planned and executed everything under his own superintendence. However, Gregory was a sick man by this time and may not have been disposed to be as forthcoming on the subject as he had been with

4. Probate of the will and codicils of Gregory Gregory, dated August 1, 1854. Christie, Manson & Woods Sale Catalogue, June 17, 1878, gives details of such of the Gregory heirlooms as were then sold.
5. Lincolnshire Archives Office, Ref. 1 P.G./2/1/28/2.

30. Harlaxton Manor, pencil perspective.

Loudon in 1840.[6] He had told Loudon that he had decided on the style in 1822, which shows him to have been very much ahead of architectural thinking of that time, and as so little had been published at that date on medieval domestic architecture, he visited houses of his chosen period throughout the country. Having settled its main characteristics to his own satisfaction and decided what details could be borrowed from existing buildings or from engravings of those that had been demolished, he employed Salvin "to embody [his] ideas in such detail as to fit them for the practical builder."[7] He had in fact inspected Elizabethan and Jacobean houses indiscriminately, and Harlaxton is, as might be expected, a composite of architectural features of the late sixteenth and early seventeenth centuries.

The evolution of Salvin's design for Harlaxton may be reconstructed through a series of perspectives that have fortunately been preserved (Fig. 30). The first in the sequence shows a treatment of the entrance facade, which is already quite close to its final form. A house built around courtyards, as many were in the Elizabethan period, had even then been recognized as inconvenient, and the sequences of interconnecting rooms lacking in privacy; the alternatives adopted were either a rectangular core with angle towers, like Wollaton and Blickling, or a house with an H or E plan: a cross-range with wings projecting forward, or both forward and to the rear, usually with the main entrance set in a central bay or tower rising the full height of the building. In the drawing it can be seen that Harlaxton was to be a rather irregular H in plan, with an attached range one bay wide on the garden front. Once again Salvin based the main entrance on that at Hengrave Hall, an oriel window between polygonal towers, which he had made a story higher than the model. Octagonal towers with ogival roofs stand at each corner of the building, and the projecting wings have shaped gables and great two-story bays. A central lantern tower is reminiscent of that at Hatfield. The courtyard is enclosed by a wrought-iron screen and a pair of single-story office ranges,

6. Sir John Bernard Burke, *A Visitation of Seats & Arms* (London: Colburn & Co., 1853.) Gregory died on June 15, 1854, of "Gout Exhaustion."
7. Loudon, *The Gardener's Magazine*. Gregory visited: Bramshill, Littlecote, Brereton, Hardwick, Hatfield, Knole, Cobham, Burghley, Castle Ashby, Deene Park, Rushton Hall, Kirby, Apethorpe, Wollaton, Blickling, Cowdray, Longleat, Westwood, and Temple Newsam.

31. Harlaxton Manor, pencil perspective.

and the fall in the ground to the right is clumsily dealt with by a buttressed retaining wall. A later attempt has the offices and the ironwork removed and the slope terraced at two levels (Fig. 31). A stable courtyard was to be entered through an arch at the left of the entrance court, and the oriel is now crowned by a triumphal arch motif similar to that on Northumberland House, but here free-standing between octagonal cupolas with ogival roofs.[8] The garden front still extends a bay but now has a central entrance porch and bay based on that at Harlaxton Old Manor.

Salvin's final design is shown in four very fine perspectives in watercolor, which are no doubt the work of James Deason, who had joined Salvin's office by this time, and G. A. Fripp, the same pair who painted the perspective of Scotney Castle for the Royal Academy Exhibition in 1838 (Figs. 32, 33, 34, 35). These show the entrance court enclosed by the garden wall rescued from Harlaxton Old Manor, entered through a single-story gatehouse and with a pair of garden houses like those at Montacute placed at the angles. Gatehouse and gazebos all bear armorial achievements decoratively framed and pinnacled, which clearly owe their inspiration to seventeenth-century church monuments such as that of the Sandys family at Wickhamford in Worcestershire.[9] The stables still flank the courtyard, but the entrance front has now become symmetrical, the range on the garden front having been eliminated; that front now has three two-story bays, one with a central porch, and all of different design. At the rear the recessed central part has a massive chimney stack, and the oriel and other windows of the great hall set between projecting ranges are identical to those on the entrance facade. But these watercolors are also interesting for what they do not show: there is no conservatory, and the single-story and rather plain stables bear no resemblance to the large kitchen court and entrance archway that were built in their place.

Salvin's design is almost entirely lacking the Renaissance detail that is a feature

8. Dr. Jill Franklin (private communication) suggests Brereton as a source for the triumphal arch, particularly as the crenellated towers there originally bore another story with ogival roofs very like Harlaxton. At Brereton however, the arch is not free-standing.

9. I have to thank Dr. Franklin for drawing my attention to this.

32. Harlaxton Manor from the southwest, watercolor perspective.

33. Harlaxton Manor from the northwest, watercolor perspective.

34. Harlaxton Manor from the northeast, watercolor perspective.

35. Harlaxton Manor from the southeast, watercolor perspective.

of the Elizabethan and Jacobean prodigy houses upon which Harlaxton is modeled. Longleat, Burghley, Kirby, Wollaton, Bramshill, and Hatfield, to mention a
few of those visited by Gregory, all incorporate classical architectural details, used
not structurally but purely as decoration. Facades are articulated with columns,
half-columns, pilasters, and entablatures, the proper function of which is often
misunderstood. Balustrades, swags, and *putti* also appear, but Salvin's perspectives
and the north, south, and east elevations that he prepared in 1834 are, with certain
minor exceptions, purged of such ornaments[10] (Fig. 36). This simple pre-Renais-
sance style of Tudor used at Harlaxton comes from manors such as Montacute,
and indeed, the design of the entrance front owes much to this house (not mentioned by Gregory as one he had visited). It is the source for the longitudinal roof
ridge between shaped gables, the semicircular gables above the dormers, the full-
length figures in relief set between the windows of the third floor, and the strongly
projecting string courses that mark the different floors. In Salvin's designs the
Italianate detail is restricted to the volutes and balustrade of the central tower,
which was in fact redesigned with a strapwork parapet before it was built, and the
roundels containing the busts of Roman emperors, which have a lengthy English
pedigree, having first appeared in Cardinal Wolsey's work at Hampton Court and
on the Holbein Gate in Whitehall. The other elevations are quite innocent of
classical detail.

Gregory had spent ten years planning his house, and it was to take longer to
build. The lease of the brickyard ran until 1832, and Salvin seems to have been
first consulted in June 1831.[11] Building began in 1832; but Salvin continued to
amend his designs for the elevations, for the facades just described are curiously

10. Described as north, south, and east to agree with the titles on Salvin's drawings. His north is in fact
almost exactly northwest and was so orientated that Bottesford Church might form a terminal point to the
view down the entrance drive from the house. This orientation is so accurate that a line drawn on the
ordnance survey map extending the mile long drive cuts through the symbol for the church seven miles away.
11. Norwich Cathedral MSS, Salvin correspondence, June 1, 1831.

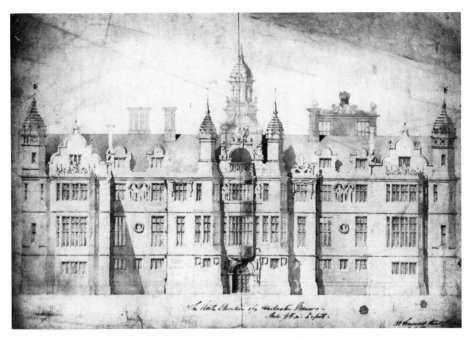

36. Harlaxton Manor, elevation of entrance front, pencil and wash.

late in the sequence of drawings, as they are numbered 102, 103, and 104 and are dated January 25, 1834. Work was well under way by that year; on May 4 Richard Watson of Rockingham Castle rode over to see his friend and to find out how things were going and wrote in his diary, "Harlaxton is wonderful, such a comfort-able and such a magnificent house." When Watson restored his castle four years later, Salvin was the architect employed.[12] The central clocktower was completed by February 26, 1836, when Gregory entertained his workmen, giving them a dinner at the Golden Lion in Harlaxton village. An account of the proceedings was published in the *Lincolnshire Chronicle,* which reported that the work had been in progress for four years and that two-thirds of the house had been built. The scaffolding that encased the tower was decorated with flags borrowed from the Corporation of Grantham; Gregory made a speech and was cheered three times three and one more. A procession then formed of the gatekeeper, watchman, the postboy, boys, masons, carpenters, bricklayers, stone sawyers, and laborers, all bearing the tools of their trade. William Weare, the Clerk of Works, who later supervised the building of Scotney Castle, marched with local tradesmen from the building site to the village, where he made a speech thanking Gregory for his generosity; at that time Weare expressed a hope that the building would be com-pleted in two years, but before that period of time had elapsed, both Weare and Salvin had been dismissed.

In 1838 the Reverend T. F. Dibdin, D.D., published *A Biographical, Antiquarian and Picturesque Tour through the Northern Counties of England and Scotland,* and the newly founded *Civil Engineer and Architects Journal* quoted his remarks on Harlaxton, which concluded: "Mr. Gregory has the *rare* merit of being chiefly his own architect, with

12. The Diaries of Richard Watson, vol. 2. Corby, Rockingham Castle MSS.

a thorough knowledge of the business in hand. Now and then, however, it is said that Mr. Blore whispers in his ear." The reviewer corrected this by stating that "we know that although both Mr. Blore and Mr. Salvin have been employed by him, Mr. Burn of Edinburgh, is the gentleman now engaged." In the next issue it is plain that either Salvin or a friend of his had seen the review and protested, and a correction of the doctor's errors and omissions was promised for the next issue. When the matter was taken up again, it was obvious that the writer had been to Salvin's office, been shown the designs and probably the Deason and Fripp perspectives, and had been quite bowled over. There is an enthusiastic description of the entrance front and of the plan "notwithstanding that it is in a style to which, as a style, we are by no means partial, we are free to confess that it is infinitely more to our taste than almost any other specimen of it we are acquainted with." The authorship of the design is then placed beyond doubt. Blore was only consulted. "The architect originally employed, when the building was commenced in 1832, was Mr. Salvin; and although the execution of the work has since been committed to other hands, his designs have been adhered to . . . and Mr. Burn, who was afterwards engaged to complete the edifice, had only to erect what remained to be done, in strict conformity with that half or portion which had been built by Mr. Salvin."[13]

No reason is given for the switch to Burn, who was a very curious choice as a supervising architect, as his practice was run from Edinburgh. At the time he took over from Salvin he had received only two commissions in England. Edward Blore might have seemed a more likely choice, but as we know, he was an old friend of Salvin's and might have been more squeamish about taking over a major work by another architect, particularly as there must have been some unpleasantness involved. It seems most likely that the disagreement arose over Gregory's wish for major additions to the original plan, namely the large kitchen courtyard and the conservatory. Salvin has all the offices in the basement, and the removal of these to a separate courtyard, where they might be more conveniently arranged, corresponds with what we know of Burn's ideas on house planning. He had established a fashionable reputation as a planner of country houses, which Gregory would have known of; Gregory had already shown himself aware of architectural trends when he chose Tudor and Salvin to build it, and now he was following another. But even if we can credit Burn with the construction of this courtyard, the stables, and other outbuildings, it is clear that another personality has entered into the process of design.

What was put up under Salvin's supervision is clear from his drawings and from one of the many tracings made by the young John Loughborough Pearson when he was an assistant in Salvin's office in 1841. It is of the principal floor plan of Harlaxton, and on it Pearson has marked and made a note of what was erected under Salvin's direct supervision, which is the whole house, except the conservatory, including the main staircase and the screens passage of the great hall, but none of the service accommodation beyond this. There are no Salvin drawings for the kitchen courtyard or for the other buildings in the immediate proximity of the house, such as the courtyard pavilions, the summer house up the hill in the garden, the gatehouse down the drive, or the gateway on the main road. There are no Burn

13. *The Civil Engineer and Architects Journal* 1:392; 2:5, 39.

37. Harlaxton Manor,
the Cedar Staircase.

drawings whatsoever for Harlaxton, and if one considers his house at Stoke
Rochford, in the next parish, begun in 1839 and to some extent a pastiche of
Harlaxton, there must be considerable doubt as to whether the man responsible
for that could have possibly designed the Baroque courtyard pavilions, let alone
the interiors of the great hall or the Cedar Staircase (Fig. 37).

But it must also be said that there is no parallel in Salvin's work for this sort of
thing, and it may well be that he found himself here in a similar position to the one
he assumed at Alnwick Castle twenty years later, when, having restored a border
stronghold, he was given the job of supervising Italian craftsmen who produced
the most elaborate seicento interiors in imitation of those that the Duke of Northumberland had seen and admired in Rome. Gregory had in his library at
Hungerton Hall both Wendel Dietterlin's *Architectura und Austheilung der V Seulen* and
Variae Architecturae Formae by Vredeman de Vries.[14] Published respectively in
1594–1598 and 1601, both are pattern books for a style that combined north European strapwork with classical architectural details in the wildest possible manner.
If this sort of thing was to Gregory's taste, it was just what Salvin had not
provided, and it was probably at his instigation that Salvin spent five weeks in
Germany in 1835, that is, at just about the time when both might have been
expected to be giving serious thought to the decoration of the interiors.[15] His
journey took him to Munich and Nuremburg; in the former city he purchased a

14. Loudon, *The Gardener's Magazine.*
15. Norwich Castle MSS. Salvin to Revd. Preb. C. N. Wodehouse, September 1, 1835. He does not mention
Gregory but says, "A few days since I returned from a 5 weeks trip into Germany my object being to see the
new buildings at Munich. We ought to take shame to ourselves that the King of a small territory should so far
surpass us in taste."

copy of Karl von Graimberg's work *Heidelberger Schloss,* which contains engravings of that German Renaissance palace, and in the latter he would have seen the sculptured decorations of the Pellerhaus and the 1616 additions to the Town Hall. If he actually visited Heidelberg he would have found similar work on the facade of the Friedrichsbau, and this type of decoration, together with Dietterlin and de Vries, were the models for the next phase at Harlaxton.

But whatever Salvin saw on his journey, and however capable he might have been of assimilating these weird German designs, it seems unarguable that someone else was called in to execute, and to a large extent to provide designs for, the Harlaxton interiors. Salvin may well have recruited the craftsmen required in Bavaria, as there seems some doubt as to whether there was anyone in England who could have undertaken such a project at that time. The 1841 census is unfortunately too late to help here; there are no men with German names living in the vicinity, although it does reveal the presence of about twenty Scottish carpenters and plasterers, who were presumably part of Burn's workforce. There is not the slightest probability that Gregory designed his own interiors. Amateur architects lack the ability to think in three dimensions without a good deal of practice, and Gregory's only other possible architectural work is the decoration of Harlaxton village, which would not have sufficed.

Until some other evidence by way of drawings or documentation turns up, the identity of this other presence at Harlaxton and his relationship with Salvin and Burn remains unknown. But whatever intervention there may have been later by others, in the great reception rooms and in the placing of trophies and sculptured groups on Salvin's plain shaped gables, the plan is his and was regarded as unique at the time. If he had been of a less retiring disposition and had tolerated publication of his designs, a good deal might have been written about this house during his own lifetime. But as it happened, it was left to William Eden Nesfield when he was writing the obituary notice for *The Builder* to draw attention to Salvin's idiosyncratic arrangement of the main rooms in his great houses. Nesfield mentions Keele Hall, the mansion rebuilt by Salvin for Ralph Sneyd in 1855–1863; he called it one of the best-planned houses of its time and drew attention to the way in which it was adapted to the slope on which it stood. This good use of different levels was a singular feature of Salvin's major houses; it occurs at Thoresby, for example, and the scheme was worked out for the first time at Harlaxton. The site selected was halfway up the hill, and the approach was arranged so that the visitor proceeded from the gateway on the Grantham Road downhill and across a small lake by a stone bridge, then up a gentle rise through a stone gateway, through courtyard pavilions, to be confronted by the towering entrance facade, four stories high. The effective height is achieved by excavating the courtyard and adding the basement, not usually visible, to the other floors. This enabled him to devise a spectacular entrance; at Harlaxton, as at Alnwick and Thoresby, the front door leads into a relatively low, plain, and dark hall; from this the stairs lead up to the first floor and the principal rooms, and in each case the decoration of the staircases increases as one climbs higher. At Harlaxton, stone walls, stone trophies on a massive scale, and wrought iron strike a somber note that is dispelled at the first bend of the stair, when a very ornate Jacobean plaster ceiling with pendants comes into view; this is a foretaste of what is to come. From the landing, the great hall is reached through a

38. Harlaxton Manor,
the garden front.

39. Harlaxton Manor, view from the terraces.

screens passage, and from here one goes on to the Cedar Staircase hall, and then into the anteroom and dining room on the right, the Gold Morning Room on the left and the Tapestry Gallery straight ahead. The gallery windows and garden door open out onto the terrace; on the garden front the height of the building is only three stories and the scale more domestic than that of the entrance front (Fig. 38). At the rear the ground is again excavated, enhancing the height of the great hall and giving it more importance than those rooms in the wings to either side (Fig. 39). This opening up of the facades to the front and rear had the additional advantage of allowing light and air to the service accommodation in the basement without recourse to the unsatisfactory expedient of areas.

Gregory was able to move into his house some time before 1851, when the census records his presence there, attended by a staff consisting of a housekeeper and seven maids, a butler, two grooms and three footmen. He died three years later. For Salvin he had provided an opportunity to design a house on the grandest scale, and he had sent him on his first European tour; what Salvin saw then was shortly to be of the greatest use to him, as we shall see later. Losing this commission after eight years and parting with Gregory in who knows what disillusion and acrimony must have been a bitter blow. Harlaxton must have given Salvin some prestige, but not as much as he might have expected, and this was Gregory's doing; the latter was confessedly antisocial, and his park was closed to all but his closest friends and the most distinguished excursionists, such as the party from Belvoir, whom it might have indeed been difficult to keep out. This meant that there are few references to it in contemporary writings. One survives, however; although it was written ten years after Gregory died, it gives us some idea of what the house was like when all the Gregory heirlooms were still in place. W. G. Rogers, the carver, wrote to Ralph Sneyd of Keele Hall from Belton: "I . . . have turned the visit to a good account by spending a few hours at Harlaxstone Hall (G. Gregory) whom I knew 30 or 40 years past—such a marvelous collection of marbles jaspers Cabinets porcelain of fabulous value Buhl with Gouthier mountings, rare sculptures delicate carvings costly lac and Italian furniture tapestries all in glorious and unreadable confusion, but the lack of symetry [*sic*] is made up by the exquisite beauty of each fragment and help make up a wonderful whole."[16] Here we must leave Harlaxton.

Salvin was a fairly persistent and unsuccessful entrant in architectural competitions until 1844, when he won, and was quite unfairly denied, the commission to rebuild the Carlton Club House. Competitions and exhibiting at the Royal Academy were two certain ways in which a young architect could make himself better known. Salvin's "Design for an Exchange, North of England" was shown at the Royal Academy in 1825 and may well have been for either the Leeds Commercial Buildings, which were built by John Clark of Edinburgh in 1826–1829, or for the Corn Exchange in Leeds, put up by Samuel Chapman of Leeds. However, there is no record now of a competition for either building, apart from the reference in the Barry biography. His designs for the refitting of Magdalen College Chapel have already been described; here he lost to L. N. Cottingham, whose restoration and removal of James Wyatt's classical furnishings won the praise of Pugin: "I can truly say [it] is one of the most beautiful specimens of modern design that I have ever seen, and executed both in wood and stone in the best manner." It was no disgrace to be defeated by a design that Pugin thought so well of.[17] After this he entered no competitions for six years; indeed he must have been very much occupied with the works at Mamhead, Moreby Hall, and Harlaxton, to which were increasingly added other smaller commissions; but in 1834 he made another attempt when the University of Cambridge decided that something really had to be done about the Fitzwilliam Bequest.

16. Keele University Library, Sneyd MSS, S 2765.
17. Benjamin Ferrey, *Recollections of A. W. N. Pugin* (London: Edward Stamford, 1861), p. 86.

Viscount Fitzwilliam had died in 1816 and left paintings, engravings, a library, and the sum of £100,000 in New South Seas Annuities for the establishment and building of a museum for the university. Difficulties over a suitable site were not resolved until 1834, and on July 21 that year the syndicate advertised for architects to submit, without fee, plans and estimates for a building in which the Fitzwilliam and other collections owned by the university could be displayed. It was stipulated that as only the middle part of the site would be available the following year, that on either side being still subject to long leases or encumbered by buildings, the museum was to be so designed that the center part could be built first; this was not to exceed the sum of £40,000. All entries were to be in by November, although this was later extended to April 1835. The syndicate received thirty-six sets of drawings, which were exhibited at the Pitt Press; in October it was announced that George Basevi was the winner with a handsome classical design. Salvin's was Gothic.

Once again it is a tracing by Pearson that records, very roughly, what Salvin proposed. The entrance front on Trumpington Street was to be a long, low range with the doorway set off to the right under a tower that was to be square for three stories, octagonal for two, and topped by a spire. On the left there was to be an octagonal pavilion with a pointed roof, lancet windows, and buttresses, which is derived from Salvin's design for the vestry of St. John's Church, Keswick. There are numbers of pointed windows filled with tracery, gables with pinnacles and finials, a pierced parapet, oriels of different shapes, and a skyline broken with tabernacles and statues. There is both a lack of cohesion and a touch of wildness in the way all these architectural features are assembled, but Pearson's tracing is a very hurried effort, and the original may not have looked quite so odd. Before the closing date for the Fitzwilliam Competition, the great fire of the night of October 16, 1834, gave rise to another, which no architect of any ambition could afford to ignore.

The election campaign for the first Parliament to be assembled after the passing of the Reform Bill was fought in October and November 1832, and when the Members took their seats for the first parliamentary session, they found themselves quite inadequately housed in a group of buildings put up at a variety of periods. Five hundred and thirteen members of the Commons had sat in St. Stephen's Chapel since the sixteenth century. It had been altered by Wren in 1692, and again in 1706 when the Act of Union had added forty-five Scots members to their number; the Lords, one hundred and eight English and sixteen Scots, had their own chamber in Parliament House, but this became too small after union with Ireland added thirty-two Irish Peers, and they were obliged to move into the old Court of Requests. One hundred Irish members of the Commons were accommodated by cutting away part of the walls of St. Stephen's, mutilating the fourteenth-century wall paintings. Overcrowding was acute. Wyatt and Soane had both built additions, but to little advantage. As soon as it had assembled, the newly reformed Parliament had elected a Select Committee chaired by the Radical Joseph Hume, which heard evidence from thirteen architects, nearly all of whom advised that the old Palace be pulled down and entirely new buildings be erected, in order to accommodate properly not only the members of both houses, but also interested members of the public, and of course the press. Ventilation and acoustics were considered, and designs by Decimus Burton, James Savage, Sir John

Soane, Francis Goodwin, and others were examined. And there matters stood on October 16 when two Irish laborers burning wooden tallies started the fire that destroyed the major part of the Palace of Westminster, including both the House of Commons and the House of Lords.

The first expedient was to patch up what little remained for immediate use. Sir Robert Smirke, who had worked for the old Board of Works, reroofed the House of Lords for the use of the Commons, and the Lords moved into the Painted Chamber; he was then instructed to prepare plans for the rebuilding of the whole of the Palace, which he did, producing a design in a very plain and dim Gothic. Smirke's architecture was not generally admired; the appointment smacked of interest and was quite at variance with the principles of the new reformed Parliament. Joseph Hume was in favor of the selection of an architect by competition; so was the Tory Sir Edward Cust, and in this they were supported by Members of all parties. Another Select Committee, for Rebuilding the Houses of Parliament, was appointed in March 1835, and on June 5 it published the terms of a competition by which the architect of the new Palace would be chosen. It was to be open to all; the style was to be Gothic or Elizabethan; entries were to be on a scale of twenty feet to one inch and in monochrome; Westminster Hall was to be preserved, and the accommodation required would be specified and a plan issued to each competitor. Three perspectives from viewpoints in Abingdon Street, Parliament Street, and the Surrey side of Westminster Bridge would be allowed, but no models. No estimates were required, and indeed there would scarcely have been time to prepare them, as all entries were to be in by November 1, although the closing date was extended later to December 1. A commission of amateurs with architectural knowledge would choose a minimum of three and a maximum of five designs from which the winner would be selected, and these would earn a premium of £500 each; if the winner was not entrusted with the building work, he would receive an additional £1000.

The commissioners announced their decision at the end of January; the chosen designs were those of J. C. Buckler, David Hamilton, and William Railton. Charles Barry, of course, was the winner. There had been ninety-seven entries in all, very few of which have survived. After the adjudication, the unsuccessful competitors met at the Thatched House Tavern and resolved that all the entries should be put on exhibition. J. C. Loudon's *The Architectural Magazine* devoted many pages to contributions, criticizing the choice of style; the fact that the commissioners' names had been revealed, and that they were therefore theoretically open to lobbying; the conduct of the competition in general and reviews of the designs.[18] Two such articles were "Remarks on the Unsuccessful Designs for the New Houses of Parliament" by "B," and "Scraps of Criticism on the Designs for the Houses of Parliament" by "Candidus" (the pen-name of W. H. Leeds); these and a review in *The Gentleman's Magazine* make it plain that Salvin's designs were particularly noticed[19] (Fig. 40). The first article comments, "Britton's *Antiquities of Great Britain* appears to have been ransacked for precedents by the competing artists," which was scarcely surprising, as Britton's volumes were virtually the only published source for domestic architecture of the required period, most research and specula-

18. *The Architectural Magazine* (May 1836): 201; (July 1836): 298.
19. *The Gentleman's Magazine* (1836) 1 :523.

40. The Palace of Westminster, view from Westminster Bridge, pen and ink perspective.

tion by that date having been confined to the study of the development of ecclesiastical Gothic. Of the many books that were to be published on Tudor architecture before the mid-century, only three appeared in time to aid the competitors.[20] This article goes on to mention fifteen entries, fairly briefly, and Salvin's design is spoken of as possessing "a good deal of originality, and some grandeur, it would look infinitely better as a state prison or hospital, than as a senate house: there are some picturesque parts about it, and it is in a style that would suit some moderate size dwelling, but hardly a public building, and more especially one like that in question." Considering the model Salvin had taken for his design, this was a very curious judgment. Candidus discusses only six entries, namely Barry's, those of the premium winners (Hamilton, Buckler, and Railton), Rhind's, and Salvin's, from which one must suppose that Salvin's was one of the more outstanding among the failures. This is confirmed by Eastlake, who was writing nearly forty years later; he recalled: "Among the outsiders whose plans found favour may be mentioned Rhind, who had apparently borrowed his details from the architecture of Hatfield, and Salvin, whose towers were suggestive of Heriot's Hospital," a model that was also presumed by *The Gentleman's Magazine*. Candidus was nearer the mark in identifying a Continental source, which he supposed to be Flemish, or perhaps German: "It has been said to resemble a prison, but it has far more the air of being a vast 'hostellerie,' of the same class as those which figure so conspicuously in the 'grande Place' of many Flemish and Italiantowns."

At the time the competition was announced, Salvin was probably the only architect actually to be engaged in putting up a really large Elizabethan house. For this reason he would have been more than aware that an attempt to expand this kind of building into something of the size required for Parliament was only likely to be achieved by putting up a conglomerate of separate buildings, as in the design submitted by J. Gillespie Graham, or by the repetition of a series of features, as in that of Buckler.[21] There was no surviving Tudor palace. We know that Barry sought a model in Belgian town halls and that he crossed the Channel to study them, particularly those at Brussels and Louvain; but little of this research appears

20. They were: T. F. Hunt, *Exemplars of Tudor Architecture adapted to Modern Habitations* (London: Longman, Rees, 1830); T. H. Clarke, *The Domestic Architecture of the Reigns of Queen Elizabeth and James I* (London: n.p., 1833); J. Hakewill, *An Attempt to Determine the exact Character of Elizabethan Architecture* (London, n.p., 1835).

21. For details of the competition and the various entries, see *The Houses of Parliament*, ed. M. H. Port (New Haven and London: Yale University Press, 1976).

in his prizewinning design. No doubt some of the other competitors also made a trip to Europe. What there was in this country, which we can assume that Salvin knew well, was the Joris Hoefnagel drawing of Nonesuch Palace in the British Museum.[22] This primitive sketch cannot have been of much practical help, but it may have suggested to him the use of massive corner towers and complicated gables set in the roofs of the ranges between. At this point, in late July, Salvin went on his trip to Germany; he would have had the competition very much in mind, whatever he may have been doing for Gregory, and he made a point of looking at the new civic buildings put up by Ludwig I in Munich. These he admired, but as they were classical in design they had little relevance in his search for a model; it was on his return journey that he came across the building that was to provide him with the pattern for his Palace of Westminster design (Fig. 41).

The Palace of Aschaffenburg had been built by George Ridinger of Strasbourg for the Archbishop of Mainz in 1605–1614, and it is clearly from this building that Salvin took his five huge towers, four at the angles of the embankment facade and the fifth, more elaborate in design, dominating the central courtyard and containing the Sovereign's Entrance. As at Aschaffenburg, the towers are square in plan, have their stories strongly marked by string courses, and have a projecting balcony and balustrade, above which there is a further square story before the corners are broached into an octagonal plan, all topped by ogival cupolas and vanes. The elaborate window frames and dormer gables and the heavy quoins are all copied from the German original. No plan of Salvin's proposed Palace has survived; indeed all we have are the three perspectives allowed by the rules of the competition. However, it does seem from these that he did not make the best use of the ground available, as did, for example, Barry (Fig. 42). Old Palace Yard has been enormously enlarged by stripping away the old Court of Common Pleas and adjacent buildings to reveal four bays of St. Stephen's Chapel; abutting and concealing the fifth is a nine-bay block with a recessed center flanked by turrets. The Lords were to enter through a triple arched loggia. The west end of Westminster Hall has also been cleared of later additions and given a new porch, and it is interesting to see that Salvin not only intended to keep the Royal Courts of Justice on the north side of the hall, which had survived the fire, but that he proposed to rebuild the part that had been damaged to match, Palladian windows and all. On New Palace Yard he duplicated on the south of the hall the Gothic screen that had replaced Soane's neoclassical facade (Fig. 43). Beyond this was to lie the House of Commons, appropriately simpler in design than the Lords, but with a similar three-bay entrance loggia with an oriel above. These designs are, so far as the new buildings on the north are concerned, sensible and not extravagant. The fireworks are all reserved for the terrific design of the front on the River Thames.

Salvin did not enter the competition that was announced by the Gresham Trustees after the Royal Exchange burned down in 1838 and thus had no part in the confusion and chicanery that led eventually to a noncompetitor, William Tite, obtaining the commission through influence. C. R. Cockerell had produced a splendid design but had been outmaneuvered; he was, however, to succeed with his designs for the Ashmolean Museum.

22. "Nonesuch Palace," by Joris Hoefnagel, 1568, British Museum Print Room.

41. Aschaffenburg, Unterfranken, view of the Schloss.

42. The Palace of Westminster, view from Abingdon Street, pen and ink perspective.

43. The Palace of Westminster, view from Parliament Street, pen and ink perspective.

The situation at Oxford was somewhat similar to that at Cambridge five years earlier. The university had been given certain works of art and had no building in which to house them. In July 1839 a competition was advertised for designs for the Taylor and Randolph Building, which was to house the Taylorian Institute, the Arundel Marbles, and such other collections as the university might own. The institute and galleries were to be kept separate, but it was hoped that their buildings might be treated as a whole. Twenty-seven entries had been received by the time the competition closed in October, but of the architects who submitted these only Cockerell, James Elmes, T. L. Donaldson, and Salvin were of national reputation, the rest being, probably justifiably, unknown. By November five entries had been selected for further consideration: those of Cockerell, George Mair and E. H. Brown, John Plowman, Henry Hakewill, and Salvin.[23] At this stage the competition committee decided they needed professional help and called upon Sir Robert Smirke to advise as to "The Practicability, Advisableness, Durability and probable Amount of expense" of each design. Smirke reported in December strongly in favor of Cockerell, not only for his beautiful design but also for the adequate lighting, which was obtained by arranging the building around a courtyard opening into Beaumont Street. Mair and Brown's design in neo-Greek was too big for the site and poorly lit; Plowman's had "more of the character of a distinguished residence, rather than of a Collegiate Establishment." Hakewill's had "no striking character of design" and was poorly lit. Salvin's was badly drawn: "These drawings represent the designs for the exterior of the Buildings in an unfavourable manner, being covered with a uniform dark tint which obscures the details and deprives them of the relief and effect that would probably be given by the bold projecting cornices and other parts of the two fronts." Salvin had designed his building around a courtyard, but to the rear, where it might at some future time be darkened by adjoining buildings; Smirke also complained about steps in the corridors and deficient lighting of these. Cockerell won, and Plowman was placed second. Despite all the criticism, Salvin thought well of his design, to the extent of having a lithograph made of his perspective (Fig. 44). He had a portfolio of such things, mostly of his ecclesiastical works like St. John's Church, Keswick, Holy Sepulchre, and Arley Hall Chapel, which he distributed to his prospective clients. He gave a print of his Ashmolean design to Edward Hussey. This may have been mishandled in its transfer to stone, but as it stands it is a singularly ham-fisted essay in the Palladian manner. Why he abandoned his preferred Gothic in Oxford of all places cannot now be known, but there are two possible explanations: he had seen a classical design chosen for the Fitzwilliam Museum, and in Oxford the major exhibits to be housed were the Arundel Marbles, and he may have had some doubts as to how they would look in a Gothic building. In any event, it was a style to which he was not accustomed, and it is employed here with a number of solecisms, such as the entablature of a giant order breaking forward above the windows, and not above the pilasters and columns where it might be acceptable.

Salvin won the next two competitions that he entered. The first, in 1843, was for a new church at Torquay, which will be described later. There were seventeen entries for this, and he was chosen out of a short list of four, which included Wyatt

23. Oxford, Bodleian Library; Oxford University Archives TL/M/1/1.

44. The Ashmolean Museum, lithograph perspective.

and Brandon. This church became a disappointment and a worry due to the Building Committee's inability to raise requisite funds, and matters dragged on until 1857, when his account was finally paid. A year after this yet another was announced, for the Carlton Club House, and the events that ensued here were almost as extraordinary as those attending the selection of the architect for the Royal Exchange. The club's premises stood on the corner of Pall Mall and Carlton Gardens. In 1844 the members decided to purchase two adjoining houses in Pall Mall and thus enlarge their building. A general meeting held in March resolved that fourteen architects be invited to submit plans and elevations; they were chosen there and then: Barry, Sidney Smirke, Basevi, Philip Hardwick, Cockerell, Lee and Bury, Pugin, Railton, Blore, M. D. Wyatt, Poynter, Hopper, and Salvin. The entries were to be in by May 1. Architects, however, were becoming increasingly disenchanted with competitions, and they resented the fact that the winners often failed to receive instructions to put up the building concerned. Many of those invited declined to compete; only eight sent in plans, and the club received four unsolicited entries. A committee consisting of the Marquess of Salisbury, Henry Gally Kight, and Henry Hope was appointed to report to the members, which they did on May 11. None of the committee was better than amateurs, and their somewhat naïve approach was demonstrated by their division of the entries into three classes, depending upon the proposed position of the front door, whether centrally placed in Pall Mall, in Carlton Gardens, or in Pall Mall but off-center. There was only one entry in the last class, that of Salvin, who was awarded by ballot the first premium of £200. Thomas Hopper came second with a design based upon that of the Banqueting House in Whitehall. Whatever may have been the shortcomings in presentation of Salvin's Ashmolean design, he now produced a most handsome set of plans and elevations and a quite stunning perspective, which seems again to be the work of Deason and Fripp (Fig. 45). It is full-blooded Jacobean, with lots of strapwork and Wollaton towers and with some recollections of the trip to Germany. The more-than-life-sized figures in shell niches are derived from those on the Ottheinrichsbau at Heidelberg, and the elaborate entrance porch closely follows the entrance to the first floor of the palace, which is illustrated in Von Graimberg. But the committee still felt some doubt as to whether such a design was suitable for the position it was to occupy in Pall Mall,

45. The Carlton Club, pen and wash perspective.

and whether it would withstand the corrosive atmosphere of coal-fired London. They conceded that it gave the opportunity to divide rooms of inconvenient width or breadth and that it allowed windows to be inserted in bays without spoiling the elevations. But they objected to the arrangement of the waiting rooms, the shape of the staircase, and the position of the entrance, which was also disliked by the owner of the adjoining house. Their report concluded with the extraordinary statement that "the Committee desire to observe that the Club, having acquired the property of these two plans, are entitled, if they should think fit, to make use of them, without employing either Mr. Salvin or Mr. Hopper as their architect, which is perfectly understood by these gentlemen." This was contrary to professional practice, and nothing of the sort had been suggested in the instructions to competitors or the correspondence. Neither Salvin nor Hopper was given the opportunity to amend his scheme to meet the committee's objections. By this time canvassing was proceeding on behalf of some of the unsuccessful entrants to such an effect that club members were persuaded to set aside entirely the results of the competition and to choose an architect by ballot. The outcome of this was that Henry Roberts, Nelson, Beazeley, and Blore got 1 vote each; Philip Hardwick 2; Railton 4; Burn 5; Cockerell 6; Taylor 9; Hopper 57; Salvin 89; Barry 210; Basevi and Smirke 220. The respective architects of the Reform and Conservative Club Houses had to all intents and purposes fought it out alone.[24]

Three years later, in 1847, the members of another London club also decided to build themselves a new club house. The Army and Navy was in St. James's Square, and after buying an adjoining site they announced an open competition to

24. Salvin's letter to the committee is in the Drawings Collection of the British Architectural Library. He apologizes for incomplete drawings due to lack of time, and estimates a cost of £31,800. Other estimates varied from £22,000 to £40,000. The full story is told in *The Builder* (May 4, 1844, and May 11, 1845).

be judged by a committee of members with prizes of £200 for the winner and £100 for the runner-up. After the Carlton Club fiasco, it is astonishing that Salvin should have ventured to compete again. He did, however, and was one of the sixty-nine whose entries were hung in the club's rooms in late April. The winner was George Tattersall, who is probably better known as a sporting artist, and second was an obscure partnership, F. Fowler and Fisk. There had already been reports in *The Builder* that a member of the club's committee had most improperly visited the offices of certain of the competitors and had had to be asked to step down; now further lobbying took place, and as in the case of the Carlton, the result of the competition was set aside.[25] The six architects who had mustered the most votes were each asked to send in fresh designs; they were G. Somers Clarke, F. Fowler and Fisk, C. O. Parnell and Alfred Smith, H. B. Richardson, Sydney Smirke, and George Tattersall. At this point Somers Clarke had some sort of accident and Salvin took his place, submitting a classical design that was not successful. The winners were Parnell and Smith, and again Salvin's not inconsiderable labor in preparing two sets of designs was thrown away. The prestige of being the architect of one of these near-palaces whose members held great political power must have been the factor that induced Salvin and so many others to compete, but now he plainly decided that the game was not worth the candle. He never entered another competition.

25. *The Builder* (January 2, May 8, June 12, 1847).

5

Life at Finchley

The Salvins lived a happy rural life at Finchley. They took the lease of Elm
House at East End on November 31, 1833; Salvin had wished to buy the freehold,
but this proved impossible, so he took a lease for sixty years at an annual rent of
£100 and no premium. It is a measure of the extent to which Finchley was being
colonized by those whose business was in London that, when Salvin wanted to sell
the remainder of his lease in 1867, he was able to obtain the sum of £850.[1]

Elm House was rechristened Elmhurst. It was small, badly built, and in sad
need of repair, but it had a large garden, stables and coach houses, ten acres of
paddocks enclosed in a quickset hedge, and views over a local beauty spot, Bishop
Wood. It was also convenient for the London omnibus. Into it moved the family,
which at first consisted of Salvin, Anne, and the two eldest children. The two
youngest, Eliza Anne and Osbert, arrived shortly after the move, and Miss Caldecleugh was then summoned from Brancepeth. The General and old Mrs. Salvin
came to live with them; Salvin's half-sister, Mrs. Anne de Lisle, was a constant
visitor; and various members of the Nesfield family often came for stays of a month
or more. The house had to be put in good order at the start; a new drawing room
and dining room were added, the garden was taken in hand, and overhanging
trees were cut back, all during the summer of 1834 when the family went to stay at
Windsor and Virginia Water to get away from the builders, who finally departed
in December. The new rooms were inaugurated with a theatrical evening and a
performance of "The Scapegoat" before family, friends, and the new neighbors.[2]

Salvin soon began to buy other pieces of land in the neighborhood, and he and
William Nesfield bought adjoining plots in Fortis Green Road, on which they built
a pair of semidetached houses designed by Salvin in the Italian villa style. Nesfield
laid out the grounds, landscaping the formal gardens near the houses as a single
unit and organizing a small sheep-rearing enterprise in the meadow beyond.
Loudon saw this in 1838 and was so impressed that he published an illustrated
article: "Fortis Green, Muswell Hill, The Villa of W. A. Nesfield, Esq., . . . we
prevailed upon him . . . to furnish us with an account of his mode of manag-
ing. . . . Sheep are kept at Fortis Green, in preference to a cow, because the family
is small, and, the neighborhood abounding in farms, the supply of milk and butter
is cheaper than were it the produce of three acres, considering the constant attendance, risk and trouble incidental in cow-keeping; whereas sheep are very
ornamental, and give no trouble worth naming."[3] Salvin, however, did keep a cow

1. Durham University Library, Salvin MSS.
2. Eliza Anne Salvin, *Reminiscences and Notes of Bye-Gone Years.* London Borough of Barnet Library Services.
MSS. Acc. 6787/7.
3. J. C. Loudon, *The Gardener's Magazine* (February 1840).

for his family's milk and butter supplies and was engaged in farming activities on a somewhat larger scale than those of Nesfield. Some deeds relating to his land transactions have survived, and from these it appears that he bought and then sold for building various fields and still had more than fifty-eight acres there in 1878, long after he had left the district. These he sold to the Ecclesiastical Commissioners. Eliza Anne wrote: "My father had bought a good deal of land in the neighborhood. He had built two houses, one rented to Mr. Ewart, the other often changed occupants. He also had a farm near the High Road, but as he knew nothing about farming and had to trust the bailiff, it was no doubt an expensive amusement." Still, they obviously all enjoyed it. Eliza's diary, written when she was about eight years old, records family outings: "We took a long walk and saw all Papa's lambs"; and later: "We went also to see Papa's bull at Fortis Green."

Salvin let his villa there, but Nesfield lived in his until he became the Drawing Master at Eton College. He had married Emma Anne Markham in July 1833 and spent a brief honeymoon touring Somerset and Herefordshire on the tops of various coaches. "My wife went outside the whole way, and it rained every day and what is lucky she prefers it [i.e., the outside]."[4] They then posted to Brancepeth to see old Mrs. Nesfield. The rector had died in 1828, but arrangements had been made for her to continue to live at the rectory, and Salvin had taken over the management of the Nesfield finances. There was a certain improvidence about all the Nesfields where money was concerned; Mrs. Nesfield was on this occasion very short, and William had only £10 to see him through to Christmas; there was to be trouble later with Charles. Now Salvin was appealed to for immediate help; he already handled their investments and dividends through his own banking account at Hoares and remitted cash as required to the Nesfields' bankers in Durham.[5]

The period up to 1850 saw Salvin's practice expand rapidly. Apart from the continuing work at Mamhead, Moreby Hall, and Harlaxton, he received more than forty-five commissions for substantial alterations and additions to country houses, for clients who were fairly evenly divided between the aristocracy and the landed gentry, with a few exceptions such as the banker Daniel Gurney, and Robert Field, who was a stockbroker. The five new houses that he built in the 1830s were in two cases for landed gentry, one for an Irish Peer who had married an English heiress, one for a minor member of the royal family, and one for his sister-in-law. His only new house in the 1840s was Peckforton Castle, a truly remarkable effort, which is discussed later. He had been entrusted with the rearrangement and restoration of Norwich Cathedral choir and designed twenty-five new churches. His famous restoration of Holy Sepulchre Cambridge for the Cambridge Camden Society led to a lucrative practice in church restorations. He carried out urgent repairs at Newark, Carisbrooke, and Caernarvon Castles, had converted Durham Castle Keep into accommodation for students, and built other lodgings there for the newly founded university. He was exceedingly busy.

---

4. Salvin MSS.

5. Hoares Bank in Fleet Street have preserved all their clients' account ledgers for the nineteenth century, from which we see that Salvin opened an account there on February 19, 1827, with a deposit of £834, which was only closed on his death. Every transaction is recorded, but these are surprisingly unhelpful for the purposes of architectural history.

His office remained at 32 Somerset Street until 1844, when he moved first to 21 Savile Row, and again in 1852 to 30 Argyle Street, since demolished to make way for Sir Henry Tanner's department store for Dickens & Jones. Here he stayed until 1862, when he assigned the remainder of his lease to his nephew, William Eden Nesfield, who shared an office with Richard Norman Shaw. Salvin, who had by then left Elmhurst and moved to 11 Hanover Terrace, Regent's Park, practiced partly from his home and partly from 4 Adam Street, which remained his London office until he retired. He traveled into town from Finchley by horse-drawn omnibus, apart from those times when he was off into the country visiting his works in hand, and he did not return home until late evening. His letters give some idea of the extent of his journeys, written as they are from all parts and giving instructions as to where correspondence might be directed to him next. Early in his career he refers constantly to the times of coaches, and then increasingly to Bradshaw as the railway network was built up. Eliza's notes and diaries are full of his comings and goings: "My father was so much taken up with his business and so frequently away from home that more of the care of the family fell to my mother's share than usual." After a holiday in Tenby: "Our return to London was accomplished with greater ease—Mama managed everything as she was accustomed to do, my father being so constantly away on business." This continues throughout the 1830s: "Papa went at the same time and will not return until the day after tomorrow"; "Papa has been staying at Mamhead and has not returned"; and "Papa went this morning to Oxford—as soon as he came home he came into us at Mr. Herring's [a neighbor] we were much surprised at seeing him as we did not expect him until 12 o'clock." When he was actually in the office the pressure was considerable, with designs to be made, working drawings to check, and many appointments. A letter excusing some delay when he was working on Norwich Cathedral complains of "people constantly calling." Edward Hussey may be taken as an example of what a wealthy and demanding client might expect when we recall the thirty-two conferences with Salvin before any start was made on Scotney Castle, and there is no reason to suppose that he was in any way exceptional.

We know very little about who he had to help him. Frederick Caldecleugh, who must have been a relative of the family governess, was working for Salvin from the Mamhead days. Caldecleugh was succeeded as chief draftsman by William Harroway, who seems to have come in the 1850s and who stayed with Salvin until he retired. We find J. L. Pearson working in the office for a six-month period beginning in March 1842, during which time he was paid two guineas a week. Pearson came from Durham and had worked briefly for George Pickering, a local man whom Salvin was to use as supervising architect for his work for the university. Willie (as he was called by his family) Nesfield came in 1853 after three years with William Burn and stayed for four years; R. N. Shaw joined them in July 1856 and left to go to G. E. Street in 1859. There must have been many others, both young men starting on their careers and ordinary draftsmen, but their names are unrecorded. Anthony Salvin, Junior, however, did not move on; he began with his father in 1848 and stayed until ill health obliged him to give up in the late 1870s; he died exactly eight months before his father in 1881.

He had been sent to boarding school in Ripon for a year and was then moved to a less rigorous establishment in Hove. Badly spoiled as a child, he was miserable at both, became rather ill, and was eventually brought home. He and Osbert were then sent to a school in Finchley as day scholars, until Osbert was old enough to go to Westminster School, from which he went in 1853 to Trinity Hall Cambridge. Both the Salvin boys were skilled carpenters and engineers, and while Osbert was still at Westminster they built and fitted out two steam launches, which were later sold and sent out to India. Osbert was briefly employed in an engineering firm when he came down, which he did not enjoy. He was already a distinguished ornithologist and made collecting expeditions to Tunisia and Guatemala. Eliza and Emmie were educated at home. With a governess and a houseful of relatives who could look after the children, Salvin was able to take his wife with him on some of his tours of inspection. There is an account by Anne of one such trip to Mamhead, which must be typical of many.[6]

They set off on September 18, 1838: "Left home at 7 o'clock Anthony being very fussy to get us off in good time and arrived at the railway station three quarters of an hour before the train started." They took the train to Woking, from whence they posted to Farnham, eating a picnic of cold chicken in the carriage; and then by Arlesford to Winchester, where they saw the cathedral, the college chapel, and the library and cloisters. They reached Romsey at half past seven in the evening, and there they spent the night. They consulted the map and decided to go on by way of the New Forest instead of Salisbury, and got up at six o'clock to see the abbey before starting. They saw Broadlands, Lord Palmerston's house, from the road, and traveled by way of Ringwood, Wimborne (where they had a fifteen-minute tour of the minster while the horses were changed), Wareham, Corfe Castle, and to Weymouth by four o'clock. Here they changed horses again and went on to Bridport, which they reached by half past seven. There they spent the night. The following morning they were off at half past six and had breakfast at Lyme Regis, where a horse threw a shoe and nearly ruined their chances of getting to Mamhead that night. However, they pressed on, taking four horses at Sidmouth because the road was so bad. "Anthony much amused at his own grandeur," but these were sent back at Exmouth Ferry, as he did not wish to appear presumptuous by arriving at Mamhead in a carriage and four. They collected seashells while waiting for the Ferry—"a great many, though none very rare"—and got to the house at half past seven, having eaten nothing since nine that morning. Salvin was constantly making journeys of this kind, stopping off on the way for site inspections and consultations with clients, and returning to the office to face the arrears of work and an accumulation of problems that had arisen while he was away. It was to have a detrimental effect on his health over the next ten years and to result ultimately in a serious breakdown.

At Mamhead they found that their hosts had already dined, but another dinner was ordered for them. During the next few days excursions were arranged to Exeter Cathedral, Teignmouth, Dawlish, Powderham, Starcross, and the local village of Ashcombe, where the sixty pupils who attended the little school designed by Salvin read and recited for the visitors. On one wet day Anne occupied herself with sketching in the gallery (Fig. 14). She allowed herself a little whimsicality in her diary: "The house is magnificent, in some parts gorgeous, and in everything

6. London Borough of Barnet Library Services. MSS 6797/6.

exhibits the taste and munificence of its owner. He must have been very fortunate in the choice of his architect who, had he nothing else to raise his reputation might venture to rest it alone on the perfect structure before me. Query—I wonder who he is?"

The return journey was made by stage, via Collington, Wellington and breakfast, Taunton, Glastonbury, and Wells, where they had just time to look at the cathedral; then on to Bristol, tired and hungry after seventy-five miles on the way. The next day they saw the quay, Queen's Square, and the cathedral, and "Whilst Mr. Salvin went back for the carriage, I went to a Toy shop and bought some presents for my darlings and some pears and biscuits for ourselves." From Bristol they went to the Clifton Zoological Gardens and then crossed the Severn by steamer into Monmouthshire, where they saw Chepstowe Castle, Tintern Abbey, and Monmouth, where they spent the night. On the following day, a Saturday, they went to Ross-on-Wye, by Goodrich Castle, Malvern, Worcester Cathedral, "a fine specimen of Roubillac's sculpture in a monument erected to Bishop Hough," and Alcester. On Sunday they went to Stratford-upon-Avon to see Shakespeare's birthplace and attended a service in the parish church ("Mr. Salvin purchased a print of its exterior"); they moved on to Warwick, but the castle was closed. From there they went to Kenilworth: "Here we spent the remainder of the day, being the first dinner we had tasted since we left Mamhead." On Monday they visited Kenilworth Castle and St. Mary's Hall in Coventry, where they caught the 1:30 p.m. train, arriving in London at seven and getting home to Finchley at half past eight, "having fasted 12 hours." They had hot mutton chops and warm tea and were glad to be home. "Where a young and beloved family is left behind the heart is almost too much divided to enjoy the full extent of the travelling."

This happy family circle was disrupted in the early 1840s. General Salvin's only surviving sister, who had accompanied him to France and shared his imprisonment in Luxembourg, died in 1840, and Miss Caldecleugh died in 1842 after a long illness. In the same year Nesfield left the villa in Fortis Green and moved to Eton College. His work as a landscape gardener was steadily increasing, due to no small extent to introductions to Salvin's clients; we find him working with his brother-in-law on the gardens of houses such as North Runcton Hall and Oxon Hoath to begin with, and later on large projects such as the planting of an arboretum at Keele Hall and planning the grounds at Thoresby, which came to nothing as he did not get on with Lord Manvers. On March 22, 1844, he wrote to Sir William Hooker at Kew, who had asked him to make drawings of some trees there, for which he had no time, "as Painting is now almost a dead letter and I am really overwhelmed with land. gardening engagements." He was then collaborating with Decimus Burton in planning the layout of the Royal Botanical Gardens.[7] General Salvin died in April 1844 and Mrs. Salvin two months later. In early 1845 it became plain that Salvin himself was far from well. Eliza wrote: "It was about this time that his health was in a very unsatisfactory state, he was constantly ailing, and an accident which he had shook him very much." Salvin was accustomed to riding to town on a seat beside the driver of the Finchley omnibus, and a collision toppled

7. W. A. Nesfield to Sir William Hooker. Hooker Correspondence, XXII:135. Library, Royal Botanic Gardens, Kew.

him off. The only physical damage was a cut finger and a split nail, but he was one of those who cannot stand the sight of blood (and indeed had fainted on his honeymoon when he cut himself shaving), and he had to be brought home by a neighbor in a fly. In October his aunt, Mrs. Jeffrey Salvin, died and was buried at Kensall Green Cemetery. "My father attended the funeral. His health was in a very unsatisfactory state, the system deranged without being able to assign any particular cause, for no complaint was apparent. He was nervous, constantly uncomfortable and lost flesh." Standing at the graveside in cold weather after years of incessant work, missed dinners, and journeys from one end of the country to another exacerbated whatever it was that was wrong; he had written that year: "I have been much engaged this Summer in travelling to various parts of the Country an occupation much increased by the facilities offered by the railways."[8] But he could not go on, and something had to be done, so in November he went to Leamington Spa to consult the redoubtable Dr. Henry Jephson.

Jephson had been largely responsible for the town's becoming a spa. "Patients from all parts of the Kingdom, from the Colonies and from the Continent of Europe thronged to Leamington. His time was occupied almost night and day. He received summonses, rare in those days, to all parts of the country for consultations and he had a specially contrived travelling carriage made for these journeys. The income he made is almost fabulous, and we have reason to know that for several years together it exceeded £20,000 and that it once reached £24,000 in one year."[9] Jephson believed that most illness could be attributed to overindulgence in food and wine, that the remedy was strict diet and abstinence and the liberal use of spa waters for both bathing and drinking. He also insisted that his patients take outdoor exercise in all weathers, going so far from time to time as to drive them into the country and then put them out of his carriage so that they were obliged to walk back. The regime did not cure all, and it did not agree with Salvin. "Dr. Jefferson's [*sic*] system did not suit my father, and he came home worse than he went, but a more generous diet and less exercise soon effected a change for the better." He seems to have been over the worst by May the following year: "Mr. Salvin is now in Devonshire recruiting his health—and I hope it is the finishing touch to his perfect recovery."[10]

As the children grew up, the family became more mobile, and indeed they became a group of dedicated sightseers. The summer of 1843 was spent in Ramsgate; the following year they went on a sketching tour in Kent, going down the Dover Road to Canterbury and returning by way of Romney Marsh. In 1845 they went on a visit to Tenby in south Wales, a choice of resort dictated by the fact that Salvin was then working on the designs for Peckforton and wished to study the castles at Pembroke, Manorbier, and Carew. In 1846 he took Anne to Ireland to stay with J. H. Smith Barry at Foata House near Cork. Salvin was to design the Royal Cork Yacht Club House at Queenstown for Smith Barry in 1854 and to make alterations to Marbury Hall, his seat in Cheshire; but at this time he does not seem to have been employed professionally. Both Smith Barry and Lord

8. Trinity College, Cambridge, Whewell MSS.
9. *The British Medical Journal* (May 25, 1878): 775
10. Frederick Caldecleugh, May 18, 1846; Howard of Naworth MSS. Department of Palaeographic and Diplomatic, University of Durham.

Midleton, however, were developing their properties at Queenstown, Lord Midleton with the help of Decimus Burton, so Salvin may have been there to give
advice. From Foata they made an excursion to Killarney and Muckross Abbey.
Here again one feels that Salvin must have had business reasons for this journey;
however beautiful the Lakes of Killarney may be, it seems inconceivable that
anyone would have traveled for pleasure in the southwest of Ireland during the
second year of the Potato Famine, which was reaching its grisly climax. In the
autumn they returned to Ramsgate with the children.[11]

In 1851 Salvin took Anne and their two daughters on their first trip abroad, to
France. They traveled from London to Dover by steamer, from thence by train to
Folkestone, and then by steamer to Boulogne. From there they took the train to
Paris, where they were joined by Thomas Henry Wyatt, whose behavior on this
jolly excursion rather belies his later reputation for being hardworking, upright,
and dull.[12] What they saw during their seven-day stay would do credit to tourists of
any period; it included three churches that were in the process of being restored by
E. E. Viollet-le-Duc: Notre Dame, the Sainte Chapelle, and St. Denis. From here
they went to Rouen, with Wyatt being very amusing on the train, and there they
saw the cathedral, St. Ouen, and the Cathedral Abbey of St. Amand. They then
went to the theater, returning afterward to the Hotel d'Angleterre, where "Mr.
Wyatt would do nothing but dance and nearly upset the chambermaid." They
took a boat to Caudebec, Harfleur, and le Havre, went on to Caen, sketching the
whole time, and then returned to Southampton. This was the first of a number of
such tours. In 1853 they went to Scotland, and in 1855 they returned to Paris for the
Exposition Universelle des Beaux Arts, accompanied this time by Willie Nesfield.
Salvin was an exhibitor: "The Peckforton model is exhibited in this [the architec-
tural] Gallery, it has a stand to itself and looks very grand," wrote Eliza, who
ended her account by observing that the French "excel us in architectural drawing;
there are some beautiful buildings by Felix Duban and Viollet-le-Duc." The
following year Anne and her two girls traveled with friends in Switzerland and
Germany.[13]

They probably traveled on their own because Salvin would not take the time off
his work. Despite the warning illness ten years before, he was doing no less, and
the next year the inevitable occurred. The family, apart from Osbert, who had
gone to Guatemala, were staying with the Boynes at Brancepeth Castle, when they
heard from young Anthony that Salvin had become ill at Warwick Castle. "There
were a few shaky lines also from Papa. Lord and Lady Warwick were most kind
but he wished to get home and the doctor thought it quite safe." They left for
Finchley immediately and arrived to find the invalid already there. "He was quite
cheerful and composed, one arm is as yet powerless. The mouth is somewhat
drawn on one side. The left leg which was also affected is nearly well." Recovery
from a stroke in Victorian times was uncertain and took a good deal of time. The
doctor prescribed rest and quiet and no business, so Anthony, Willie, and Shaw
took over the running of the office. There was much for them to do.

11. British Architectural Library Drawings Collection: Salvin family topographical sketches.

12. John Martin Robinson, *The Wyatts* (Oxford: Oxford University Press, 1979).

13. *Journals of Foreign Tours by Eliza Anne Salvin. Copied in 1860.* London Borough of Barnet Library Services.
MSS 6787/5.

6

The Country House Practice

We have already remarked on the astonishing fact that in the twenty years leading up to the middle of the nineteenth century, Salvin built only six entirely new country houses. The reason for this was that he came from the landed gentry himself, and most of his clients were drawn from this class, or from the aristocracy. In other words, they already had large estates and country houses, often of considerable antiquity. He seems to have had little contact with the industrial and entrepreneurial classes, whose efforts were on the one hand earning the country immense wealth, and on the other, turning the structure of society upside down. Indeed, his only clients of this type seem to have been the Marshall family of Leeds, for whom he built the churches of St. John's, Keswick, and St. Patrick's, Patterdale, and greatly extended Patterdale Hall when they removed themselves from the scene of their commercial success and settled in the Lake District. Their money came from a new process for spinning flax. He also carried some quite small works for one of the Vivians, who had copper smelting works in Swansea. Of course, some of the established county families benefited from the Industrial Revolution, as did Gregory Gregory and Lord Boyne, who had Salvin build a house in the Italian style on his Burwarton Estate in Shropshire with the money he obtained from his wife's coal-mining interests. He had married Emma Maria Russell, the daughter and on her brother's death the sole heiress of Matthew Russell and Elizabeth Tennyson. But usually the money for building or improving country houses came from agricultural rents, and for this reason work was often spread over a number of years and could be halted by periods of agricultural depression, such as the ones that occurred in the 1850s after the repeal of the Corn Laws and in the 1870s.

Salvin built eight large country houses in the next twenty-year period, and these were his last such commissions. Three have been utterly demolished: Congham High House and Stoke Holy Cross, both in Norfolk, and Hodnet Hall in Shropshire. Bangor Castle incorporates unidentified work by Burn, and Paddockhurst in Sussex, built for the contractor George Smith, who worked on many of Salvin's most important commissions, was much added to by Sir Aston Webb in 1897. Keele Hall, Thoresby Hall, and the smaller Crossrigg Hall remain much as when they were built. All were Tudor or Jacobean in style, and most of the old houses that Salvin was brought in to improve also dated from these periods. The requirements of those who came to him for such improvements were fairly standard and reflected both changes in society and improved domestic technology. The nineteenth century saw an increase in the desire for privacy on the part of the master and mistress of the house. There was also a polarization of the occupants into groups determined by status, sex, and occupation, which created a series of clearly defined spaces where certain activities took place, and nowhere else. Early houses might have splendid sets of rooms where the family conducted their lives, but which were also the only route for servants passing from one part to another, the venue for children at noisy indoor games, and open territory to any guest who might be staying in the house. This disorder was replaced by the rigid division of the household into family and servants, and further divisions within these groups, who all required specific accommodation. If we look at the gentry side first, they are separated into three: master and mistress, their children, and their guests. All three are further subdivided by sex.

The lady of the house ran it from her boudoir, which was generally upstairs, adjoining her bedroom and dressing room. If there was a morning room, which was desirable, she and her lady guests would use it as a sitting room, and this was where she would receive callers. Her husband worked at estate business in his study, and he and his male guests used the library as a sitting room. A billiard room might be built near this, billiards being an invaluable resort on long wet weekends. A cloakroom could also be added, forming a self-contained male suite in which smoking might be allowed. The drawing room was the general meeting place, and from here family and guests would move in procession to the dining room for their meals. Throughout this period the hall became larger and was increasingly used as a sitting room open to all sexes, despite the fact that servants could sometimes be seen from here, proceeding with slop-pails from the bedrooms above. The children had their own set of rooms: a schoolroom and day and night nurseries, placed near the boudoir and their parents' bedroom. Bachelors and spinsters, whether resident or visiting, were carefully separated, the bachelors often sleeping in small rooms with their own staircase in a bachelors' wing.

The arrangements for the staff were equally complicated. It was usual for the main part of the house to be separated from the offices by the butler's pantry and the housekeeper's room and sometimes by the master's study, which had a secondary entrance for the bailiff, tenants, and others calling on estate business. There was inevitably a servants' staircase, which became a vital part of an alternative circulation designed to ensure that the staff and family never met when the former were carrying out their duties. "We always had to work as if we wern't there," said a gardener trained at a big house in Suffolk; "if a maid was in a passage and Lordship or Ladyship happened to come along, she would have to face the wall and stand perfectly still until they had passed."[1] Salvin often showed considerable ingenuity in inserting corridors running parallel to the main rooms of an old house, which enabled the servants to move about unseen. The housekeeper's room had to be big enough to serve as a sitting room for the senior staff and a store for the best china; next door was the still room, where cakes and preserves were made. The butler's pantry was the place where wine was decanted and the silver washed and polished, and it usually had a large plate safe opening into it. The kitchen had to be removed some distance from the principal rooms of the house, as all cooking smells were then regarded as intolerable. This was often done by building a separate kitchen court, as was the case at Methley, where it was isolated with its related sculleries and pantries, the game, fish, and pastry larders, vegetable stores, bakehouse, and dairy. The servants' hall was also placed at a distance, in case of

1. Ronald Blyth, *Akenfield* (Harmondsworth: Penguin Books, 1977), p. 199.

46. Mears Ashby Hall.

noise, and as far as possible from the house were those rooms used for dirty or
smelly operations: the lamp room, laundry, brushing room, brewhouse, coal-hole,
and dustbins. Domestic staff slept in, the maids usually in attics reached by their
own stairs, the male servants either in a carefully segregated part of the attics or in
the basements. Imposing nineteenth-century domestic arrangements on houses
built up to three hundred years before demanded both great skill in planning and
great tact, so as to ensure that the often large additions looked as if they had
always been part of the old house.

An example of what happened in the case of one of the smaller houses with
which Salvin was concerned may be seen at Mears Ashby Hall in Northamptonshire (Fig. 46). Captain Henry Stockdale married in 1858, and the
following year Salvin carried out essential improvements to his family home. This
had a fine E-shaped front of 1637, which had been added to an earlier building, but
the rooms were by no means large and the ceilings low. Salvin added a new west
wing that contained a large drawing room and dining room for entertaining, and
two bedrooms and dressing rooms above. This two-story addition was joined to
the old three-story house by a recessed square staircase tower with a pyramidal
roof, which disguises the transition from two stories to three. A new kitchen and
scullery were built at the back of the house and corridors and a servants' hall
carved out of the old offices. The new stonework is a good match with the old, and
the new west gable is of the same pitch as those on the old house. Mullions,
pinnacles, chimney stacks, and string courses are copied from the originals—
attention to detail that helps to unite the new fabric with the old seventeenth-
century building.

Marriage was frequently the event that precipitated improvements. Another
was the owner's appointment as Deputy Lieutenant or High Sheriff of his county,
positions that entailed a certain amount of official entertaining; another event was
of course the succession of the heir. The third Earl of Mexborough came into his
title, estates, and fortune in 1830, and Salvin spent the next six years working on
his country house, Methley Hall, in the West Riding, now demolished. The old
house had consisted in the fifteenth century of two ranges running north and
south, linked by the great hall on the south side. The eastern range had been
replaced at some time before 1778 with a seven-bay block with pediment, roof

balustrade, and sash windows, which Salvin pulled down. East of the great hall he built a large library, anteroom, and drawing room, basing his design on the entrance front of Heath Old Hall, a sixteenth-century house a mile or so to the south, which has now also been demolished (Fig. 47). To the north of the great hall he put a small courtyard, a staircase, and a large dining room. Up till then the kitchen had occupied the same position as it had since the house was built, that is, opening into the screens passage and just to the left as one came in through the front door. As we have already noted, cooking smells were not to be tolerated, and cooking smells, when there was much roasting at open fires and much boiling up of everything, were quite formidable and unacceptable so close to the principal entrance. The old kitchen and buttery were therefore converted into a billiard room and the butler's pantry, beyond which Salvin placed the housekeeper's room and still room, the servants' hall and kitchen, with the kitchen courtyard beyond. Thus, those parts that caused the worst smells, the brewhouse and laundry, were as far away from the reception rooms as possible. Salvin's work at Methley was in a practical, plain, and accurate Tudor, and it is clear that he has benefited from his employment on a series of great Tudor mansions such as Somerhill in Kent of around 1603 and at Parham, where he worked for Baroness de la Zouche.

Parham was a perfect sixteenth-century manor that had been allowed to get into a terrible condition internally and had acquired externally sashed windows and segmental gables on the south front (Fig. 48). What the owner desired here was not only the restoration of the house to its former appearance but also privacy for the family, from the many servants who shared the house and equally from unexpected and possibly unwelcome visitors. The front door was on the south or garden side, which meant that someone enjoying the flowers ran the risk of meeting anyone who cared to call. The solution was to transfer the entrance to the north front, opposite the stable block. Salvin's first design for this shows a keep-like tower and a four-story gabled porch (Fig. 49). The final version has a massive two-story porch with octagonal angle buttresses topped by ogival roofs, within which a flight of stairs rises from ground level to that of the great hall. The tower now stands to the left of

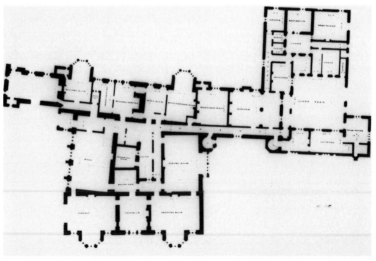

47. Methley Hall, ground plan.

48. Parham Park,
watercolor by
Stebbing Shaw, 1790.

49. Parham Park, elevation of north front, pencil and wash.

50. Parham Park, from the northeast, watercolor by H.S.H., 1855.

this and contains a service stair, which together with a new corridor taken out of
the library allowed the servants to get across the house and from one floor to
another without going through any of the main rooms (Fig. 50). On the south front
the eighteenth-century accretions were removed, the eaves lowered and the gables
rebuilt, the sashes removed, and the chimney stacks sorted out and rebuilt in
groups (Fig. 51).[2]

2. Salvin moved the position of the front door from the garden front to the rear on at least two other
occasions, at Tabley House in 1845 and Encombe House in 1871.

51. Parham Park, from the southeast, watercolor by H.S.H., 1855.

At Rufford Abbey the eighth Earl of Scarborough succeeded at the late age of forty-seven. He was unmarried, so there was no new mistress seeking to make changes to his house, but he was to become Lord Lieutenent of Nottinghamshire and Custos Rotulorum, which may have led him to undertake major improvements. These began in 1837 and were a general refurbishing, which included a new grand staircase and complete redecoration throughout a building that had begun as a Cistercian abbey, and to which Elizabethan and Georgian additions had been made. The total spent was £13,167, of which the largest accounts were those of Thomas Willement for painting and of Frederick Crace and Son for carving, gilding, paperhanging, and painting, by craftsmen sent down from London. Salvin's commission, which included minor work at two other houses owned by the earl, came to £839.9.11d, a considerable sum. His work at Rufford has now been demolished, as is the case with Flixton Hall in Suffolk, where he went after one of those fires to which houses were so liable in days of open grates and oil lamps. This was in 1846, and here he undertook almost a total rebuilding of the hall, with the addition of large new offices, and he had fun improving upon the original appearance of the house by adding molded brick chimney stacks, pinnacles, and pretty wrought-iron vanes (Fig. 52). The Flixton commission gave Salvin an intimate knowledge of East Anglian brick buildings of the late sixteenth and early seventeenth centuries, built on the E plan with mullioned and transomed windows, stepped gables, and polygonal angle shafts. He used this style in two houses, both of which have unfortunately been demolished; they were Stoke Holy Cross, a new house for the banker Henry Birkbeck begun in 1852, and Campsea Ash High House, a major rebuilding for J. G. Sheppard in 1863 (Fig. 53).

It is not possible to mention here more than a few of the houses restored and adapted to contemporary ways of life, and we now turn to the castle work, for which Salvin was best known. Leaving on one side for the moment those that came under Her Majesty's Office of Works, which will be dealt with in a later chapter, he carried out major restorations at no less than ten castles that were still privately occupied.

At Greystoke he built a new house for Henry Howard in 1837-1845 around the fourteenth-century pele tower and restored this, making further additions after a fire in 1868 (Fig. 54). At Rockingham he was again called in twice, once in 1838

52. Flixton Hall, watercolor of the offices by Anne Salvin.

53. Campsea Ash High House.

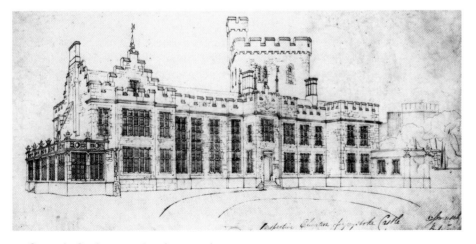

54. Greystoke Castle, pen and wash perspective.

when Richard Watson had just acquired the castle and was anxiously putting it in order for his new bride, and again in 1849 when he added the gallery tower and the keep tower. At Naworth Castle he was summoned by another member of the Howard family after the fire of 1844 had gutted the south range and the Dacre Tower, part of Lord William's Tower, and badly damaged the great hall. Letters survive from Salvin to the Clerk of Works that show his care that the new work should marry as nearly as possible with the old; the masons "may prepare stone for the windows, and make the new ones an <u>accurate copy of the old ones</u> and not <u>make believe</u> copy as that of Lanercost's chimney." He made no attempt to recreate the famous paneled ceiling of the great hall, which had been painted with portrait busts of the kings and queens of England. Instead he put in a massive open timber roof with collar and arched braces resting on plain stone corbels. The kitchen department, though not affected by the fire, was improved, and a new tower, the Morpeth Tower containing extra bedrooms, was built on the east wall adjoining the great hall.[3]

At Warkworth in 1853 he constructed living quarters and accommodation for the manorial court within the great keep for the Duke of Northumberland, who was at this time employing him at Alnwick. At Thornbury in Gloucestershire he carried out a major restoration in 1854 for Henry Howard of Greystoke, turning what was little more than a shell into a comfortable hunting lodge. Warwick Castle was another building to which he returned more than once. The fourth earl succeeded in 1853, and in 1856 Salvin extended the domestic range toward Caesar's Tower by an additional room, hall, and staircase and remodeled some of the adjoining rooms. In 1863 he was called in again, perhaps to put in more family accommodation. All this was destroyed by a fire in 1871, which broke out in Lady Warwick's boudoir and rapidly took hold despite the efforts of fire brigades summoned from all the nearest towns, and proceeded unchecked until it was stopped by the west wall of the great hall. The shell was externally more or less intact, but the roof of the great hall, the main staircase, two libraries, the breakfast room, the boudoir, sitting room, three state bedrooms, and sixteen other rooms were burned out. The contents were mostly saved, due to the efforts of the servants and townspeople, and the governess made a spectacular rescue of two Greville children from the nursery floor. The cost of rebuilding was quite beyond the resources of the earl, and a public subscription was opened, which raised £9,651.5.9d. towards the cost, which came to a grand total of £26,423.7.1d.[4]

Salvin worked at Muncaster Castle, Cumberland, in 1862–1866 for the fourth Baron Muncaster, and ten years later he carried out more substantial alterations for the fifth Baron. Few drawings for this survive, and it is not certain what was done on each occasion; but it is clear that he restored the old pele tower and put in new windows and that he built a new tower of roughly similar dimensions at the north end of the west front. He fitted a new main entrance in the angle between the pele and the late eighteenth-century octagonal library and added bay windows to the garden front. The old pele became a family suite, with the schoolroom on the ground floor, Lady Muncaster's dressing room on the first floor, and the nursery

3. University of Durham, Department of Palaeography and Diplomatic, Howard of Naworth MSS C/575/9.
4. Warwick Castle Archives.

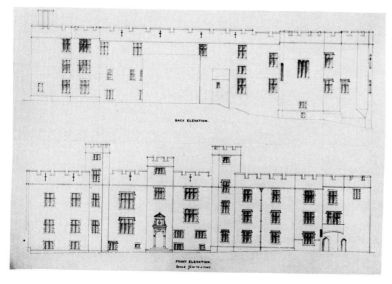

55. Dunster Castle,
entrance front and
rear elevations.

and maids' rooms above. The north end of the house was reorganized, the butler
and housekeeper as usual living between the main part of the house and the
kitchen, scullery, and larders. The servants' hall occupied the ground floor of the
new tower with its only window on the north side, so that the staff could not
overlook the private gardens. The octagonal library was magnificently refitted and
decorated by the Italian craftsmen and their English assistants, who had worked
for Salvin at Alnwick.

If Muncaster Castle has a fault, it is its uninterestingly flat skyline; even the old
and new pele towers are pitched at much the same height as the rest of the
building. The situation was the same at Dunster Castle in Somerset, where there
was a major recasting of the exterior and rearrangement of the interior, which is
fortunately well documented by both drawings and correspondence. When Salvin
went there the castle had three slender towers and symmetrically arranged
mullioned windows under a perfectly level battlemented roofline (Fig. 55). The
aspect of a romantic medieval castle was achieved on the entrance front by building the kitchen tower with an attached octagonal stair turret copied from that at
Markenfield Hall, and by putting a new doorway with a large carved coat of arms
above, by inserting new windows of differing designs, quoins, and arrow slits and
rebuilding the battlements (Fig. 56). The south front was enlivened by the addition
of the drawing-room tower, a keep-like mass of irregular plan (Fig. 57).

Internally the rooms were rearranged in accordance with current requirements.
An outer hall was created out of two small rooms, and the inner hall was
remodeled, retaining the Elizabethan ceiling but removing a triple arcade of
Corinthian columns between the hall and staircase, which Salvin held to be
inappropriate. A pair of large stone arches replaced them, the intention being that
the visitor would assume "the walls and arches to be of the earlier date into which
the style of Elizabeth has been introduced."5 The morning room was above the
inner hall, and the drawing room reached from the outer hall and led in turn to a

5. Somerset County Record Office, Dunster Castle MSS, DD/L/EOC, Salvin to Luttrel, November 4,
1869.

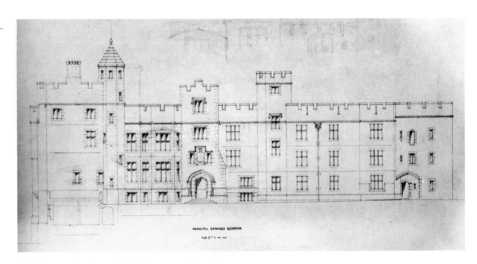

56. Dunster Castle, principal entrance elevation.

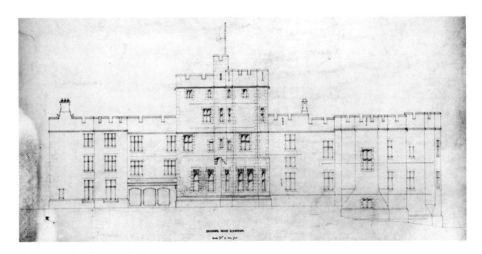

57. Dunster Castle, rear elevation.

conservatory. At the west end of the building, the rooms that would have been used by the male members of the family and their male visitors are grouped together: the justice or business room, the library, and the billiard room. The butler's rooms, a particularly comprehensive arrangement, were on the ground floor of the kitchen tower adjoining the dining room. They were the butler's bedroom, pantry, pantry lobby, cleaning room, strong room, and the serving room. Meals came up the turret stair from the kitchen, which with its associated sculleries and pantries was housed in a semibasement running north to the fifteenth-century gatehouse, which was put to use as larders. They were invisible from the entrance courtyard, but due to a steep fall in the land to the east, Salvin was able to put in plenty of windows, giving light and air to these steamy premises.

However, the castle as rearranged still had its inconveniences, such as the position of the morning room, which was the only route from two sets of bedrooms to the main stairs and so lacking privacy and quiet. It was inevitable that this was commented upon, and Salvin wrote in reply toward the end of the work, acknowledging part payment of his account and adding: "For my part I do not expect or care to find suites of rooms in a Castle such as you naturally expect in a modern house."[6]

When the fourth Earl of Radnor inherited Longford Castle, it had long been abandoned as uninhabitable. This was the result of misconceived attempts to enlarge the 1580 three-towered triangular building, first by James Wyatt and then by Daniel Alexander. Three new towers with connecting ranges had been added before the work was finally stopped. Salvin was required to unify these uncomfortable additions with the old part of the house and to bring the whole up to a lavish standard of comfort and convenience. What he did was to close the kite-shaped area created by Wyatt's addition on the south by building a new single-story dining room, leaving a small open court in the middle, converting the whole of this part of Wyatt's building into offices. He then roofed in the triangular central courtyard in the old part and added circular stair towers at each of the angles; the main reception rooms were then arranged around this central hall on both the ground and first floors. He also remodeled the entrance front, which was of eleven bays with a five-bay open loggia on the ground and first floors, a continuous balustrade at roof level, and many-paned sash windows. Salvin brought forward the three bays on either side of the loggia and built gables with volutes and pediments above these and above the central section. These help to conceal the fact that the angle towers are now no longer the same height. Mullions replaced the sashes. The garden front was given a couple of new bays with shaped gables and smaller gables between.

Inverary Castle in Argyllshire was Salvin's last private castle commission. The castle was, and essentially still is, a square building with round towers at each corner and a central lantern rising two stories above the parapets. It was designed by Roger Morris, who began work here in the mid-eighteenth century, and it was largely destroyed by fire in October 1877. Quite a number of Salvin's designs for the restoration survive, from which it can be seen that he wished to alter the building completely, abandoning Morris's symmetrical arrangement (Fig. 58). His recasting involved raising the height of the building by a story, adding a vast keep-like block at one angle, and improving the round towers with pointed and gabled roofs, bartizans, and Franco-Scottish architectural details (Fig. 59). The result would have been imposing and highly picturesque but must have added considerably to the cost of the restoration. In any event, Salvin was restricted to his single additional story, which was lit by ranges of five identical dormers on each elevation, and topping the towers with high conical roofs and chimney stacks.

Although work at Alnwick began in 1852, so that it falls chronologically between that at Naworth and Warkworth in the sequence just described, it has been left till the end because it was Salvin's restoration of this castle that attracted most attention from antiquarians and architects. Also, it was during the course of a meeting of the Royal Institute of British Architects, at which several papers were read dealing with the castle and its history, that Salvin for the the first and only time in his life spoke in public about his work, and was severely criticized by, among others, Gilbert Scott. What everyone was particularly upset about was what was

6. Dunster Castle MSS, DD/L/EOC, Salvin to Luttrel, June 23, 1870.

58. Inverary Castle, pencil sketch of preliminary design.

59. Inverary Castle, elevation of north front, pen and wash.

being done inside the castle, although there were some complaints about the restoration itself.

Alnwick, the "Windsor of the North," consisted in medieval times of a shell keep to which a fourteenth-century Percy had added seven round towers and a square gateway tower. It had been improved by the Yorkshire baronet, Sir Hugh Smithson, who had married the heiress to the Barony of Percy and their Northumbrian estates. Smithson found the castle rather derelict, and in about 1756 he had employed James Paine on a restoration, Robert Adam on the interiors of the saloon, drawing room, and library, and "Capability Brown" about the park. The result of this campaign may be seen in the plan of the castle as it was in 1760 (Fig. 60). The castle had been rearranged with the main entrance on the opposite side of

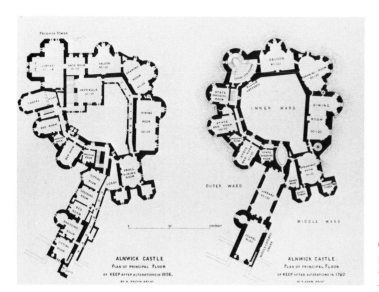

60. Alnwick Castle,
ground plans in 1856
and 1760. *RIBA Transactions
1856–57*, p. 15.

the inner bailey to the gate tower. This led into a rebuilt round tower containing the grand staircase, which led in turn to the state apartments of the first floor. On the east were ranged the saloon, drawing room, and dining room, each taking up the whole floor area of one of the round towers, and the breakfast room in the middle gateway. These rooms interconnected and could only be reached by passing through one to another. The three towers on the west contained a state dressing room and two state bedrooms, which were reached by a corridor running around the courtyard and which led to a secondary oval staircase adjoining the middle gateway. Both the breakfast room and the dining room were served by a circular stair up which all food had to be carried, after it had first been conveyed across the gateway on its way from the kitchen. This was highly inconvenient, and it was not unknown for guests and the dinner to reach the arch at the same time. There was no separate circulation for servants. Externally the castle, like Dunster, lacked impact and verticality. Unbroken lines of battlements crowned the round towers and the intervening walls, all of the same height and broken only by low turrets and the apotropaic figures that were regularly spaced on each tower. As for the decoration of the interior, we know that the dining room and drawing room were "done in a very good Gothic style of Stucco," which had been introduced "out of complaisance to the Duchess," and that the saloon had been given a fan-vaulted ceiling.[7]

Algernon, the fourth Duke of Northumberland, had succeeded his brother in 1847 and "found a great absence of domestic comfort and a deficiency in those modern conveniences requisite in the residence of a nobleman of His Grace's rank. The considerable transformation which it had undergone in the last century . . . had caused it to lose many striking features, important parts having been reduced in size and consequence, depriving it of much of that original dignity and variety of effect, which it had doubtless possessed in ancient times."[8]

7. J. Macaulay, *The Gothic Revival 1745–1845* (Glasgow: Blackie & Son, 1975), pp. 56–82.
8. *Royal Institute of British Architects. Papers* (1857), pp. 1-26.

Salvin's reorganization was drastic. The entrance remained in its former position, but the round staircase tower was pulled down and replaced by the massive Prudhoe Tower, which rises well above the rest of the castle (Fig. 61). A vaulted porte cochère projects into the courtyard and leads into an entrance hall that opens onto the grand staircase (Fig. 62). As at Harlaxton, this hall is low and gloomy in contrast to the well-lit state rooms above. The staircase leads up to the guard chamber and then into an anteroom that has on one side the library, occupying the whole of the first floor of the Prudhoe Tower, and on the other the sequence of intercommunicating state rooms. Salvin has added a service corridor to these, corbelled out on the courtyard side and leading to the breakfast room. The tower on the west next to the Prudhoe Tower was rebuilt as a chapel, and the family's private sitting rooms, bedrooms, and dressing rooms were placed in the middle gateway range. There had been an earlier proposal for a free-standing chapel, but this was abandoned (Fig. 63). The problem of communication between the two dining rooms and the kitchen was aggravated, as Salvin built a new kitchen standing on wine and beer cellars outside the curtain wall beside the middle gateway. The small dining room, as it was now called, could be served by a dumbwaiter up to the corridor giving access to the rooms in the private suite; food destined for the state dining room, however, was wheeled out of the kitchen through a white-tiled tunnel under the middle bailey to a serving room beneath the south wall of the dining-room tower, whence it was taken up by another service lift. The counterweights of this can still be seen against the tower wall, and the path of the tunnel followed across the grass by its glass roof lights.

Externally the eighteenth-century windows were picked out and replaced with groups of tall cusped lancets. Some of the apotropaic figures were removed, and the heights of the round towers varied. The mass of the Prudhoe Tower and the steep lead roof of the chapel now dominate the whole of the inner bailey. Much work was done about the middle and outer baileys by way of reconstruction and

61. Alnwick Castle.

62. Alnwick Castle, pencil sketch of inner ward.

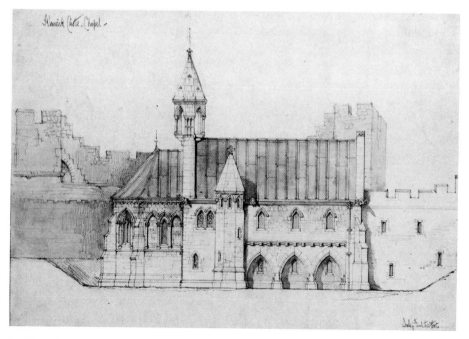

63. Alnwick Castle, elevation of chapel.

additions; the curtain wall was repaired, the Falconer's Tower rebuilt, and the Warder's Tower added, but a long stretch of wall and the Armourer's Tower were demolished to improve the view.

In 1854, with work well under way, Salvin received a letter from the duke, who was then in Rome, in which he announced that the internal decorations were to be in the Italian style of the fifteenth and sixteenth centuries. The duke had been greatly taken with Roman palazzi and also by the fact that seicento furnishings were there to be found in medieval buildings. As Scott was to write later: "Whether the princely Lord of Alnwick thought he had no alternative between the debased Gothic of Windsor and (what I hope I shall be pardoned for calling) the mimic feudalism of Peckferten, [*sic*] I know not; but the result was this—that, happening at the time to winter in Rome, his Grace became enamoured of the interiors of Renaissance palaces, and fostered the infelicitous idea of making his ancestral residence a feudal castle without and a Roman palazzo within."9 Salvin made his view of the matter quite plain to the assembled Members of the Institute: "I had great doubts of the propriety, as well as the practicability, of introducing Italian art into a Border Castle. My own wish would have been to devise Mediaeval decorations to a plan consistent with modern requirements, and that would have accorded with the exterior as well as the associations of the place. I must here observe that I do not for a moment admit, what many opponents of the style urge against it, that because the doors, the windows and the ceilings are Mediaeval, therefore, the floors must be covered with rushes, and the furniture benches."10

The duke, of course, had his way. He sought the advice of Commendatore Canina, an eminent Italian archaeologist and a specialist in antique architecture. Canina spent much of a visit to England at Alnwick but managed to get to the Crystal Palace, which had just reopened at Sydenham. Salvin, C. R. Cockerell, and T. L. Donaldson spent a day with him, visiting the Geological Museum in Jermyn Street and Henry Hope's house in Piccadilly. Canina prepared a schedule of the proposed decorations but unfortunately died on his way back to Rome, so that the work was carried out by the Signori Montiroli and Mantovani, apart from the wood carving, which was done by Leoni Bulleti with the help of locally recruited craftsmen. They were all under Salvin's supervision. In the end the dichotomy between the Edwardian exteriors and the seicento interiors was not as obvious as it might have been. For example, Salvin so designed the windows that they are round-headed on the inside, despite the cusping without. The transition from one style to the other is carefully calculated: the entrance hall has stone walls with a plain plaster ceiling and simple marble fireplace; the lower staircase hall has a little marble decoration, the staircase has walls lined with marble; the guard chamber has a coved and coffered ceiling, a frieze of the Hunting of Chevy Chase, and a marble floor imported from Rome. It is in the next room, the anteroom, that the visitor first encounters the splendid and quite overwhelming decoration of the state rooms. Alnwick was Salvin's biggest undertaking and is said to have cost about £100,000. The number of men employed is known from the testimonial signed by all and presented to Salvin upon his recovery from his illness in 1858.

9. G. G. Scott, *Remarks on Secular and Domestic Architecture, Present and Future* (London: John Murray, 1857), p. 235–37.

10. *Royal Institute of British Architects. Papers* (1857), pp. 1–26.

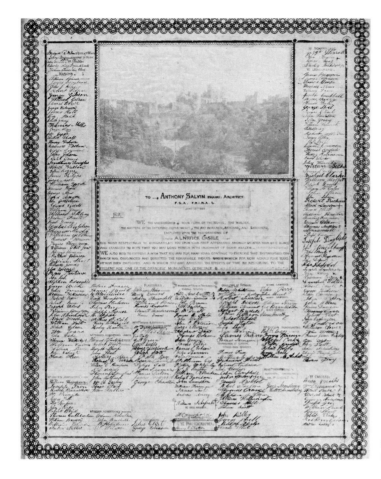

64. The Alnwick Castle
testimonial.

Even with Frederick Wilson acting as Clerk of Works, and Wilson was an architect
on his own account, the task of supervision was immense, and it was by no means
the only thing Salvin had in hand at the time. He collapsed when the work was in
full swing, and the strain of controlling the Italian craftsmen and integrating their
work with his own no doubt contributed to his breakdown (Fig. 64).

We now come to Salvin's last great mansions, Keele Hall and Thoresby Hall.
Keele is to all intents and purposes a new house, although its plan was in part
dictated by that of the sixteenth-century house that occupied the same site (Fig.
65). When work began on alterations to this, the initial demolition revealed that so
much of the structure was rotten that in the end everything had to come down. It
was built for Ralph Sneyd in 1854–1860. He was a bachelor, and this was reflected
in the planning. The house is L-shaped, with a squat staircase tower at the angle of
the two ranges. Once again the entrance courtyard is lower than the land on the
garden side, so that an impressive approach is contrived; the basement offices
receive light and air, yet the main rooms open straight onto the garden terraces.[11]
Sneyd's bachelor status is reflected in the particularly comprehensive set of rooms
for the use of his male guests and himself. The front door led into a screens

11. W. E. Nesfield, writing Salvin's obituary notice, particularly mentions Keele Hall as being cleverly
adapted to the ground and one of the best-planned houses in England.

65. Keele Hall, entrance front.

66. Keele Hall, the great hall.

passage, the great hall lying on the left and Sneyd's private rooms on the right; these consisted of a study, a sitting room, a smoking room, a billiard room, and a conservatory. Beyond the great hall and in the other range were the library, drawing room, breakfast and dining rooms, the staircase tower, and the offices, some of which are housed in a lower extension, with the laundry and brewhouse at a distance from the main building. The interior decoration was eclectic to an extreme and very expensive (Fig. 66). Indeed, the whole undertaking seems to have been embarked upon regardless of cost. Sneyd had a very able agent who had made him a lot of money by dealing cautiously with the estate affairs, the purchase and sale of land, and the leasing of farms and coal mines; this affluence was demonstrated even in the contract with the builders, which was written on vellum and bound in red morroco. Sneyd's signature was witnessed by Salvin, and those of James Paton of Ayr and James Paton, Junior, by Richard Norman Shaw.

Built of the local red and cream sandstone, Keele is a curious house and only partially successful. The entrance front is quite satisfactory, with the flight of steps climbing up into the three-story entrance porch with an oriel above, and the rather overpowering glass windows of the hall on the left balanced by a three-story canted bay window on the right. All this is overshadowed by the massive staircase tower in the corner. The south front is also rather grand; it has a two-story three-bay central section with a loggia on the ground floor, all faced in cream sandstone, above which is a third story in red sandstone, which originally bore a two-story octagonal pavilion roof similar to the one that survives at Oxon Hoath. This is flanked by narrow three-story extruded corners that used to have pyramidal slate roofs, and beyond these broad bays with the unique shaped gable copied from the old house. These are in red sandstone, and the contrast between the two building materials is effective. The eastern or garden front is not attractive, however; it is too long for its height, and the length is accentuated by a series of identical gabled dormers. The polygonal bay of the drawing room does little to rectify the horizontality of the design (Fig. 67).

Thoresby Hall was Salvin's last great house, and it seems more than likely that he obtained the commission through Sneyd's recommendation; certainly he saw all the original designs and made suggestions for their improvement, which were adopted. Sydney Pierrepont, third Earl Manvers, came into the title and estate in 1860. He succeeded also to a house designed in 1767 by John Carr of York, of brick with stone dressings, three stories by seven bays with an Ionic portico. It was a somewhat outdated design even when it was built, and to Manvers it must have seemed quite inadequate for a man with his position to maintain, which could be one of some magnificence on an income in excess of £50,000 a year. Planning began in 1863, and by this date to select Salvin was to make a very conservative choice. His kind of archaeological Tudor and Jacobean with clearly identifiable precedents had been quite overtaken by later developments in the Gothic Revival. Gilbert Scott's Kelham Hall, just twelve miles to the south, had been built in 1858–1862 and epitomizes High Victorian Gothic, with borrowings from Continental models and a violent constructional polychromy that Salvin never used in his

67. Keele Hall, elevation of the garden front.

life. Two other houses of this type that were completed at just the time Thoresby was begun are S. S. Teulon's Elvetham Hall in Hampshire of 1859–1862 and Ettington Park, Warwickshire, built in 1858–1863 by John Prichard. Furthermore, Salvin was equally untouched by the English Vernacular Revival, of which he would have heard a good deal, Shaw and Willie Nesfield having both been in his office. Leyswood and Kinmel, spectacular houses by these young men, were being built at the same time as Thoresby, and it was this development that was to transform English domestic architecture and carry it forward into the next century. But Salvin was not tempted to adjust himself to new fashions. At Thoresby nothing of novelty was required, and what was put up was in accordance with the tried formula that Salvin had worked out in his first great house forty years before; here it was also applied on the grandest possible scale.

A model of the proposed house has survived in a rather battered condition, and this was no doubt made as an aid to the discussion between architect and client. This is more elaborate than that for Scotney Castle and is made of painted wood instead of plain white card. It has two alternative versions of the staircase tower, but apart from that it differs little from the house as built (Fig. 68). Work began in May 1864. The main contractors, George Smith and Co., received their first payment in September, and from then on small items in the accounts tell us how work progressed. The shell was roofed in by the middle of 1868 at the latest, as the clock and bells in the entrance tower were paid for in October that year and the lightning conductor was paid for in January 1869. The carved pendants for the roof of the great hall, the kitchen fittings, chimneypieces, wrought-iron gates, and fencing arrived in 1870, the painter Charles Smith was paid off in 1872, and work on the roads and terraces, stone lions and vases, encaustic tiles, and gas brackets appear in George Smith's accounts for that year. The books were closed in August 1873, showing that a total of £171,015.4.3 ½d. had been spent, of which Salvin's commission and expenses came to £6,617.11.3d. The stables were also very expensive and were put up in 1873–1877 at a cost of £27,978.3.4 ½d., in itself the price of a large house. For Manvers the total for house and stables was just four years' income.[12]

Once again the entrance and central courtyards are excavated, and the basement is used to add an extra floor and a towering effect to the entrance facade, which is here increased by the terrace walls on the left, and a single-story service range on the right (Fig. 69). Again the main rooms on the garden front open straight onto the gravel paths, that part of the basement beneath them being used only as cellarage. Here is the usual small low hall, from which a flight of not very grand stairs lead up to the screens passage from which the visitor enters the great hall, three stories high. Although Salvin had used this sequence so many times before, with variations, it is nowhere so effective. The contrast of light and size is immensely theatrical, and the impact of this space, which still retains many of its original furnishings, is quite stunning (Fig. 70). The main reception rooms lie on the left; at the far end the great staircase rises in three flights to a corridor running around and opening into the hall at first-floor level, and this gives access to the

12. University of Nottingham Library, Manuscripts Department, Thoresby MSS. Quoted by permission of the Trustees of Earl Manvers.

68. Thoresby Hall, the architectural model.

69. Thoresby Hall, entrance front.

state bedrooms. The family quarters, that is, the billiard room, garden room, boudoir, Lord and Lady Manvers's dressing rooms, bathroom, and bedroom, are on the ground floor set behind the stairs, and a private stair goes up to the nurseries, governess's rooms, and schoolroom above.

In design Thoresby is a careful balance of symmetry and asymmetry. The apparently symmetrical design of the entrance front, a central clock tower flanked by two pairs of dormers and lateral towers, is upset by the fact that the towers are to two quite different designs. The same thing happens on the garden front, where the three regularly spaced two-story bay windows are all quite different, a feature

70. Thoresby Hall, the great hall.

that Salvin has recalled from Harlaxton (Fig. 71). The clock tower and the staircase tower balance each other but are in no way alike. Finally, there is great attention to detail. Gables, dormers, and chimney stacks all show a great diversity, and there is a continuous contrast between the rough-cut stone of the walls and the smooth finish of the bays and the architectural detail generally. It is a measure of Salvin's competence, helped by the sheer bulk of the place, that it all hangs together. The stables are equally monumental (Fig. 72). A rock-faced range with octagonal towers flanking a central entrance, and dormers built like garderobes over the hayloft openings. Within are the usual coach houses, loose boxes, stalls and tack rooms, and a riding school with a timber roof of extraordinary construction, namely kingposts resting on flattened arches built of brick.

All the buildings mentioned so far in this chapter were built or remodeled by Salvin in the style for which he was best known, firmly based on a painstaking study of the best example of English medieval, Tudor, and Jacobean houses and castles. But there were a few instances when his clients insisted on his working in a different and possibly uncongenial manner. The house at Burwarton that he built in 1835–1839 for the Honorable G. F. Hamilton, later to become Viscount Boyne, was in the rural Italian villa style and looked much as if it had been put up by a pupil of Decimus Burton. This was later enlarged and has now been partly demolished. A somewhat more interesting use of this style occurs in two houses, both in Wales, both begun in 1846 and clearly influenced by what Thomas Cubitt and Prince Albert had built at Osborne.

At Hafod in Cardinganshire, Salvin's client was Henry de Hoghton, who had bought the estate from the Duke of Newcastle. Hafod was, of course, Thomas Johnes's house and an important item in the history of the Gothic Revival.[13] Given

13. Elizabeth Inglis-Jones, *Peacocks in Paradise* (London: Faber & Faber, 1950).

71. Thoresby Hall, garden front.

72. Thoresby Hall, the stables.

that it was Gothic, it is curious that the large additions should have been in the Tuscan vernacular; but de Hoghton had spent the previous year in Italy on his honeymoon, and this, quite apart from what Cubitt was doing, probably influenced his choice (Fig. 73). Salvin's additions more than doubled the size of the old house and lay on the west of it. There was a new library, and a courtyard containing the gentlemen's rooms, a sitting or smoking room, an office, the clerk's room, and a cold bath and a shower. These last were fed from tanks in the belvedere tower. Behind this court was another for the kitchen, scullery, larders, storeroom, pastry larder, lamp room and oil cellar, servants' hall, rooms for brushing clothes and cleaning shoes and knives, and sheds for turf, wood, and coal. The stables and the main part of the house were untouched; Salvin simply added on those extra

73. Hafod.

rooms that were then required. Work was never completed; two years later de Hoghton's wife ran away with a captain in the India Company's service, and when his client, after further domestic tragedies, put Hafod on the market in 1855, Salvin's additions there were still unfinished.

Pennoyre in Breconshire was completed, but at such expense that Colonel J. L. V. Watkins was obliged to close his house and to live cheaply in a local hotel. Watkins was the local Member of Parliament and in 1847 became Commandant of the Brecon Militia and Lord Lieutenant of the county. In this instance the existing house was partly rebuilt in the Italian villa style, given a belvedere entrance tower, a loggia running around on the ground floor, and a new conservatory with a large glass dome. The inside was rearranged, grand rooms for entertaining provided, and new service accommodation added, although the extent of this is obscured by later alterations (Fig. 74).

Salvin's two houses in the French style are as surprising as it is to find him building Tuscan villas. The first of these was Oxon Hoath in Kent, which he altered in 1846–1847 for Sir William Geary Bart. It had been preceded only by Wrest Park, built by Earl de Grey to his own designs with the help of the professional architect James Clephan in 1834–1839; we do not know why the future president of the Institute of British Architects chose this style. Geary, on the other hand, was a Francophile and like Gregory collected French eighteenth-century furniture. Oxon Hoath had been built in the seventeenth century and was largely rebuilt in the eighteenth. Salvin added the Mansard dome over the central bay and the tower, with a pavilion roof, quoins, balustraded balconies, and open arches on the ground floor (Fig. 75). Another sketch shows a high hipped roof above the entrance and a tower with a tall pyramidal roof, but it does not seem that these were built (Fig. 76). There are no French interiors; they are, oddly enough, Jacobean with woodwork incorporating Flemish sixteenth-century carvings as at Scotney Castle. The garden was laid out with parterres by William Andrews Nesfield.

At Marbury Hall in Cheshire Salvin undertook an even greater transformation

74. Pennoyre.

75. Oxon Hoath, design
for alterations to
garden front.

for J. H. Smith Barry (Fig. 77). This house dated from the eighteenth century, and
the paintings and antique statuary that Smith Barry's grandfather had collected in
Rome in the 1770s were displayed here. Salvin turned the old house into a château
in 1856–1858, and the model for this is plainly the style of the Second Empire,
particularly Visconti and Lefuel's new buildings at the Louvre, begun in 1852 and
seen by Salvin when he went to Paris in 1855 (Fig. 78). Of these four unusual
commissions, Hafod and Marbury Hall have been demolished, but Pennoyre and
Oxon Hoath survive in good condition to show what Salvin could do when he had
to adopt an unfamiliar style.

76. Oxon Hoath, design
for alterations to
entrance front.

77. Marbury Hall, north front.

78. Marbury Hall, from
the southeast.

7

Peckforton and Other Castles

Long before any legislation for the protection of ancient monuments was passed, there was concern in England for the state of old buildings. The Society of Antiquaries had long been regarded as the standard-bearer of preservation and had been particularly critical of operations like James Wyatt's swingeing restorations at Salisbury and Durham Cathedrals. By the early 1840s the Oxford Society for Promoting the Study of Gothic Architecture and the Cambridge Camden Society had both been founded and were showing increasing anxiety about the treatment of medieval buildings; their interest was chiefly in the parish churches, but there was a parallel interest in secular buildings and the remains of castles, which was all part of early nineteenth-century enthusiasm for medieval times mentioned before in connection with the restoration of Brancepeth Castle. By 1844 Lord Lincoln, the First Commissioner of Woods and Works, was well aware of the damage done to ancient buildings by "misjudged reconstructions under the name of restoration and repair."[1] But nothing could be done about those in private hands until the passing of the first Ancient Monuments Protection Act (1882), and even then, such was the reluctance of Parliament to interfere with the rights of property owners that this piece of legislation had to be strengthened by a series of succeeding acts that went onto the statute book during the first half of the twentieth century. Lord Lincoln, as we shall see, took steps himself to preserve in the most conservative way three castles that belonged to the Crown.

One that had been Crown property but had been handed over to the county authority in 1806 was that at Norwich, and this was Salvin's first restoration of a publicly owned castle. His experience up till then had been restricted to the work on Brancepeth while he was still a pupil, the replica pele tower at Mamhead, and some remodeling of Bayons Manor in the castle style. Norwich differs from all his other castle work because it was still in use as the county jail. In 1832 the twelfth-century keep, which was all that survived of the original building, and a large addition put up by Sir John Soane in 1824–1825, housed about two hundred prisoners, but the older fabric was in a ruinous condition. Not only were there fears that the building was getting to a state when it could no longer keep convicts in, but the core of the outer walls was also being exposed by the decay of the Caen stone facing, which fell from time to time, endangering the safety of prisoners being exercised below.

In 1834 the Visiting Justices instructed Francis Stone, the County Surveyor, to reface the south and west walls of the keep, and there were at once protests from local antiquarians and artists who preferred its then very picturesque condition. A public meeting was held at the Guildhall, when those assembled called upon the

---

1. Manuscripts Dept., University of Nottingham Library, Newcastle MSS 12030.

justices to stop the work. Shortly after this a section of the south front collapsed, and it was decided that the justices should seek the advice of Edward Blore. He conceded that the work must be continued, but recognizing the indignation that had arisen in the city, recommended that as much as possible should be preserved, "not only to satisfy the minds of those persons who from local associations have an affection for the old Building, but as an unanswerable reply to those cavillers who after the work of Restoration is completed may be disposed to doubt its authenticity." Arguments and patching with Bath stone continued until Francis Stone died in 1835.[2]

The Dean of Norwich had been among the protestors and had asked Salvin, who was at this stage just completing his restoration of Norwich Cathedral, for advice. This Salvin felt himself unable to give without first making an inspection, which he clearly could not do while Stone was employed, but he saw only too well the difficulties of reconciling antiquarian and artistic interests with the practical matter of keeping the building standing. "No one can have a greater admiration for a fine old ruin than I have, or could be more unwilling to have it disturbed in any way . . . [but] we should therefore be careful to prevent an interesting building from entering that state when we can no longer attempt to preserve it from further dilapidation."[3] Now, within a week of Stone's death, he was taken on by the justices' building committee.

Salvin approved of Stone's work so far, subject to some strengthening, and carried on, using more substantial blocks of masonry; but he took a more serious view of the castle's condition after he had made a proper survey. Eventually the justices recorded that he had convinced them that "no part of the old facing could have been safely retained." The facades were therefore all rebuilt, following the design of the originals as closely as possible, until roof level was reached. All trace of battlements and whatever else had been on the roof had disappeared by the early eighteenth century.[4] Salvin took the view that the keep must have had turrets standing above the circular stairs at each angle, and he investigated possible models in great detail, sending the building committee sketches of Bamburgh, Richmond, Durham, Castle Hedingham, and Brougham Castles, and of the Seal of the City of Rochester on which that castle was shown as it was before it was ruined. In all he was able to name sixteen castles with angle turrets, but despite this the committee stubbornly took the line that there had been no such thing at Norwich. Salvin had taken considerable pains to assemble his evidence and had made a point of visiting a number of castles in the north during his professional journeys and of making a special trip to Castle Rising, the closest to Norwich both geographically and in design. He was not at all happy when asked to prepare three alternative schemes for finishing the roof. One member of the Cathedral Chapter who had been much involved with the restoration work there and who had got

2. Norfolk and Norwich Record Office, Norwich Castle MSS. Visiting Justices' Minute Book; Repair and Restoration of the South, West and North Sides of Norwich Castle, as by Order of the Quarter Sessions April 11th 1834.

3. Norwich Castle MSS. Salvin to Revd. Preb. C. N. Wodehouse September 8, 1834. He had written before on January 25, showing that he knew full well the castle's perilous condition: "In a Norwich paper I saw you made an effort to get the Castle restored the arguments of the uncontents are odd for their extreme anxiety to keep the old work as it is and I fear it will not consent to please them by remaining in status quo."

4. Prospect of Norwich Castle by Samuel and Nathaniel Buck, dated 1736.

to know him well felt obliged to write and to try to pacify him: "I wish to assure you that nothing can be further from my wish than to press you to give in a plan which you do not approve—in a case like the present I feel it would be particularly unfair towards you."[5] Salvin eventually capitulated and sent in three alternatives. These were "A," with angle turrets five feet high; "B," with low angle turrets like those at Castle Rising; and "C," with battlements and no turrets. The last, which we may assume was the cheapest expedient, was the one chosen.

It must be admitted that the fears of the "uncontents," as Salvin came to call them, were more than justified. Norwich was his most unsympathetic restoration and is not helped by the fact that the Combe Down stone, chosen by Francis Stone and approved by Blore, as "it came nearer to Caen than any other," has not mellowed in the hundred and fifty years since. The carved detail is mechanical, and the flat roof diminishes what ought to be a dramatic profile on the skyline. Salvin learned much from the mistakes made here.

France had set an example to all Europe in the care of historic monuments by the government; Lord Lincoln was aware of this and aware also that the learned societies were unlikely to contribute much in the way of practical restoration work, both through lack of cash and even more so through their habit of getting themselves into controversial positions, as did the members of the Cambridge Camden Society over their restoration of Holy Sepulchre. He therefore took the responsibility, in his capacity as First Commissioner, for the restoration of three ruinous castles, and in each case Salvin was the architect employed. By the time work on these was completed, attitudes had changed, and it was generally accepted that the state had a duty to maintain "other remnants of fuedal times," and a program of consolidation and repair was put in hand that continues to this day.[6]

The first castle to be tackled was Newark in Nottinghamshire, which was a ruin and in the process of collapse. Salvin surveyed this in May 1844 and found much of it to be unsafe; work began in October and consisted of clearing out an accumulation of earth and rubbish from the gatehouse, strengthening the foundations, and pulling out the mixture of brick and rubble that blocked old arches and windows. This, and the laying out of the grounds as a public park, was completed by the provision of another amenity for the townsfolk: new public baths built in the gardens and designed to look like a park keeper's lodge. Carisbrooke on the Isle of Wight was the next to be taken in hand. This was partly inhabited and had for years been one of the governor's residences but was now in need of considerable repair. It was begun in 1845, but what was in fact done has been obscured by the work carried out by Philip Hardwick in 1856. Caernarvon was a very much greater undertaking.

In his obituary in *The Builder,* Salvin is said to have influenced "high quarters" to get this castle repaired.[7] He had visited it while on holiday in Wales in August 1844 and made a study and a number of drawings of the ruins. Others were worried about their condition; the Central Committee of the British Archaeological Association had taken the matter up, and there had been "the strenuous

5. Norwich Castle MSS. Wodehouse to Salvin, September 21, 1836.
6. *The Builder* (February 16, 1850): 80. It refers particularly to the Welsh Castles: Conway, Beaumaris, Harlech, Rhuddlan, Criccieth, Carew, Caerphilly, and Pembroke.
7. *The Builder* (December 31, 1881): 809–10.

representations made to the Government by Mr. Justice Coleridge." Then, in the winter of 1844, part of the Queen's Gate collapsed, and Salvin was immediately called in. Heavy snow prevented even so much as a survey being made before March, but work got under way in July. The Queen's Gate was cleared of rubbish, turrets and battlements were restored, holes in the wall were filled in, windows and loops were repaired, and the masonry was rebuilt where the old and by then demolished town walls had abutted the Eagle Tower and the North-east Tower. All was complete in 1847, when it was found that some of the money voted for the restoration remained unspent. With Lincoln's approval, Salvin used this on a small excavation, which revealed some underground vaults.

The conclusion of the work was celebrated at the Second Annual Meeting of the Cambrian Archaeological Association, which was held at Caernarvon. An exhibition was mounted in the National School, consisting of Elevations and Sections of Roman and British Remains, by the Reverend C. H. Hartshorne; Views of the Principal Castles in South and North Wales, fifty in number, by A. Salvin Esq.; Plans and Elevations of Caernarvon Castle and other Welsh Castles, by Hartshorne; Mediaeval Remains found in Caernarvon, by Salvin, who also read a paper on the history of the castle and conducted the members around the building in a downpour. At a *Table d'hôte* dinner given at the Sportsman Hotel before the evening meeting, Lord Dungannon proposed "that this Meeting wishes to express to A. Salvin Esq., its highest approval of the efficient and careful manner in which he had supervised the restoration of Caernarvon Castle; also of his close adherence to the style, and the pure architectural and military character of the building." He was seconded by Hartshorne.[8]

Gilbert Scott never made any secret of his disapproval of Peckforton Castle and was man enough to express it in Salvin's presence at a meeting of the Royal Institute of British Architects on November 17, 1856, when discussion of the restoration work at Alnwick Castle was resumed: "For the last half century it has been the fashion to build new castles; and, although Mr. Salvin had built the most complete one—a perfect model of a Mediaeval fortress—that gentleman must excuse him for expressing his opinion that building castles was one of the greatest fallacies that could now be carried out."[9] He enlarged on this in print in 1857, and it is worth quoting what he had to say in full:

> The equally monstrous practice of Castle-building is, unhappily, not yet, extinct. The Royal Academy exhibitions continue periodically to show specimens of it, and the largest and most carefully and learnedly executed Gothic mansion of the present day is not only a castle in name,—it is not a sham fortress, such as those of twenty years back, whose frowning gateway is perhaps flanked on either side with a three foot clipped hedge,—but it is a real and carefully constructed mediaeval fortress capable of standing a seige from an Edwardian army,—a bulwark against the inroads of a Llewelyn or a Glendower. No pains or outlay have been grudged to render the fortress impregnable under mediaeval conditions, and against an army of five centuries back. . . . Now this is the very height of masquerading. The learning and skill with which the pageant has been carried out reflect the highest credit upon the architect; yet I cannot but feel it to have been a serious injury to our case, that so unreal a task should have been imposed upon him; and a misfortune of no ordinary kind that so much knowledge and skill should not have been directed to the

8. *Archaeologia Cambrensis* 1 (1846): 80; 3 (1848): 351.
9. *The Royal Institute of British Architects Papers* (1857): 23.

adaptation of the noble style in which he was working to the genuine requirements of the nineteenth century, though I am assured by those who know the house well, that, in spite of all, it is most convenient, and thoroughly comfortable as a modern residence.[10]

Now Scott was writing a good fifteen years after the event, and it is at least possible that he mistook the entire circumstances that led to the building of Peckforton Castle. John Tollemache was no medieval romantic like Charles Tennyson d'Eyncourt. He was probably one of the most formidable men of his age. The elder son of an equally formidable admiral, he was born in 1805 and had been page to Lord Blessington at the coronation of George IV. A first-rate athlete as a young man, he twice beat the champion of England over a hundred yards, though he was kind enough to remark afterward that the champion was past his best. He was a keen horseman and drove his carriages expertly. He married twice and had one of those Victorian families that were causing his contemporaries to greatly enlarge their houses: twenty-four sons and a daughter, of whom twelve sons and the daughter survived him. Tollemache succeeded to a 26,000-acre estate in Cheshire in 1837, and three years later he inherited Ham House at Richmond and another 7,000 acres with Helmingham Hall in Suffolk. He also owned five West Indian sugar plantations.

He entered Parliament in 1841, standing as Member for Cheshire South until 1868, and for Cheshire West from then until 1872. In 1876 he was created first Baron Tollemache of Helmingham, and he died in 1890. In Parliament he was a Tory and a Protectionist and one of those Members who defied Peel and opposed to the last ditch the repeal of the Corn Laws, although as a rule he contributed little to the day-to-day proceedings of the House. As he said himself, when speaking of the need to help West Indian planters who employed free labor and were at a serious disadvantage when competing with the sugar growers of Cuba and Brazil who still used slaves, he "very rarely troubled the House with any observations."[11] When he did speak, it was almost invariably on a matter to do with agriculture, and he had usually been provoked to do so by someone making ill-informed statements. In February 1846 he rose to protest about the state of the farming industry in Cheshire, which he described as being "so pressed down . . . by local and general taxation as to make it utterly impossible for the British farmer to compete with the foreign farmer," and went on to say that he was disenchanted with a Tory government that adopted a Liberal program, that he disapproved of their actions in connection with Dissenters' Chapels, academic education in Ireland and the College of Maynooth, and of course, the Corn Laws; that he could no longer support the government in Parliament and was going to vote against repeal. He concluded that he did not believe that the relaxation of tariffs improved trade, which like the landed interest also needed protection; and if this was not given "when the season of depression in the manufacturing districts arrived—and arrive it occasionally would—there would be nothing to fall back or rest upon, and the most fearful consequences would be the result to every interest in the Kingdom."[12] He no doubt had vivid recollections of what had happened five years before.

Salvin had first worked for Tollemache at Helmingham Hall, soon after it came

10. G. G. Scott, *Remarks on Secular and Domestic Architecture, Present and Future* (London: John Murray, 1857), p. 14.
11. *Hansard* 99: 1441.
12. *Hansard* 83: 1223.

into his possession. It had not been lived in for some years, and what was required was the same pattern as for many other clients: larger rooms and more domestic comfort and privacy. The hall ceiling was raised, a dining room and drawing room created by knocking together some small rooms, and an oak staircase put in. The stables and lodges were rebuilt, and the main gateway was hung with some wrought-iron gates from Ham. The bridge across the moat was repaired. Helmingham's moat had never been filled in with silt and rubbish and could still protect its occupants from intruders; once the gateway was blocked, the house was safe. There was no house on the Peckforton estate, and there is good reason to suppose that when Tollemache decided to build there the castle style was chosen just because he thought he might need a home that could be defended.

Building operations began in 1844, and it was in the autumn and winter of that year that Friedrich Engels wrote *The Condition of the Working Class in England.* Engels's knowledge of the state of the workers in industrial towns in the early 1840s came from a stay in Manchester in 1842–1844, when he was working in his father's textile firm. In his book he describes the factory system, labor movements, and the recent strikes, which he took as evidence that the inevitable uprising of the oppressed masses would shortly begin: "The decisive battle between the proletariat and the bourgeoisie is approaching," and he was certainly correct in anticipating political upheavals where the continent of Europe was concerned. Engels was a foreigner and a Communist, and he had lived in a town that had seen a great deal of civil disturbance; but what was going on was not lost on others. Charles Greville, aristocratic Clerk to the Privy Council who mixed with the highest in the land, had the matter plainly explained to him in November 1842. "Lord Wharncliffe and Kay Shuttleworth, who are both from the north, have given me an account of the state of the country and of the people which is perfectly appalling. There is an immense and continually increasing population, deep distress and privation, no adequate demand for labour, no demand for anything, no confidence, but a universal alarm, disquietude, and discontent. . . . Certainly I have never seen, in the course of my life, so serious a state of things as that which now stares us in the face."[13]

Consider the events of the years immediately before the construction of Peckforton was begun. There had been a financial crisis since 1837, but by the early forties the depression had reached critical proportions. In late 1839 there had been widespread Chartist riots, and that November the mob at Newport in Monmouthshire had only dispersed after being fired upon; in January 1841 there were mass meetings at Merthyr Tydfil and Clerkenwell Green. By 1842 the situation in Bradford was such that only two out of nineteen broadcloth manufacturers were still in business, and the west of England was equally badly hit; in April a riot at Rowley Regis over a wage cut had to be quelled by troops from Birmingham, and there was worse trouble in the Potteries, which was put down by the 3rd Dragoons. In August a mob from Stalybridge and Ashton closed the mills and marched on Manchester armed with sticks. On the tenth of that month there were mobs out at both Manchester and Salford, and the Riot Act was read three times in the course of that day. Three hundred special constables were sworn in. Dudley and Wed-

13. *The Greville Diary,* ed. Philip Whitwell Wilson (London: William Heinemann, 1927) 2: 175.

nesbury saw marches, and "several thousands of men and boys armed with bludgeons" tramped from Stockport to Macclesfield. Congleton was invaded by ten thousand men also armed with bludgeons; Huddersfield, Skipton, and Bradford suffered major demonstrations. In the end the riots extended from their point of origin in Lancashire and Staffordshire to Cheshire and Yorkshire, to the Welsh mining valleys and the industrial towns of Scotland; they were stopped by turning out the troops, mass arrests by the police, and a proclamation by the Queen against the offenders. Nonetheless, discontent simmered on, although the attention of the government was distracted from the Midlands by the Irish Famine, which began in 1845. When 1848 came, bringing revolution in Europe, the Chartists became active again, calling a meeting on Kennington Common, from whence it was intended that the crowds should march to Westminster and present a Monster Petition to Parliament. Remembering the events of four years before, Londoners panicked; seventeen thousand special constables were sworn, and the Duke of Wellington was commanded to defend the city. Fortunately for all concerned, rain stopped play.

Peckforton is thirty miles from Manchester, the chief scene of the disturbances in 1842, twenty-four miles from Macclesfield, and only twenty from Congleton; any one of these and other distressed towns in the area was barely two days' march away if determined bands set out to create trouble in the countryside, or to find food, for most of them were starving. From his remarks in the House, Tollemache obviously feared that such scenes would recur whenever there was industrial recession, and that "fearful consequences" would ensue. He had a wife and a young family; his duties as the local Member of Parliament and as a major landlord obliged him to spend much time in Cheshire. In Ireland there were many instances where houses had been attacked, and the mobs there had been able to lay their hands on firearms; this could happen in England, but up till then the rioters had, as we have seen, been armed only with sticks and bludgeons: medieval weapons that medieval walls could keep out.

Salvin was not, in fact, the first architect to be consulted. Tollemache began with George Latham of Nantwich, an architect with a very small business in Cheshire who is known only for some minor church work, an addition to the court house at Preston in Lancashire, and for Arley Hall near Northwich, designed for Rowland Egerton Warburton, who also abandoned Latham for Salvin when he built himself a private chapel. If a castle-style dwelling was envisaged from the very start, and this was later maintained by members of the family, it would soon have become apparent that someone of Latham's limited talent and experience was unlikely to produce what was required. Having decided upon the change, Tollemache treated him very handsomely, paying him £2000 for the work he had done and in compensation for the loss of the commission. Nothing quite like this had been tried before; the castles of the early nineteenth century, Belvoir, Eastnor, Penrhyn, Goodrich, and Gwrych, were the products of Romanticism and were all great glass windows and lack of conviction. Peckforton was intended by its owner to be capable of withstanding siege by rowdy elements of the population. Once the portcullis was down and the massive wooden entrance gates shut, Tollemache, his family, and domestic staff would have been able, if properly supplied, to remain safely inside until rescued by the police or the army (Fig. 79). There are no weak

79. Peckforton Castle, the barbican.

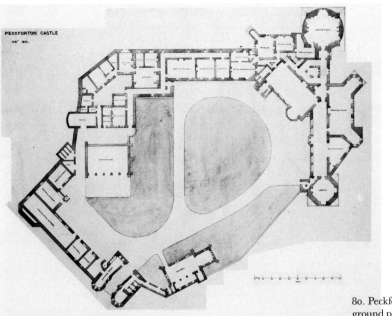

80. Peckforton Castle,
ground plan.

spots in the considerable circumference of the castle walls, apart from a sallyport that led into the dry moat and could be defended; all basement and ground floor windows are arrow slits, and attempting to scale the walls to the first floor level would have required ladders and been very hazardous. There was no way in without the use of artillery or explosives, which were unlikely to be obtained by a mob. Salvin's encyclopedic knowledge ensured complete authenticity and security.

Salvin turned to Brancepeth Castle as a model when he came to plan Peckforton (Fig. 80), not the Brancepeth of the Nevilles, to be sure, but the Brancepeth that had become the seat of the Russells as remodeled by Paterson (Fig. 2). It cannot be a coincidence that the organization of both castles has so much in common. Both are arranged irregularly around an inner ward and approached through a bar-

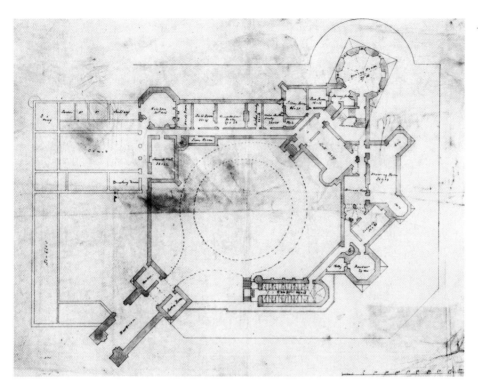

81. Peckforton Castle, early ground plan.

bican of impressive aspect; directly opposite this the principal reception rooms are arranged in an L-shaped block, with the great hall placed diagonally across the junction of the two ranges. Salvin has a more archaeologically correct great hall, with a porch leading into a screens passage and the dais end lit by an oriel window. Paterson had the entrance to his through a centrally placed porte cochère; at both the entrance leads through the hall to the main staircase, which is tucked into the triangular area between the hall and the flanking ranges. Peckforton's keep is roughly in the same position as the Neville Tower at Brancepeth, and the huge angle buttresses built by Paterson, which contain recesses opening into the rooms they support, recur in the boudoir and the drawing room at Peckforton, where they are enlarged into bay windows.

An early drawing shows how Salvin tightened up his planning (Fig. 81). Here the castle is shown as a vast rectangle with the barbican and great hall on a diagonal axis. Hall, staircase, dining room, and drawing room occupy their final positions, but there is no gallery, which now forms the ceremonial route from one end of the principal rooms to the other, the library cutting into this space behind an awkwardly contrived billiard room. The boudoir is far removed from the other private family rooms between the hall and the service and bedroom wing, and a chapel with a semicircular apse squares up one side of the bailey. Removing this to a position near the barbican and turning it onto a liturgically correct east-west alignment makes for a more picturesque grouping of this, the gateway and the stables, now in a pair of diagonal ranges. Indeed, the plan as finally worked out is a pattern of diagonals imposed upon a rectangle. The private rooms, boudoir, bathroom, sitting room, and schoolroom are grouped around a private stair that leads to the children's bedrooms off the cathedral corridor. These rooms, and the offices that occupy the ground floor of this range, are iron framed with segmental fireproof ceilings above. The seemingly solid oak frames are cast iron boxed with thin wooden planks. Perhaps the most impressive part of the interior is the arrangement of the stairs in the restricted triangular area behind the hall. The stairwell is a top-lit polygon with large lancets opening onto and lighting the steps, part of which lead up very grandly from the gallery to the dining room.

Peckforton stands on a hill about three hundred feet above the low-lying Cheshire countryside. Salvin was clearly thinking out his designs while on his holiday in Wales in August 1845, and there are a number of watercolors showing variants of the castle in its setting that may have been made for Tollemache before it was begun. There is also the large cork model that, as already mentioned, was sent to the Exposition Universelle in 1855, where it would have been seen by Prince Albert, who was in Paris that year to join with the Governor of the Tower of London in drawing up a comprehensive scheme for the restoration of that castle,

82. Peckforton Castle, the architectural model.

83. Peckforton Castle,
detail of stonework.

84. Peckforton Castle,
entrance front.

which was put under Salvin's direction (Fig. 82).[14] Salvin was to make cork models to illustrate his proposals for the tower, cork being more rugged in finish than paper or wood and giving a better impression of rough stonework. The Peckforton model, which survives at Helmingham Hall in the original glass case on its stand, is beautifully made, and the more finely cut architectural details such as the framing of the windows are indicated by carving these out of boxwood and inserting them in the cork of the walls. Minor differences in the fenestration show that it was made to show Tollemache what was intended; it is a model for, not a model of, the castle. Peckforton was completed in 1850 and has a lively silhouette dominated by the round keep, and there is a lot of nicely calculated contrast between the roughly cut masonry and the finely worked and stippled dressings (Fig. 83). The exterior is splendidly rugged, and so is the inside (Fig. 84). Lionel Tollemache, one of the twelve surviving sons, wrote, "The singular hue of antiquity is given to this 'John of Gaunt Castle' by the fact that in the hall, the dining room, and some of the passages, the walls of red sandstone are left bare; and it should be added that on those rocky walls the traces of primaeval waves are plainly visible."[15] Architectural detail throughout is kept simple; the windows are shouldered or cusped lancets that are used singly or in groups, and only in the great hall is there anything more elaborate. Internally the detail is kept very plain in the fireplaces and paneling, and the effect of the interiors is chiefly through what detail there is being overscaled. This is particularly the case in the great hall, the only large area that Salvin ever attempted to roof with a stone vault; this is quadripartite and divided into three sections by pairs of transverse ribs rising above the edge of the dais and the screen. The ribs are supported on massive corbels bearing pairs of shields, in both scale and handling very reminiscent of the trophies in the lower hall at Harlaxton. The only color or pattern is in the red, cream, and black of the Minton tiled floor.

The character of Tollemache's new house was dictated by his fear of civil unrest. His wishes in another respect were also obeyed. No central heating was put in during his lifetime; the castle was warmed throughout by open fires. He seems to have been well known to be quite impervious to cold, and it was a matter of remark at his clubs if he wore a waistcoat. Clearly a castle of this design could not be seen to be discharging smoke at random from the battlements. This presented Salvin with a considerable problem, which he solved by piping the smoke in metal flues across the flat roofs to a few large chimney stacks away from the outer wall. This could not be done for the fireplaces in the round keep, which has four stacks and a number of ventilator ducts incorporated in the battlements. One can only hope that the flues that ran horizontally for a considerable distance provided sufficient draft. Salvin was to encounter similar problems at Alnwick when he worked there.[16]

The building of a private chapel at Peckforton was no doubt due to Tollemache's extreme religious views (Fig. 85). It was not at all usual to include a chapel in a

14. *The Builder* (March 31, 1855): 149.
15. Lionel Tollemache, *Old and Odd Memories* (London: Edward Arnold, 1908).
16. *The Builder* (February 8, 1862): 89. "There are, too, other oddities peeping over the battlements— common red tile chimney pots. In explanation of this incongruity, we learn that in spite of the application of every modern appliance, the smoke nuisance cannot be overcome. The smoke-curing doctor at one time applied a device which made the parapet appear to be covered with rooks."

85. Peckforton Castle, the chapel, stables, and kitchen tower.

new house, and it has been pointed out that of a group of 380 houses put up in 1835-1914, only 21 had such a thing, and in 7 cases they were built for Roman Catholic families.[17] Disagreements with the local clergy could be the reason for the owner's incurring such expense. Egerton Warburton built his at Arley Hall because his parish priest would not tolerate the introduction of ritual. Tollemache's chapel was unlicensed so that the Bishop could not interfere and was intended for services of quite a different kind. He was strongly evangelical and opposed to any elaboration, preferring the plainest possible form of worship and short sermons, which he timed, watch in hand. His entire family and all the servants were obliged to attend morning and evening prayers, and this alone in a place as remote as the Peckforton hilltop made the chapel a necessity.[18] At Brancepeth one had been fitted up in one of the towers, but by this date such an expedient was no longer accept-able: "Ancient canons forbid the placing of living apartments *over* a consecrated building, and reverence would equally counsel against their standing under them."[19] It was for this reason that the chapel at Alnwick, which had been above the middle gateway, was removed to a separate building adjoining the Prudhoe Tower.

   The defenses of Peckforton were never to be put to the test, but its forbidding aspect was never softened as a concession to late Victorian or Edwardian taste: "No flower-beds soften the ruggedness of the rock-fortress; but the wild growth with its wealth of bilberries and broom, stretches to its very base. The two small gardens are situated—not very conveniently—at the foot of the hill."[20] It is all Salvin at his most grim and most successful.

   17. Jill Franklin, *The Gentleman's Country House and Its Plan, 1835–1914* (London: Routledge & Kegan Paul, 1981).
   18. Tollemache, *Memories.* There were no hot meals on Sunday, and white wine was drunk instead of champagne.
   19. *The Ecclesiologist* (July 1845).
   20. Tollemache, *Memories.*

8

Church Work

John Keble was born in 1792, Edward Pusey in 1800, and John Newman in 1801. Thus the most prominent members of the movement that began in Oxford for the reformation of both the university and the Church of England were Salvin's immediate contemporaries. Three years before Keble's birth, the established order in Europe had been shattered by the French Revolution; for the next twenty years England was committed to a Continental war aimed at curbing the power of France. At the same time, the Industrial Revolution got under way. Farm laborers deserted the fields for the factories, a move that was given impetus by the agricultural depression that followed the Napoleonic Wars. Consequently, the population of northern industrial cities such as Manchester, Leeds, Sheffield, Bradford, and Blackburn doubled between 1801 and 1831 and continued to increase enormously during the next twenty years. No provision was made for housing this influx of people, who lived in miserable tenements or at best in back-to-back houses; there were no sewers and no pure water supply. The appalling rate of mortality was inflated by frequent epidemics of diseases such as cholera, and the spiritual welfare of this new urban working class was as neglected as their physical condition.

The process of Church reform during the nineteenth century cannot be described in detail here, but it may be recalled that Newman became a tutor at Oriel in 1826 and that Keble published *The Christian Year* in 1827. Keble publicly voiced the concern of those who perceived the decay of the established Church in the Assize Sermon of 1833, when his subject was "The National Apostasy," and Dr. Arnold published *The Principles of Church Reform* in that same year. The intellectual approach was set out by Hurrel Froude, Pusey, and Newman in the *Tracts for the Times;* the last of these, *Tract XC,* written by Newman in 1841, entitled *Remarks on Certain Passages in the Thirty-Nine Articles,* caused such a storm of protest that further publications were suspended. Newman and his followers found no alternative to the Church of Rome. Those of the Oxford movement who remained Anglican were accused of Romanism, ritualism, and the perversion of the Church of England, and the opposition party, organized as "The Church Association," founded in 1865 to counteract High Church Popery, was powerful enough by 1888 to present a petition to the Archbishop of Canterbury and thus place on trial no less a person than the Bishop of Lincoln, who was accused of certain illegal acts, namely taking the eastward position during the recitation of the creed, placing lighted candles on the altar, and making the sign of the cross, among other things, during the service of Holy Communion. This, however, was in the future.

Returning to the first part of the nineteenth century, disquiet at the spiritual condition of the Church, as expressed by its own members, was greatly surpassed by the dislike and indignation that its entrenched privileges aroused elsewhere. Its opposition to the Catholic Emancipation Act in 1829, and the defeat of the 1831 Reform Bill, which was popularly attributed to the fact that twenty-one bishops had voted against it in the House of Lords, provoked great anger in two sections of the community.[1] Once they had been provoked, the Church itself supplied the ammunition for vicious attacks on its organization; poor town parishes were neglected by the clergy, and wealthy but underpopulated country parishes were much sought after, frequently obtained by simony or influence, and when obtained often held *in commendam* and in plurality. The nonconformist sects agitated against the payment of Church rates by their members, and the immense income derived from the endowments of some cathedrals was considered a national scandal; the threat of government intervention led in the case of Durham to the founding there of the university, financed by income that had previously gone to the Bishop and canons. But, in general, the Church resisted all attempts at reform from outside as Erastianism.

Such action on the part of the Bishopric of Durham demonstrated an increasing awareness on the part of the clergy that if the Church persisted in its old ways the government might find itself with no alternative but to interfere. This, with a new sense of its responsibilities stimulated by the reformers within, led to an immense effort during the nineteenth century to deal with the increase in population and the drift to the towns. At the turn of the century there were 10,300 clergy to man 10,500 parishes, of which no less than half had an annual value of less than £50. Before the District Churches Act of 1843, the creation of new parishes was legally very complicated, but the passing of the Church Building Act of 1818 and the provision of a million pounds for building new churches set in motion an astounding outburst of activity. Coincidentally, the Church Building Society, privately financed and insisting from the outset on the provision of a certain proportion of open seats for the poor in every church it contributed to, was founded this same year. Between 1811 and 1820 only 96 churches were built or rebuilt; in the following decade the number rose to 308, and between 1831 and 1840 it had virtually doubled at 600; during the next twenty years 1,749 churches were built, and between 1861 and 1870 the number was 1,110. Between 1840 and 1876 the sum of £25,603,220 was spent on the building and repair of churches, and £1,093,340 was spent on the cathedrals; but the efforts of all concerned to provide places for those who wished, or should have wished, to attend Anglican worship were doomed to failure by the rapid growth of the population. In 1800 it had been estimated that nearly half could be accommodated, but fifty years later this was down to less than a third, and of those who lived in the towns only one-fifth could have found a place. An undignified scramble for seats, which might have been expected from these statistics did not, however, occur, as the lower orders showed a marked reluctance to attend.[2]

The motives of those who provided all this money were not entirely altruistic; the Church was widely regarded by the well-to-do as a method of controlling, if not

1. Supporters of the Reform Bill knew their enemies and took care that the public at large know them also. Posters were printed: "Black List! Being the Annual Amount of Pickings of the Peers and their Families, who voted against the Reform Bill, in the House of Lords, on Saturday, Oct. 8, 1831." Lists follow, then "Total amount of the above £2,161,867, which only includes about one half of the Peerage. Printed, published & Compiled by W. P. Chubb, & sold at the *London Spy Office.*"

2. *The Church Builder* 53 (January 1875).

repressing, the potentially revolutionary poor. In 1875 *The Church Builder,* the publication of the Incorporated Church Building Society, as it had become, said: "There is no statesman, be his party politics what they may, who will underrate the value of an Established Clergy as a moral police. Certainly the behaviour of the Lancashire workmen during the cotton famine, as contrasted with the troubles of 1843, bore witness to the effects of improved education and increased church work in the interval."3 This attitude was reflected in the obligatory church attendance demanded by the middle classes and gentry of their servants, an attitude that persisted in rural areas into the depression years of the 1930s, when receipt of relief was often dependent on churchgoing.4

Six years after the passing of the Church Building Act, a further £500,000 was granted to the commissioners; after twelve years 134 commissioners' or Waterloo churches, as they were generally called, had been completed. The total number was to be 214, of which 174 were in the Gothic style. They proved to be the watershed between the fanciful Gothic of eighteenth-century churches such as Francis Hiorne's St. Mary's Tetbury, completed in 1781, and the Gothic reality insisted upon by Pugin and the Cambridge Camden Society, and a forcing ground for the development of archaeological Gothic in ecclesiastical architecture. Practically every architect of competence who was in practice in the 1820s and 1830s built his commissioners' church, and Salvin was no exception. The architects, and indeed the commissioners themselves, had inherited attitudes to church buildings that had been current since the seventeenth century but that were shortly to be vigorously, not to say venemously, challenged. The Book of Common Prayer required the participation of the congregation in the service, and it had to both see and hear what was going on. This led to rectangular buildings without chancels, and as it was desired that as great a number as possible should be seated, to the provision of galleries. They had none of the furnishings that were to be considered necessary later in the century, such as a reredos, a sedilia, or a chancel screen; and where there was stained glass it was such that James Fergusson, who was no admirer of the Gothic Revival, could remark nastily: "where painted glass is introduced, good drawing and elegant colouring had to be employed, after the fashion of Sir Joshua Reynolds's window at New College, Oxford, or West's at Windsor."5

The commissioners' task was to seat as large a congregation as possible as cheaply as possible, and when they came to consider the various styles open to them, they expressed a preference for Gothic, chiefly, it seems, because Roman or Grecian styles required large stone porticos that swallowed up a disproportionate amount of the funds allowed. It also required some ingenuity to adapt the classical style to a Christian church in the form then understood, whereas Gothic models were to be found throughout the country and needed little manipulation. What seems to have been one of the most popular was the type of Perpendicular found at St. Augustine's Skirlaugh, built by Bishop Skirlaw in 1401, but with monumental west porches replacing the classical porticos. Examples of this sort of thing are James Savage's St. Luke's Chelsea and Charles Barry's St. Peter's Brighton, both

3. R. A. Soloway, *Prelates and People* (London: Routledge & Kegan Paul, 1969).
4. The Reverend A. D. Dean of St. Paul's Over Tabley, private communication.
5. James Fergusson, *History of Modern Architecture* (London: John Murray, 1902).

built in the early twenties. The architects who built the churches of the early part of the nineteenth century, Savage and Barry, Rickman, Ambrose Poynter, Blore, Burton, and Salvin himself, were overtaken by two factors with which they were unable to come to terms. The first was Tractarianism, which transformed the doctrine and the rites of the Church of England; the other was the writings of Pugin. That a man so pragmatic and indeed commercial in his approach to architecture as Scott could regard himself as being "morally awakened" by these gives a fair idea of their impact on the younger generation. Their elders were not so easily moved; men like Blore, Burton, and Salvin continued to build churches as they had always done, the chief differences in design being dictated more by the amount of money available than any development of style.

Salvin's churchbuilding practice began as a result of his Durham connection, and the first five church commissions he received were all in the north. They had their origin in the rapid industrialization of this part of the country and a consequent increase in population. They are the Church of the Holy Trinity Ulverston, St. Paul's North Sunderland, Holy Trinity South Shields, St. John's Shildon, and Holy Trinity Darlington. Ulverston was an iron-smelting town and exported copper and slate; North Sunderland was a center for the North Sea fishing fleet and traded in fish, lime, and corn; South Shields had shipbuilding and was a coal port; Shildon and Darlington both expanded following the opening of the Stockton and Darlington Railway in 1825, which had extended as far as Shildon by 1830. Ulverston was a commissioners' church and was built there because the town had expanded from 4,962 inhabitants in 1801 to 7,250 in 1831 and the single parish church was inadequate; in North Sunderland the numbers for the same period were from 496 to 860; South Shields, loading the larger colliers and with thirteen dry docks building up to thirty ships a year, had a population of nearly 9,000 by the 1830s and a dissenting majority who attended chapels opened by the Primitive, Wesleyan, Independent, and New Connexion Methodists, the Baptists, the Presbyterians, and the United Seceders, all of whom were actively recruiting adherents at this time.

All these churches, apart from St. Paul's, were in a rather misunderstood Early English style, and the reason for this was economy. Alexander James Beresford Beresford Hope, one of the founders of the Cambridge Camden Society, wrote: "The Lancet style enjoyed extensive popularity with the fabricators of cheap churches on account of the happy reputation which it enjoyed of surviving more starvation than any other. It was emphatically the cheap style, and in the hands into which it fell as often emphatically proved itself to be the nasty one."[6]

It must be confessed that Salvin's early churches tend to confirm this condemnation (Fig. 86). Ulverston is a typical commissioners' church: nave and aisles, a large west gallery, no chancel, the altar being simply placed against the east wall and flanked by the pulpit and reading desk. A northwest tower and spire have some pretty cusped corbelling and a rather handsome clock, but Salvin is clearly unfamiliar with his chosen style; there are mean external buttresses, some extraordinary timberwork in the aisle roofs, and, most curious of all, a flat ceiling above the nave. It is clumsy, as is Holy Trinity South Shields, a larger building with a short chancel, transepts, and west tower, but again giving the impression that the

6. A. J. B. Beresford Hope, *The English Cathedral of the Nineteenth Century* (London: John Murray, 1861).

86. Holy Trinity Church,
Ulverston, lithograph.

87. Holy Trinity Church, Darlington, pen and wash sketch.

architect was struggling with the detail and with a very short purse. Darlington is more accomplished (Fig. 87). Again there is no chancel, and nave and aisles are under a single roof, with lancet windows forming part of a continuous arcade along the north and south sides. The tower is slightly to the west of center on the north side and acts as a porch; it has angle buttresses and triple lancet louvres to the bell chamber. It was quite the best thing Salvin had done up to this date. There

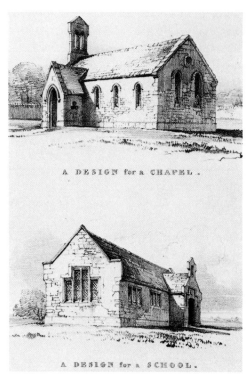

88. St. John's Church,
Shildon, pen and
wash sketch.

89. Designs for a chapel
and a school, lithograph.

is, however, no doubt that Early English is most happily employed by him on a small scale, as in the little church at Shildon, now much altered (Fig. 88). He uses it also in an unpretentious and pleasing design for a chapel, which appears in a lithograph with a school in the Tudor style, which Salvin had drawn before Queen Victoria came to the throne (Fig. 89).

His first encounter with the peculiar problems of restoration work began with his appointment to Norwich Cathedral in 1830, having obtained the position through letters of recommendation from Colonel Cust, Thomas Lister Parker, and the Reverend W. N. Darnell, one of Lord Crewe's trustees who was at this time his client at North Sunderland. He was retained at an annual fee of £50 and worked at Norwich for four years. He began in the south transept. The ruins of the slype and other buildings between the cathedral and the chapter house were cleared away, exposing the lower part of the transept's south facade. This was refaced, following generally the design of the north transept: three bays and a central door. Above the door Salvin placed a clock, for which he designed the inside and outside faces. The face on the outside was the same as the one at Ulverston, but the inside face has curious Romanesque beasts and foliage and was much admired by his fellow members of the Society of Antiquaries before it was sent up to Norwich on a cart. Within the transept some partitions were taken away, fire-damaged stonework repaired, and the east arch blocked in. A monument to Dean Joseph Turner, also designed by Salvin, was inserted.

The rearrangement of the choir was a more complicated matter. A change in the manner of worship was causing trouble at nearly every cathedral in the land; the problem that Salvin now faced at Norwich, and later at Durham and Wells, was essentially the same. The naves of cathedrals were only very occasionally used for services, and the laity were admitted to the choir. A congregation in the nave could not see the service, and as the prayers were not intoned as they still were on the Continent, they could not hear, either. The choir was therefore crowded with worshipers, who at Norwich sat in large box pews abutting the choir stalls; above these there were galleries reached by wooden stairs in the north and south aisles, which had canopies, screens, and windows fitted with leaded lights to keep out the drafts. It was all most unsuitable. This was cleared away, and a good deal of discussion, not to say argument, then ensued as to what could be done to provide sufficient seating. The chapter suggested that extra sittings might be placed east of the crossing; Salvin thought that the presbytery should be kept uncluttered and wrote saying that the Bishop of Carlisle had been consulted and agreed with him. Then there was a proposal that galleries should be built in the transepts and the organ placed in that on the north side; Salvin could not agree. Next the chapter decided that part of the transepts should be thrown into the choir, and a sketch of this arrangement as carried out at Tewkesbury was obtained from R. C. Carpenter. Salvin responded that Tewkesbury had been reordered in 1796 and was not an acceptable precedent; annoyed that they had gone to Carpenter, he also suggested that the chapter should employ another professional person on the choir, as he was unable to agree with any of their proposals. Four months later the Reverend Prebendary Wodehouse, clearly much disturbed at the delay, wrote on behalf of the chapter, asking him to continue in any way he thought proper.

Stone screens with tracery windows filled with glass were built between the pillars of the two bays west of the crossing, and similar screens shut off the transepts from the aisles. The old oak choir stalls and their misericords were stripped of paint and reused, with two new rows of stalls placed in front of them; the deal canopies were replaced with new ones in oak to Salvin's design. The pulpitum was rebuilt, and the organ was given a new case and placed upon it. A new royal arms and commemorative inscription completed the work.[7] The final position of the organ had been the subject of yet another dispute between the chapter and their architect, but such interference as he experienced at Norwich can have been as nothing to that which Salvin faced in connection with the restoration of Holy Sepulchre at Cambridge, where he worked for a large and self-opinionated committee. It was his first parish church restoration and an event of importance both for his career and for the entire movement of the restoration of ecclesiastical buildings in the country, which must now be considered.

When Gilbert Scott's autobiography was published in 1879, it began with an introduction by the Dean of Chichester that deplored "the ruthless work of destruction which for the last thirty years has been going on in almost every parish in England under the immediate direction of our architects, and with the sanction of our parochial Clergy. . . . At the beginning of the period referred to, to seek out and to study the village churches of England was almost part of the education of the English gentleman." But after thirty years of restoration, "in by far the greater number of our lesser churches there scarcely survives a *single point of interest*."[8]

7. Norwich Cathedral MSS, Chapter Act Books and Correspondence. John Britton, *The History and Antiquities of the See and Cathedral Church of Norwich* (London: Longman & Co., 1816).

8. Gilbert Scott, *Personal and Professional Recollections* (London: Sampson, Law & Co., 1879).

The Cambridge Camden Society had its origin in just such a group of English gentlemen who systematically visited parishes in the neighborhood of their university. Their first concern had been to remedy years of neglect of the fabric of the churches by the clergy and their churchwardens, but as early as 1843 the society had become aware of another danger, arising in no little part from their own efforts in the parishes concerned: "We are entering on an age of church restoration: does it not behove us and all others to watch the first steps with the most careful interest? How sad for the church if the current should take the wrong direction! How lamentable even that one noble pile should be sacrificed, while we are yet feeling our way to the right principles!"9 And later the same year: "We have before had occasion to observe that at present our wish to restore has gone beyond our knowledge. . . . The restorations of the nineteenth century may be classed with the sacrilege and indifference of the preceding, and scarcely less dangerous to the consistency and original beauty of our ancient churches."10 But the prescience of the Camdenians was no defense against what was to come. As we have seen, the money was readily available, from the state, the Incorporated Church Building Society and similar organizations, and from private individuals enriched by industry; £25 million was spent on building and restoring eight and a half thousand churches, and the Cambridge Camden Society, which had in 1846 become the Ecclesiological Late Cambridge Camden Society, and by 1852 The Ecclesiological Society *tout court* must bear a good deal of responsibility for the ruthlessness with which the work was carried out. Criticizing Scott and Moffat's restoration of St. Mary's Stafford, they held that it was necessary "either from existing evidences or from supposition, to recover the original scheme of the edifice as conceived by the first builder, or as begun by him and developed by his immediate successors; or, on the other hand, [he] must retain the additions and alterations of subsequent ages, repairing them where needing it. . . . For our own part we decidedly choose the former . . . who can doubt that it was right to recover the *original* appearance of the church."11 From this position they were able to proceed without a qualm to recommend the removal of such things as clerestories and other windows that had been inserted to give more light to early medieval churches, and here Salvin follows them, taking out the clerestory in the chancel of All Saints Sherburn-in-Elmet and replacing Y-tracery windows with narrow lancets; he also removed two large Perpendicular windows that had been installed in an attempt to lighten the little Norman church of St. Swithin Nately Scures, and replaced them with round-headed windows modeled on a surviving original, plunging the east end once again in gloom.

By 1847 the Camden dogma of reversion to a real or supposed original had been pushed to an almost lunatic degree. *The Ecclesiologist* reviewed E. A. Freeman's *Principles of Church Restoration* and described three theories of restoration, which it christened the Destructive, the Conservative, and the Ecclectic.12 The first of these was favored by one of the society's founders, J. M. Neale, who declared himself ready to pull down Peterborough Cathedral, if it could be "replaced by a Middle-Pointed cathedral as good of its sort."13 The Conservative, which called for the

9. *The Ecclesiologist* (April 1843): 113.
10. Ibid. (November 1843): 33.
11. Ibid. (February 1842): 65.
12. Ibid. (May 1947): 161.
13. Ibid. (June 1847): 233. But Neale may have been speaking with tongue in cheek.

repair of ancient work of whatever period, found few supporters among the society's members, but the Ecclectic, which advocated a combination of restoration and remodeling as seemed desirable to the architect and to his clients, received general approval. This, in effect, gave the restorer carte blanche to replace anything he considered inappropriate with new features of his own design. The resulting destruction was enormous and the general position so unclear that a man like Scott, who definitely considered himself on the side of the angels and who had in 1850 published *A Plea for the Faithful Restoration of our Ancient Churches,* could be Ecclectic to the extent that it was the unwelcome news that he was about to begin on Tewkesbury Abbey that caused William Morris to write to the *Athenaeum* in protest, and then to form the Society for the Protection of Ancient Buildings.[14] The revulsion that Morris and the founding members of this society felt for what was going on in the name of restoration had been voiced in a work published a year before Scott's *Plea.* The formidable Ruskin, who to some extent became his generation's mentor in all matters concerning art, had put the matter quite plainly in *The Lamp of Memory:* "Do not let us talk then of restoration. The thing is a Lie from beginning to end. You make a model of a building as you may of a corpse. . . . I must not leave the truth unstated, that it is again no question of expediency or feeling whether we shall preserve the buildings of past times or not. *We have no right whatsoever to touch them.* They are not ours. They belong partly to those who built them, and partly to all generations of mankind who are to follow us."[15]

Salvin had been made an honorary member of the Cambridge Camden Society by November 1841. The reason for this was that the society had undertaken the restoration of Holy Sepulchre Cambridge, after the collapse of part of the south aisle that September. It was their most ambitious project to date, their earlier efforts having consisted merely of repairing a font and font cover and the stripping of some rough cast in three Cambridgeshire churches.[16] Salvin was appointed the society's architect despite the fact that his ecclesiastical work had until then consisted only of that at Norwich Cathedral and his rather plain new churches, most of which were in the north and not likely to be known to society members. One, however, was in the south, Christ Church, Kilndown, which he had begun in 1839 for Edward Hussey and Field Marshal Lord Beresford. This was a typically unremarkable building, small, Early English, lacking a chancel, but with a west tower and spire. Beresford Hope, the Field Marshal's stepson, an active and influential member of the society, had set about improving it ecclesiologically. He was later to obtain designs for fittings from R. C. Carpenter and William Butterfield, but at this stage Salvin was collaborating with him and proving an acceptable ally. Beresford Hope wrote to the Vicar in March 1840: "The suggestion of Mr. Salvin, of having painted glass and a stone altar which you mentioned, is so ingenious and beautiful that I have determined on adopting it." It is interesting that at this early date Salvin favored what were then very "High Church" furnishings, but his clients rarely cared for or could afford such things. He was being particularly daring in suggesting the stone altar, the design of which

14. Gilbert Scott, *A Plea for the Faithful Restoration of Our Ancient Churches. A Paper Read before the Architectural and Archaeological Society of Bucks, at Their First Annual Meeting in 1848, and Repeated at a Joint Meeting of the Architectural Societies for the Archdeaconry of Northampton in the County of Bedford in 1849* (Oxford: Parker, 1850).
15. John Ruskin, *The Seven Lamps of Architecture* (London: Smith, Elder & Co., 1849).
16. James F. White, *The Cambridge Movement* (Cambridge: At the University Press, 1962).

he based on the tomb of William of Wykeham at Winchester Cathedral; a stone altar at Holy Sepulchre was to lead the society to the Court of Arches, but that at Kilndown, installed by the most influential family in the neighborhood, still survives.[17] The stained glass at Kilndown is by Franz Eggert of Munich; it is more than likely that Salvin would have visited the royal glassworks there on his visit five years before and recommended German glass in default of any satisfactory English alternative. Clearly his ideas on church furnishings corresponded with those of Beresford Hope, who saw to it that he was employed not only on Holy Sepulchre, but also on other projects of the society, such as his designs for a model church based on the twelfth-century Norman example at Thaon, sent to Bishop Selwyn in New Zealand, and for the new Anglican church at Alexandria, which was built some time later to the designs of J. W. Wild. Furthermore, Salvin's connection with the society enabled him to pick up a number of useful commissions from the members, the most important of which was that for Arley Hall Chapel; the others were mostly for work on parish churches, and this allowed him to expand his churchbuilding and restoration practice, which until then had been somewhat limited.

The restoration of Holy Sepulchre was undertaken and financed by the Cambridge Camden Society as a practical demonstration of the correct method of proceeding with the repair of a ruinous church. The society began by setting up a Restoration Committee of twenty-one persons under the chairmanship of Archdeacon Thorpe, their president; all but three of this committee, namely the incumbent, the Reverend R. R. Faulkner, and the two churchwardens, were either vice-presidents or committee members of the society and held strong views on what should be done, which did not necessarily correspond with those held by their architect. This twelfth-century church is one of the round churches that in England were usually built by the Knights Templar or Knights Hopitallers in imitation of the Holy Sepulchre at Jerusalem. By 1841 it had undergone a number of alterations, which included the addition of a chancel in the fourteenth century, a north chancel aisle and a vestry built mostly of red brick, the insertion of large Perpendicular windows in the round nave and its tower, and the addition of an extra belfry story containing five bells, the ropes of which hung down in the middle of the congregation. The weight of this belfry, the vibration of the bells, and the undermining of the foundations by grave-digging had been responsible for the collapse of part of the nave aisle. The windows had been carved out of clunch and were badly decayed; the nave was full of box-pews, and a staircase had been built against the south wall, leading to a gallery, reached through the triforium and containing both more worshipers and the organ. The walls were whitewashed and dotted with black and white marble monuments.

Salvin's restoration follows, except for minor details, the reconstruction published by James Essex in 1782, from which it may be presumed that both architects found a good deal of evidence as to the original appearance of the building.[18] Faithful to the principles of Ecclectic restoration expounded by the society, the

17. The Dowager Countess of Pembroke, whose family was also fairly influential, was not so lucky. The Cosmati work altar she had brought from Italy for her son's new church of St. Mary and St. Nicholas at Wilton, begun in 1840, was absolutely forbidden by the bishop of Salisbury.

18. James Essex, "Observations on the Origins and Antiquity of Round Churches; and of the Round Church at Cambridge in Particular," *Archaeologia* 6 (1782): 163.

90. The Church of the Holy Sepulchre, Cambridge, after restoration, lithograph.

round nave was ruthlessly stripped of later additions, apart from the fourteenth-century chancel. The central tower was reduced to its original height and given a conical roof; the windows in both tower and aisles were replaced by new round-headed windows copied from one surviving Norman example in the clerestory. The aisle was reroofed. A new south chancel aisle provided sittings to replace those that were lost when the pews and gallery were cleared out of the nave, and a new vestry and bell tower were built on the north (Fig. 90). Internally the intrusive marble memorials were taken down, the stonework cleaned of whitewash and repaired, and the floor relaid with encaustic tiles; various well-wishers, including Salvin, gave stained-glass windows. The font was given an elaborate wooden cover, and a credence table and stone altar were installed.

The Reverend Faulkner was a nonresident incumbent and clearly of a Low Church persuasion. His first attempt to rectify such papistical excesses was overruled by the chancellor of the diocese, but his case was upheld in the Court of Arches. Stone altar and credence table were thrown out into the churchyard, and "the incumbent, having sufficiently defaced its beauty, by re-erection of monuments on the walls, the 'formation'—to use his own term,—of a reading and clerk's pue, the introduction of a table, with flimsy buttresses to its legs and cockney spandrils,—of chocolate-coloured commandment boards, and useless benches between the piers of the nave, proceeded to give notice of its re-opening."[19] The society was humiliated and in considerable debt, which it took a few years to discharge. Salvin made the best of an unfortunate start in church restoration by publishing, by way of advertisement, a lithograph of the newly repaired Holy Sepulchre, which he distributed to his clients, actual and potential.

The experience of working on this twelfth-century building was as beneficial to Salvin's attempts in the Romanesque style as working on old manor houses had been for his development as a designer of Tudor country houses; his study of Thaon, undertaken when preparing the designs for Selwyn, must also have

19. *The Ecclesiologist* (September 1845): 217.

91. St. Paul's Church, North Sunderland, from Wilson's *Archdeaconry of Lindisfarne.*

helped. His first essay in the Norman style had been for the little church of St. Paul, North Sunderland. The plans for this were approved in late 1830, and the church opened for services in the summer of 1833. It consists of a nave covered with a plaster tunnel vault and lit by four round-headed splayed windows on the north and south sides. There is an apsidal chancel and a west door with a double bellcote on the gable above (Fig. 91). Salvin also designed the parsonage here, and both buildings show a number of unconvincing Norman features, such as squashed cushion capitals and tall round chimney stacks. His next attempt at this period was in an equally small church, that of Holy Trinity Sewstern. Less pretentious than St. Paul's, it consists of a nave but no chancel, with four round-headed nook shafted windows on either side and similar windows flanking the west door. This is incorporated in a buttress which rises to a single bellcote (Fig. 92). Salvin built only two more churches in neo-Norman, which was at its most popular in the early 1840s but thereafter fell out of favor. They are St. Andrew's South Otterington of 1844–1847 and St. Michael's Cowesby of 1846, which stand within six miles of each other in the North Riding. St. Andrew's is large, with nave and north aisle, a chancel, and a substantial west tower with a pyramidal roof. The windows are as at Sewstern but with the addition of chevron moldings, and a carved corbel table supports the eaves of the chancel and tower roofs (Fig. 93). Inside there is a remarkable set of Norman furnishings, a stone reading desk and pulpit decorated with chevron and dogtooth moldings. St. Michael's is even more impressive; it has a central tower, and again a pyramidal roof with lucarnes, chancel, and south porch. It is probably the most satisfying village church that Salvin ever built (Fig. 94).

Salvin rapidly fell out of favor with the Ecclesiologists, and their vehemence in condemning his designs so soon after the completion of the Holy Sepulchre commission is surprising, but characteristic of the intemperance and diverse views of those concerned. His next important church was St. John's Keswick, Early English and consisting of a nave, west tower, and spire, and an odd polygonal vestry on the south side (Fig. 95). Nave and tower are decorated with attenuated pinnacles, which appear again at St. John the Evangelist Grantham (Fig. 96). This was well

92. Holy Trinity Church, Sewstern.

93. St. Andrew's Church,
South Otterington.

94. St. Michael's Church, Cowesby.

95. St. John the Evangelist's Church, Keswick, lithograph.

96. St. John the Evangelist's
Church, Grantham, tower.

received by the correspondent of *The British Almanac:* "This church is in the Early
Pointed or lancet style, and it is also a favourable exception to most modern
designs professing to be in that mode of architecture. Although plain and rather
homely in character it is free from trumpery pretension and meanness and lit-

97. St. John the Evangelist's Church, Grantham, lithograph.

tleness of manner"[20] (Fig. 97). *The Ecclesiologist,* on the other hand, was disgusted: "The church erected some three years ago at Spitalgate, Grantham, is of the worst class of modern design. No one who examines either its composition or details would suppose the architect knew any thing of the Pointed style. It is not too much to say that every single detail involves a solecism, and the plan is as faulty as the design. A western tower, intended for First Pointed or Early Middle Pointed, is surmounted by pinnacles such as no ancient church ever had or could have, and has a western doorway with mouldings of the worst possible description."[21] The money for the church had been raised by the Vicar and the local gentry, and it is all too plainly an example of what Beresford Hope referred to as "starved." This was unfortunately the case with the great majority of Salvin's later churches. Very occasionally, as in the cases of St. Mary Magdalene Torquay and the very fine All Saints Runcorn, which cost £9,000, the Duke of Northumberland's large St. Paul's Alnwick, which cost £20,000, and his last church, St. John's Perlethorpe, which cost nearly £18,000, did the easing of the usual financial constraints permit him to build something really striking.

St. Mary Magdalene has a nave, north and south aisles, a polygonal apse, and a tower and spire at the southeast corner of the nave (Fig. 98). The style is an elaborate Early English, with nice touches such as the arcade at clerestory level, intermittently pierced with windows and the small flying buttresses between the pinnacles and the spire. All Saints is large and high, built of local red sandstone and covered with green Westmoreland slates; it stands on a fine site beside the

20. *British Almanac and Companion* (1841): 231.
21. *The Ecclesiologist* (July 1845): 186. Similar pinnacles occurred on the chancel of St. George's Birmingham by Thomas Rickman, 1819–1822; it is possible that both architects were using a single and now unidentifiable precedent.

Anthony Salvin

98. St. Mary Magdalene's Church,
Torquay, lithograph.

River Mersey. It has nave, aisles, chancel, and a southwest tower and a tall
octagonal broach spire with two tiers of lucarnes, these facing the cardinal points
springing from the base, and those above springing from the broach, a complicated
yet successful design (Fig. 99). The aisles are lit by pairs of lancets, the clerestory
by quatrefoils, and arcades run both across the square east end and along its sides.
Another arcade, rising from the top of the west door to eaves, level crosses the west
front and is pierced by a pair of lancets; there is a triangular sexfoil window in the
gable above. St. Paul's Alnwick, the most expensive by far, was built in the
Decorated style; it had an aisled chancel and nave, a west tower, and an east
window designed by Willian Dyce and made by Ainmuller of Munich. The last of
this group, St. John's, put up by Earl Manvers, is again Decorated and the
prettiest, with a setback octagonal spire rising behind a crenellated parapet,
crocketed pinnacles and trefoil cresting on the roof ridge, and a chancel with a
band of quatrefoils at the eaves and gabled pinnacles (Fig. 100). There is excellent
carving both inside and out and some use of colored marble shafts, but Salvin
remained a man of the 1840s to the last, and one does not find in his churches the
constructional polychromy, mosaics and wall paintings, marble and metalwork,
and the borrowings from Continental models that characterize the High Victorian
Gothic churches of the second half of the nineteenth century. Nevertheless, the
little church of St. Paul's Escholt, built at the expense of W. R. Crompton
Stansfield for the use of three hundred villagers and now entirely surrounded by
Bradford Sewage Works, and Egerton Warburton's Chapel at Arley Hall, intended
for a family at odds with their parish priest over liturgy, show what he could
achieve under very differing circumstances.

99. All Saints' Church, Runcorn.

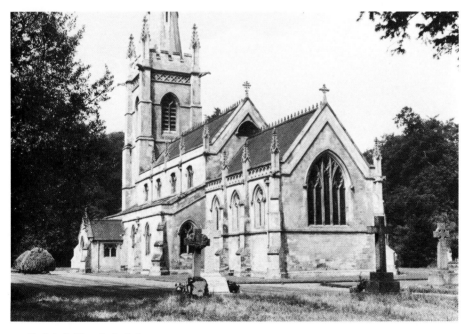

100. St. John's Church, Perlethorpe.

101. St. Paul's Church, Escholt.

102. St. Mary's Chapel,
Arley Hall, lithograph.

St. Paul's is Early English but without Salvin's usual cusped lancets, the windows here being almost imperceptibly pointed and arranged in pairs under simple hood molds (Fig. 101). The entrance is by a south door with no porch; ornament is confined to a cross on the chancel gable and the double bellcote. St. Mary's Chapel, being more expensive, is in the Decorated style and consists of a small nave and chancel with a parapet pierced in geometric patterns, pinnacles, and an octagonal bell tower with a pointed roof (Fig. 102). The fittings are in keeping with the High Church views of its owner, piscina, three-seat sedilia with cusped arches supported on half-figures of angels, and the roof braces resting on carved wooden figures of angels bearing shields on which are painted the Instruments of the Passion.

103. Exeter College,
Oxford, design
for the chapel.

Another charming set of designs were unfortunately not carried out; these are Salvin's proposals for rebuilding the chapel of Exeter College, Oxford. The old chapel occupied a cramped site and was generally not very satisfactory. In 1847 a committee was set up by the fellows that was to seek advice on the selection of an architect, and then to ask them to send in plans. Salvin's were ready by May (Fig. 103). His plan is not far from a square and consisted of a stubby nave, short wide transepts, each containing four rows of pews, and a short chancel. The entrance front had a porch occupying the base of a bell turret, rectangular at the base with a final octagonal battlemented story with gabled openings, decorative paneling, and corbel heads. To the right of this is the massive transept gable with a five-light window of flamboyant tracery. This commission went to Gilbert Scott some years later.[22]

22. S. J. Rigaud, a master at Westminster School, sent the rector a list of architects about whom he had made inquiries. They were Scott, Salvin, Hardwick, Hussey, Ferrey, Hakewill, Hayward and Butterfield, and Penrose. Salvin received his warmest recommendation:

> Salvin, is I believe about the best man of the day, take him for all in all. He thoroughly enters into his art, probably as thoroughly as Scott, but is a better man of business. He was one of the competitors for the Taylor Building, and I am inclined to think sent in the best design—I have seen it within the last day or two, & though the drawing was very small have no doubt myself on this point. He would in all probability have been employed to build it, had he not failed on the point in which he is generally particularly distinguished for excellence, namely arrangement. He was much engaged at the time & hurried over his interior, intending if successful to rearrange this, but unfortunately was rejected for this very cause. I think I may tell you however that Liddell voted for him, against Cockerell. He had been employed at Durham, and all which he had done there had been most excellent, especially in economy of space in arranging the Castle for the students. I have no doubt from what I have heard of him that his introduction to Oxford will be a public benefit, and you might be sure of his best efforts on every ground—I think much of his power of arrangement on account of the difficulties of the ground, but would not be supposed to speak of this to the depreciation of his artistic powers, which are of an equally high order. He is correct in his estimates I am told.

It would be profitless to discuss in detail the numerous commissions for restoration work that followed the completion of Holy Sepulchre. A brief note of what was undertaken in each case, is, where known, included in the Catalogue, and it needs only be said that Salvin's restorations were done as thoroughly as funds would allow. Many of the clergy who called him in were members of the Ecclesiological Society, or sympathized with its aims, and they were usually confronted with similar problems. Churches are particularly vulnerable to trouble with their roofs and windows; timbers get the beetle, and tracery decays. The former frequently required complete renewal when the stripping out of eighteenth-century ceilings revealed the true state of affairs, and the latter were usually replaced by new versions compatible with the date when the bulk of the fabric went up, either to Salvin's own designs or copied from the best surviving examples in the buildings. Interments in the churchyard caused soil to be thrown up against the church walls, causing damp; this was removed and drains laid. Interments in the church led to uneven paving and an untidy arrangement of paving and tomb slabs; all this was taken up, broken slabs repaired or discarded, and the more presentable reset in shiny encaustic tiles, which were colorful and easy to clean. Seating that had accrued through the centuries, in the form of benches, box-pews, and galleries, was removed and replaced by open pews, oak in the chancel and deal in the nave.

Although it often proved impossible to do away entirely with private sittings and pew rents, an attempt was made, encouraged by the Incorporated Church Building Society's conditional grants, to ensure that the humbler members of the congregation could at least see and hear what was going on. This was partly accomplished by enlarging the chancel arch. The pulpit, which might be found occupying the center of the chancel, or perhaps placed at one side of the nave, and usually including the reading desk and clerk's desk as part of its structure, was removed; and a more compact version of wood, or stone if the money allowed, was placed to one side of the chancel arch. Choir stalls appeared in the chancel, which was raised some steps above the level of the nave, and a suitable altar with a reredos, if possible, was installed a few steps higher yet. If the church was still too small for parochial needs, even after careful reordering of the seating, a new aisle or two could be added. All fireplaces and stoves were removed and central heating put in, with the boiler and stokehole below the new vestry. Heating was most commonly through hot water pipes that ran below gratings in the floor; a spectacularly unsuccessful variation in which hot water ran in open gullies beneath the gratings, which Salvin tried only once, filled the church with so much steam that the altar became invisible.[23]

The church had to be tidy. Antiquarian sentiment was not allowed to preserve the courses of herringbone that came to light at Aberford, nor to prevent the complete reworking of the chevron ornament on the north porch at Sherburn-in-Elmet (Fig. 104). In fact, the greatest aid to preservation was a shortage of money in the parish. Where a rich landowner shouldered the expense, like the Honorable Mrs. Howard at Elford, the whole fabric would be worked over, and a good deal of decorative detail would be put in. Elford now has a handsome hammerbeam roof in the chancel, as does Silkstone, another church where the restoration was paid for

23. At St. Mary Magdalene Torquay.

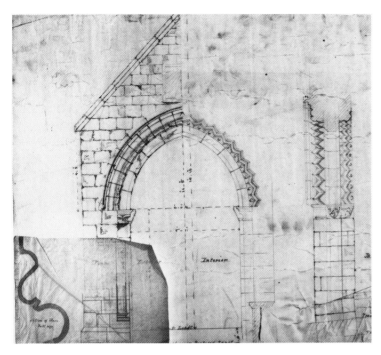

104. All Saints' Church, Sherburn-in-Elmet,
design for recutting stonework of porch.

by a wealthy lady. At Elford, Salvin was able to go to the expense of having special
tiles made instead of buying from Minton's catalogue. They are copies of a medieval example that came to light when the box-pews were removed. These are very
pretty, but there are a number of curious failures. The Early English lancets on the
south side of the nave at Lesbury are plainly all taken from the same drawing. This
is fair enough, for the design of a lancet has no variations of tracery to be considered; but the drawing has been followed too precisely. The framing blocks of stone
from which the windows are carved are identical for each window, a form of
ecclesiastical mass production quite alien to medieval work. It is doubtful whether
Salvin was enchanted when he saw it. It demonstrates the difficulty of supervising
small jobs far from the office. This was in 1846, and Salvin's care for detail and
competence in the execution of stonework improved immeasurably. St. Philip and
St. James, Rock was in the course of restoration ten years later, and Frederick
Wilson, the Clerk of Works at Alnwick, was asked to report on progress. What
Salvin learned did not please him: "Do you mean that the new ashlar at Rock is
smooth and the old not. I must have the surface size and joints of the new stone
work to match the old or I will not pass the work."24

   At the cathedrals of both Durham and Wells, the problem that Salvin had
encountered first at Norwich recurred; more worshipers had to be accommodated in
the choir. His employment by the dean and chapter of Durham was due to his local
connections. In 1841 he had prepared designs for the bishop's coach house and
stables on Palace Green, now converted into public lavatories. The following year
he was engaged on the buildings for Durham School, which had just been trans-

24. Alnwick Castle MSS.

ferred to a new site. In 1847 he supervised the restoration of the great hall of
Durham Castle, in use as the university dining hall, and he was later to convert the
Red Lion Hotel into students' lodgings and to build further sets of lodgings in the
castle keep.

He probably began on the cathedral in 1842. In all his work for the chapter he
was associated with a local architect George Pickering, who acted in the same
capacity as Frederick Wilson at Alnwick, as the man on the spot, producing survey
drawings to be sent to Salvin in London and supervising the execution of Salvin's
designs. Repairs began in the south transept, and in 1844 there was a rearrangement of the seats of the choristers, singing men and minor canons, and the wooden
feretory screen was replaced by a low stone wall. In 1845 some pews and a gallery
in the choir were removed and benches put in, and the following year there was a
major act of vandalism. Bishop Cosin's beautiful choir stalls, dating from 1665,
were broken up so that the tabernacle work could be placed above a row of stalls
set back between the piers of the choir. Behind these again were built galleries for
the ladies, entered from the aisles. In this way Salvin gained twenty-two more
stalls and thirty sittings. In 1847 the organ screen, also of Cosin's time, was
removed, opening up a most unmedieval vista from the new west door, also by
Salvin, to the Neville Screen and the high altar. The organ was put in the north
transept. This same year the large old pews at the east end of the choir, which were
used by the families of the canons and which obstructed the view of the bishop's
throne, were taken out and replaced by benches made in Durham but incorporating carved paneling and grotesque animal armrests carved in London by
Wetherall. In 1848 the three north windows of the choir were replaced by some with
Decorated tracery, copied by Pickering at Salvin's suggestion from examples at
Sleaford, Holbeach, and Boughton Aluph; and some Perpendicular windows on
the north of the nave were pulled out and appropriately Norman replacements
installed. As well as all this, there was much refacing work repairing the eroded
millstone grit on the southern exterior of the nave and repair to the clerestory
windows and the north range of the cloister. So far as the fittings were concerned,
the greatest outrage after the destruction of the organ screen and the pulling about
of the stalls was the removal of Cosin's font and font canopy. It seems that this
onslaught on the seventeenth-century woodwork must have been on the orders of
the chapter, as Salvin was careful to preserve similar work at St. Brandon's Brancepeth in 1864 and at St. Edmund's Sedgefield in 1876. At Durham he replaced the
font with one modeled on that of black Tournai marble in Winchester Cathedral,
but the scenes from the life of St. Nicholas were replaced by copies of the illustrations in Bede's *Life of St. Cuthbert,* then at Brough Hall in the North Riding, and
now in the British Museum.[25] Cosin's font has happily been returned to the
cathedral, and Salvin's is in St. Oswin's, South Shields.[26] At this time the old
wooden pulpit was also removed into the castle chapel, and one by Salvin in the
Middle-Pointed style installed, to be in its turn superseded by one in Cosmati
work designed by Gilbert Scott. The final improvement was a new altar rail,
designed by Pickering and accepted "subject to such alterations as may be sug-

25. British Museum Add. MSS 39943.
26. Brigadier R. H. Walker, private communication.

gested by Mr. Salvin, and approved by the Chapter."[27] This was of Caen stone with Purbeck shafts and was carved by White of Pimlico. Most of Salvin's work in or about the choir was removed or altered by Scott, who succeeded him as architectural adviser to the chapter in 1859.

The restoration of Wells Cathedral had begun in the early 1840s under the supervision of Benjamin Ferrey. When the Master of Balliol, Dr. Richard Jenkyns, was appointed dean, he found that the only part as yet untouched was the choir. Here walls, arches, and capitals were encrusted with plaster and dirt, and as at Norwich, galleries above the stalls on either side provided a much-needed extra forty sittings. In 1847 the chapter decided that the choir should be restored and the galleries removed and that the services of Salvin should be sought in addition to those of Ferrey. Here again the problem was how to provide for the full congregation after the galleries had gone, and the solution that Salvin proposed was that the fourteenth-century wooden stalls should be taken down and be reerected within the arches of the arcade just as at Durham, thus making room for an additional row of seats. In February 1848 the dean and chapter considered Salvin's plans and compared them with one suggested by Edward Blore in 1830 and another produced by Ferrey. They decided to adopt Salvin's scheme. Work began immediately with the scraping, repair, and coloring of the vault and walls and the demolition of the old stalls, of which only the misericords were retained and reused. Salvin designed five alternative canopies for the new stalls, and there was a good deal of discussion as to whether these should be of wood, which was cheaper, or of stone. Salvin reported that he had seen oak stalls set in the arcade of another cathedral, no doubt Durham, and thought it a failure due to the impossibility of achieving harmony and congruity between two such different materials as wood and stone. A decision on the canopies was deferred until the following year. In the meantime Salvin consulted his friend, the eminent antiquarian the Reverend C. H. Hartshorne, his fellow lecturer at Caernarvon, who preferred the more expensive alternative of stone. He wrote to the dean: "When the battle is fought he will be a valuable ally in our army and a <u>very awkward</u> opponent to the enemy."[28] Stone was eventually decided upon, and Salvin's final design is a simplified version of the canopies in the Lady Chapel at Ely. Work on the stalls was completed by 1853, and they appear to be the first major work in England of the carver James Forsyth.

The new arrangements did not meet with universal approval. One W. G. Tozer wrote to *The Ecclesiologist* objecting to the placing of four rows of seats on each side of the choir, facing each other across the aisle: "Picture to yourself, Sir, canons and 'canons' ladies,' theological students, choristers, grammar-school boys, and the good people of the cathedral 'liberty,' all packed thus vis-à-vis in one heterogeneous mass!" And later: "The present congregation, and the choir as arranged by Mr. Salvin, are totally and entirely unfitted for one another." Tozer wished the seats to be placed running across the choir, turning it, in effect, into a small church. The editor of *The Ecclesiologist* did not approve of this proposal and objected to the growing tendency to make only partial use of cathedrals by abandoning the nave and concentrating the congregation in the choir.[29]

27. Durham Chapter Act Book 1838–1847.
28. Wells Cathedral MSS.
29. *The Ecclesiologist* (February 1853): 42.

Apart from the new stalls, Salvin supervised the scouring of all traces of paint from the bishop's throne and designed a new stone pulpit, which was paid for by the dean. He also prepared a set of drawings and estimates for the removal of the fan vaulting from the crossing tower, which was fortunately not carried out, and advised as to the repair of some of the more decayed statues on the west front. His last work at Wells followed upon the gift by the Committee of the Citizens of Wells of a Henry Willis organ. It was necessary to extend the center of the west side of the pulpitum to accommodate the frame. The organ case, designed by Salvin and topped by four angels carved by Forsyth, was not a success and was subsequently described as the most hideous in the country. Dean Jenkyns died in 1854, and this terminated Salvin's connection with Wells, although work on the organ case continued until 1857.

Salvin's practice as a church restorer in no way measures up in quantity to that of a man like Gilbert Scott. His most active period was in the 1840s, when he was concerned with seventeen churches; in the following two decades he dealt with fifteen and thirteen, dropping to a mere five in the 1870s. To a great extent the process became routine, and a destructive one at that. It is perhaps unfair to blame too much of this on Salvin. Not only was there a revival of interest in ritual, which is reflected in the reordering of the interiors and the new furnishings, but restoration committees wanted their churches to be smart, with plenty of polished brass and varnished woodwork to show for their money. They liked their new altars with marble and mosaic reredoses, and brocade frontals embroidered with the monogram of Christ, the encaustic tiles in the sanctuary, the stalls for the now-surpliced village choir, the spiky wrought-iron and brass communion rail, the eagle lectern, and the handsome new pulpit. They liked the substantial framing of the new roof, which kept the rain out, unlike the old one. They liked the draft-proof windows, with or without stained glass; the comfort of the new pews, sufficient in number so that the gentry did not have to compete for the best places and even the poorest could be seated; and the warmth of the new and efficient central heating system. But set against these natural aspirations for worship under comfortable and decorous conditions, there was increasing protest at the destruction that was so often involved.

One of Salvin's last restorations, that of the Saxon church of St. Nicholas at Worth, gave rise to protests from the Royal Institute of British Architects and the British Archaeological Association, and according to a correspondent writing in *The Builder,* "the whole architectural profession and the distinguished archaeological societies were in arms at the desecration of the place."[30] Worth was indeed treated drastically, but probably necessarily so. Some letters from the builder employed have survived, and in one dated October 1869 he reports that the northeast corner of the nave had been found to be ten inches out of true alignment on the east, and one foot six inches out on the north. That the apse was in a falling condition can be seen from a sketch made in the eighteenth century by S. H. Grimm.[31] This shows it supported by massive buttresses on the east and the south, and Salvin had it taken down to the foundations and rebuilt in accordance with the

30. *The Builder* (October 29, 1870): 869.
31. British Museum Add. MSS 5673 f.49; RIBA Salvin /44/.

now long-outdated precepts of the Camdenians, whose final manifestation as the Ecclesiological Society had been disbanded the previous year. A three-light Perpendicular east window was removed and replaced by five deeply splayed roundheaded windows; the old timber belfry also went: "I think it right to inform you that its natural guardians are now taking down the tower, a curious structure, you will remember, including in its construction the trunks of four large trees of quite unknown age."[32] This tower was built above the north transept, and Salvin made one design for a timber-framed tower, which was intended for the same place, but this idea was abandoned in favor of a tower and broach spire of the plainest kind, built in the angle between the north transept and the apse. Why a broach spire? This was not in accordance with Camdenian principles. At Worth the Sompting-style helm roof that Salvin built at St. Mary's Flixton would have been much more suitable.

Cement and old plaster were stripped from the exterior, windows removed or replaced, and the north doorway blocked up. Inside, the north gallery went, but not the west gallery, which dated from 1610. The wooden chancel screen and the Commandment Boards were thrown out, the latter being replaced by a mosaic reredos of the Last Supper. The seventeenth-century communion rail was reused, as was the pulpit of sixteenth-century German woodwork, but it lost its tester and clerk's desk. The box-pews went, of course, and the north and south transept arches were rebuilt with massive square capitals.

The Society for the Protection of Ancient Buildings was founded four years before Salvin died, and its views on conservative restoration were to awaken no sympathy in him. His last restoration, of St. Margaret's Fernhurst, his own parish church, which he completed shortly before his death, was undertaken in the same spirit as his very earliest attempts. With his contemporaries, like Gilbert Scott, Salvin must bear part of the responsibility for the rape of the English parish church in the nineteenth century.

32. *The Builder* (May 14, 1870): 390.

9

The Universities, the Tower of London, and Windsor Castle

No great public commission was to come Salvin's way. His competition entries met with no success; he was not to build the Houses of Parliament, the New Government Offices in Whitehall, or the Law Courts in the Strand. These well-publicized, time-consuming, and indeed almost overwhelming commissions went to Barry, Scott, and Street, each of whom had to put up with a great deal of interference and criticism before their buildings were completed, and anxiety to a degree that it is probable that it hastened Street's death. The public works with which Salvin was concerned were on a smaller scale and consisted of the adaptation and repair of old buildings, the provision of new accommodation for lodgings and for scientific purposes at the three oldest universities, and major restoration works at the two most important castles in the land.

His university work began at Durham. The See of Durham was the wealthiest in the country and afforded princely incomes to its bishop and the cathedral hierarchy, which had come under particularly virulent attack at the time the Reform Bill was being fought through Parliament. There was talk of swingeing confiscations of Church property, which persuaded the dean and canons to decide unanimously on September 28, 1831, to found the University of Durham and to endow this with part of the cathedral revenues. The necessary bill received the royal assent on July 4, 1832, when the university was endowed with property in South Shields valued at £80,000. The Bishop contributed generously out of his own income and handed over his official residence in Durham Castle for university use. Salvin was first approached by the dean in 1834 and requested to draw up proposals for increasing this accommodation by building a hall, common rooms, and other apartments, which he proposed doing by encasing Bishop Bek's four-teenth-century great hall in four-story additions, destroying the kitchen and buttery, keeping the great hall as a dining room, and filling the undercroft with sets of bedrooms and sitting rooms for the students. This was to be carried out in a rather dreary Tudor style, and fortunately it proceeded no further. In 1839 he was called upon again, this time to convert Bishop Hatfield's polygonal, and at that time ruinous, keep. The chapter had first thought that this might be lecture rooms with a museum on the ground floor, but it was eventually rebuilt by Salvin with six sets of rooms on each of the ground, first, and second floors, and connected with the rest of the castle by a two-story range.

In 1843 the university, still seeking for room for the undergraduates, acquired the Red Lion Hotel, which Salvin was asked to adapt as Bishop Hatfield's Hall for poor students. The hotel ballroom became the dining hall, and he added two new

105. Durham University,
the Old Library,
new oriel window.

staircases leading to twenty-four sets of rooms, eight on each of the three floors.
This work was carried out in 1847–1848, and like the earlier proposals for the castle,
it is in plain Tudor, which with Salvin betrays a limited budget. At this time he was
working with George Pickering when he received commissions in the city, and
Pickering assisted him with the restoration of the window tracery in Bishop Bek's
hall, and again ten years later when he was called back to repair Bishop Cosin's
library. This was at the time when he was seriously ill, and his son was bearing the
brunt of the office work: "Agreed at a special meeting of the Chapter held this day
that Mr. Salvin's designs for the restoration of the windows of the Old Library and
the Reading Room and for the South Entrance to the Cloisters, as personally
presented to the Chapter by Mr. Salvin Junior be adopted and carried out forth-
with."[1] Here he added an oriel and a doorway opening onto Palace Green and a
staircase that allowed the public access to the library, which was used for university
ceremonies (Fig. 105).

   Salvin's most interesting job for Durham is probably the observatory. In 1838 the
Reverend T. J. Hussey of Hayes Court in Kent offered to sell his collection of
astronomical instruments, which he had assembled at great expense from all the
best-known makers in Europe. Hussey was an astronomer of note, but "a distress-
ing accident" had rendered his observatory useless to him. Professor Temple

1. Chapter Act Book 1847–1856. Chapter Office, Durham Cathedral.

106. Durham University Observatory.

Chevalier negotiated the purchase for £800, and a site was acquired just south of the city. Salvin was then asked to design an observatory that was to contain rooms for the observer on the ground floor and for the optical equipment, including a sidereal clock and transit instruments, a library, and a dome for a Fraunhofer equatorial telescope. The building was completed and the instruments were about to be installed by June 1840. Freed for once from the necessity of adding on to medieval structures, Salvin designed a small classical stone building with a rectangular ground floor and a first floor of Greek cross plan supporting the dome (Fig. 106).

In 1841 Beresford Hope came of age and into possession of his private fortune, and William Whewell became master of Trinity College, Cambridge. As we have seen, Beresford Hope was already consulting Salvin in his process of ecclesiologically improving Christ Church, Kilndown, and now in his letter congratulating Whewell on his appointment, he offered the sum of £300 toward the restoration of the oriel and mullioned windows of the master's lodge, which had been replaced by sashes during the mastership of Richard Bentley in the eighteenth century. He eventually increased his contribution to £1,000; the sum of £250 was given by Whewell, and the balance of £3,765.19.6d. was raised by subscription. The cost was much greater than at first anticipated, as it was decided in late 1842 that the oriel overlooking the master's garden on the west of this range should also be restored. The beginning of the work is described by Whewell in his diary: "Mr. Salvin the architect arrived, and under his direction and in his presence we made attempts to discover traces of the oriel which formerly existed as part of the front of the Lodge. We found the foundation of the wall of the oriel immediately beneath the surface of the ground. The plan was semi-circular."[2] The semicircular form was not adopted, Salvin's oriel being a two-story canted bay with an acute gable above (Fig. 107). The gable was an afterthought, and Beresford Hope thought it added height and dignity to the whole. He also expressed a wish to commemorate his gift by placing stained glass in the oriel windows bearing his and his wife's arms; dissuaded from this, he recorded his benefaction in an inscription that

2. Whewell MSS Add. a. 60. Quoted by permission of the master and fellows of Trinity College. R. Willis and J. W. Clark, *An Architectural History of the University of Cambridge* (Cambridge: At the University Press, 1886).

107. Trinity College Cambridge,
the master's lodge,
new oriel window.

108. Trinity College Cambridge,
design for the facade
on Trinity Street.

caused both amusement and some offense: "Munificentia fultus Alex. J. B. Hope generosi hisce aedibus antiquam speciem restituit W. Whewell May Colleggi A.D. MXLIII." This provoked Tom Taylor's parody, *The House That Hope Built,* in which Salvin comes in for his share of the ragging:

> This is the architect, rather a muff
> Who bamboozled the Seniors who cut up rough
> When they saw the inscription, or rather the puff,
> Put up by the Master grim and gruff,
> Who married the Lady tawney and tough
> And lives in the House that Hope built.[3]

Salvin carried out further work at Trinity College at the request of the seniority in 1856, when he rebuilt the facade onto Trinity Street between the chapel and the Great Gate, adding a three-story bay with a crow-stepped gable and a first-floor oriel; he also refaced the courtyard side of this range (Fig. 108).[4] For Whewell he

3. H. W. Law and I. Law, *The Book of the Beresford Hopes* (London: Heath Cranton, 1925).
4. Willis and Clark, *Architectural History.*

109. Trinity College Cambridge, the First Master's Court.

undertook two major building projects, the First Master's Court of 1857, and the Second Master's Court, begun eight years later. These stand on land opposite the Great Gate and provide extra rooms for undergraduates in Salvin's most economical Tudor style (Fig. 109).

His connection with Jesus College began in 1845 and was brief, consisting of the rebuilding of the east windows of the chapel and the opening up of old arches in the north wall of the choir and the east wall of the north transept, which in fact weakened the structure and endangered the stability of the tower. He also built a new north aisle, which returned down the east side of the north transept, to house an organ presented by John Sutton, and a vestry for the choir of boys that Sutton had introduced. Sutton was one of those who were to join the Roman Catholic Church and was probably responsible for Salvin's being replaced here by A. W. N. Pugin. At Trinity Hall he embarked on a rebuilding program after a fire had gutted the eastern range of the principal court in February 1852. To this he added an extra story and designed the whole in a classical style complementary to the rest of the college buildings and to C. R. Cockerell's University Library across the way. He was also asked to make some alterations to the master's lodge and the chapel.

His work at Gonville and Caius began in 1852 when the college instructed the master to try and ascertain the best way in which a hall, lecture rooms, and additional accommodation for students might be obtained. A committee was appointed, which approached Salvin, Scott, and P. C. Hardwick for plans for rebuilding the Trinity Street entrance front (which was in fact done by Alfred Waterhouse in 1870), along with the building of a dining hall and as many sets of rooms as possible on the site of the Stable Court. Salvin was employed by May 1853, and into the northwest corner of the college site bounded by Trinity Lane he was required to fit the master's house, the great hall, the kitchen, and all the larders and cellarage that the college needed. This was achieved by ingenious planning. The entrance is from Gonville Court through a lobby from which staircases rise and turn at right angles to left and right. That on the left for the master and fellows leads to the Combination Room, the master's lodge, and the dais end of the hall, all on the first floor. That on the right for the undergraduates leads to the body of the hall, the library, and other rooms. On the ground floor beyond the lobby, and occupying the entire area under the hall and library, are the kitchen, two larders, buttery, plate room, bakehouse, scullery, pastry and preserve pantries, the cook's room, housekeeper's room, butler's pantry, and dumbwaiters for raising food and drink to the hall. The style is Tudor, red brick with stone dressings; the hall is the most important feature, of six bays with a steeply pitched roof and a southern gable with a five-light mullioned and transomed window surrounded by stone scrolls.

The saga, for such it may be called, of the building of the new museums and the anatomical and chemical schools at Cambridge began in 1854, though the buildings themselves were only put up in 1863–1865. The major problem here was again the complexity of the planning, for reasons that will become apparent, although the matter was compounded by interfaculty jealousy.[5] The Natural Science Tripos had been established in 1848, and in 1853 Professor Robert Willis prepared a report in which he described the buildings that were required to house the newly established museums and lecture rooms. He suggested that these should be of brick and as plain as possible to save expense and arranged so that the museums might be visited with a minimum of interference to the professors and their pupils. Each professor was to be consulted as to his special requirements, and Salvin was to be employed because his work at Trinity Hall and Caius had given "proofs of his special skill in the planning of complicated and commodious buildings upon a site limited in space, awkward in form, and connected with previous structures." The twelve "literary professors" who had also to be housed only required lecture room space at the actual time of their lectures, but the scientific professors were more exacting, and as in the case of Durham Observatory, Salvin also had to provide room for their equipment. The Lucasian Professor needed a private study, a working room for experiments and apparatus, and a lecture room; the Chemical Professor a study, his own and his students' laboratories, and a balance room; the Plumian and Lowdean Professors a study each and a students' room for astronomical instruments; the Botanical Professor a museum of 1,300 square feet, a study, and an unpacking room; the Jacksonian Professor a museum of apparatus (manufacturing, steam engines, etc.), a workshop, study, a laboratory with a forge, and a furnace for smelting; the Mineralogical Professor a museum and lecture room, a study and a small storage room, and a room 40 feet by 10 feet to suit "the peculiar nature of his observations." Salvin completed his designs in time for them to be placed before the Syndicate in May 1854.

There was no money for such a project, and matters rested in abeyance until 1861, by which time Willis and Salvin had produced a second set of plans for an even larger group of buildings estimated to cost £26,475, to be built of red brick with stone dressings in a simple Italian style. This was presented to the Senate, where it "excited almost universal disapprobation." Yet another amended design was put out to tender, but the lowest quotation, put in by George Smith, was for a figure £7,000 above Salvin's estimate, and the hostile reaction in the university, due

5. Cambridge University Archives; Reports of the Syndicate. Willis and Clark, *Architectural History.*

at least in part to an antipathy to the study of science in general rather than the cost, resulted in the rejection of both tender and design. A new Syndicate was then appointed, which began by asking Salvin what his fees were to date; he replied that they were £579 on the first project, and £823 on the second, large sums indicative of the work that had been expended on such a complex building. Eventually the second design, with some reductions, was adopted in 1863, and it was all built in less than two years.

Balliol College, Oxford, was also short of room. This had been felt as early as 1841, when George Basevi had prepared some designs, and Pugin then commissioned in opposition to submit drawings for remodeling and extending the college buildings. Unfortunately for Pugin, the controversy that arose out of the activities of the Tractarians in Oxford in the mid-1840s, and his own Roman Catholicism, made his elaborately medieval proposals unacceptable to the master, Dr. Richard Jenkyns, however attractive they might have been architecturally. Jenkyns was to consult Salvin about the choir at Wells Cathedral later; now he called him in at Balliol with instructions that the college kitchen and the hall were to be enlarged and new sets of rooms built on the site in St. Giles' Street formerly occupied by the master's stables. Work on the hall began in 1853 and was completed that year, and Salvin's designs, though also medieval, owed nothing to those of Pugin, of which he seems to have thought very little, writing to Jenkyns in 1854: "I saw Petit [the Reverend J. L. Petit] yesterday after he had had a peep at Pugin's design which I smuggled for him he says what an escape they have had!"[6] The new rooms for the undergraduates were begun at the end of the term in July 1852 and were supposed to be ready for occupation the following Michaelmas, but wet weather and trouble with the foundations caused delay. This building is again Tudor and very similar in style to the two Master's Courts, with sets of rooms on three staircases, three stories high with a four-story tower on the north. Salvin was also consulted about furnishing the rooms, which the college was to undertake "with a view to adopting some mode of checking the expensive and luxurious habits of young men in the fitting up of their rooms."[7] The alterations to the hall and kitchen and some repairs to the windows of the Fellows' Common Room were all completed by 1853. Jenkyns died the following year, ending Salvin's work at Balliol, just as at Wells. When Jenkyns's successor as master began the rebuilding of the chapel in 1856, he turned to one of the next generation and a practitioner of High Victorian Gothic, William Butterfield.

The condition of the Tower of London at the beginning of the nineteenth century was little less than deplorable. It was still in use as a prison, and indeed the Cato Street Conspirators, who had planned in 1820 to murder the Cabinet, set fire to public buildings, and seize the Mansion House and the Tower itself, were confined there awaiting their execution or transportation. But interest in the old castle was growing; in 1825 John Bayley published his *History and Antiquities of the Tower of London* in two folio volumes with many illustrations. Perhaps of greater consequence, because it appealed to the general reading public, Harrison Ainsworth's historical romance *The Tower of London* came out in monthly parts in 1840, with engravings by George Cruikshank. The first to attempt some improve-

6. Wells Cathedral MSS.
7. Balliol College Minute Book.

ments was the Duke of Wellington, who was appointed Constable of the Tower in 1826. He was confronted by a thousand or so miscellaneous inhabitants who, as residents of the ancient "Liberties of the Tower," were often persons who had reason to seek immunity from bailiffs' officers, and about a hundred yeoman warders, who hired their quarters out as lodgings or public houses and who made it their business to extort money by way of tips from visiting antiquaries and tourists. The position of the latter was regularized by Parliament in 1837, when a standard admission fee of 1/– and a 2/– fee for a view of the Crown Jewels was laid down; but the duke had continuing difficulties with the holders of various leases and sinecures attached to the establishment. The state of the buildings also caused him concern, but all became insignificant when compared to the condition of the moat, which had been used for the reception of sewage and as a refuse tip for hundreds of years, so that by this time banks of ordure eight feet high prevented scouring by the tidal flow of the Thames. One of his first actions was to order the removal of 10,000 cubic feet of muck and an annual flooding and scraping of the ditch thereafter. The smell caused by the first operation was popularly supposed to have occasioned an outbreak of cholera.

In 1841, the year after Ainsworth's book came out, the Great Storehouse, which stood on the north of the White Tower, caught fire and burned down. During this spectacular blaze, the Crown Jewels, which were on display in the Martin Tower, had to be rescued by the Keeper of the Jewels and his wife, assisted by yeoman warders armed with axes. The cloth on which the regalia had been displayed was later found to have been charred by the heat of the flames. The jewels were on display again by 1844, but in a temporary building, and Salvin was some time later instructed to provide a secure and fireproof place for their safekeeping. Building activity during the duke's term of office was confined to the erection of the Water-loo Barracks on the site of the Great Storehouse, which was opened by him in 1845, and the Officers' Quarters, now the Museum. Some tenements on the west of the Salt Tower were pulled down and two adjoining arches demolished for road-widening before the duke's death in 1852 brought General Lord Combermere in as constable. He had, however, finally solved the problem of the noisome moat after another cholera epidemic in 1849, having it filled in and drains and sewers run both within the tower precincts and in the moat: "Executed as proposed, per Board's Order dated 4th March 1850," according to a drainage plan found among Salvin's drawings for the tower (Fig. 110).[8]

Quite apart from the new sewers, this plan gives a fair idea of the extent to which later buildings were hiding the medieval work when Salvin was first con-sulted. It also shows that the whole was under the control of two separate bodies, the Ordnance Office and H. M. Commissioners of Woods and Forests, shortly to become the Office of Works, between which there was a fair amount of inter-departmental jealousy. Some of the old menagerie buildings in the Barbican were still in existence, surrounded by barracks and storehouses. A guardhouse was built in on the north of the Middle Tower. The whole of the Outer Ward on the west, from the Byward and Bell Towers to Devereux Tower and Legge's Mount, was filled with officers' quarters, storehouses, and warders' tenements. The latter were

8. RIBA Salvin /18/1.

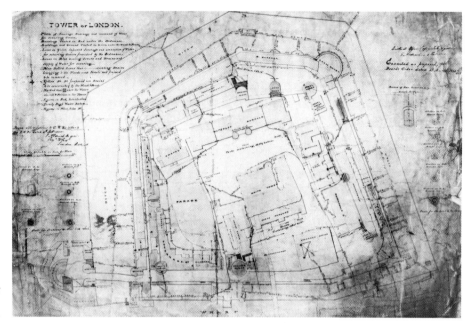

110. The Tower
of London,
drainage plan.

built against the curtain wall itself and against the lower part of the Beauchamp
Tower. Much the same state of affairs existed on the north, the area between
Legge's Mount and Brass Mount being occupied by officers' quarters and schoolroom, a canteen, a temporary military barrack, and "B" Barrack. From Brass
Mount running south were a small hospital, the governor's stables, and a storehouse between the Constable Tower and Salt Tower, with artillery officers'
quarters to the east of this. On the south the wall of the Inner Ward had entirely
disappeared between the Salt and Record or Wakefield Towers, and a large building containing a store and the Ordnance Office extended over half the area
between the line of the old wall and the large horse armory built against the south
front of the White Tower. On the outer wall the Develin and Well Towers were
pretty much intact, but the Cradle Tower had been virtually demolished, and St.
Thomas' Tower housed a steam engine.

Over the next twenty years most of these encroaching buildings were taken
away, and the Beauchamp, Martin, Salt, St. Thomas', and Wakefield Towers and
the intervening walls were restored, and most of the towers put to a new use. It was
a major commission for Salvin and brought him before the public eye, leading to
the award to him of the Royal Gold Medal of the Royal Institute of British
Architects in 1863 and also to his employment at Windsor Castle. Indeed, the
Governor of the Tower, Lord de Ros, reported in June 1865: "There is hardly any
old building in the Tower which has not been brought under Mr. Salvin's consideration, and in respect of which he has been asked for general suggestions, which
he has readily given."9

He was first consulted about the Beauchamp Tower, and there is little doubt that
he was chosen because of the restorations that he had carried out at Newark,
Carisbrooke, and Caernarvon Castles for H. M. Commissioners of Woods and

9. PRO Works 14/174.

Forests five years earlier. He made a survey in April 1851, but nothing seems to have been done until the following year, when the houses in the Outer Ward were cleared away, some on the Tower Green side removed, and the stonework repaired. This tower had been used as a state prison from the thirteenth to the sixteenth centuries, and Harrison Ainsworth had suggested that it be opened so that the public could see the commemorative inscriptions carved on the walls by the often distinguished prisoners. It had more recently been used as an officers' mess; now partitions were removed, and the basement and upper floor were turned into warders' quarters. The stonework was renewed where necessary, and the tower was given new battlements and windows of an appropriately medieval style. The Salt Tower had also been used as a prison. After the demolition of the arches and abutting houses in the 1840s, the base had been exposed, revealing considerable losses of stonework and patching in brick. This situation remained until General Lord Combermere informed the Queen of its condition, and on June 14, 1855, Prince Albert paid a visit of inspection. The Prince Consort's opinion was that all the restoration work at the tower should be subject to a comprehensive plan and carried out by a single architect, and Salvin was selected as a result of his success with the Beauchamp Tower. He was instructed to make a survey and prepare an estimate, and to have a cork model made showing the hoped-for appearance of the Salt Tower after restoration. Tenders were obtained by June the following year, and the contract was awarded to George Myers. The final certificate was sent in September 1857. The Salt Tower is of Kentish rag with quoins and vertical bands of Bath stone. At the time of Salvin's survey the ground floor was being used as a smithy, and the walls here and above had been pierced to take modern windows. Salvin repaired the exterior and put deeply splayed slits into the basement with cross slits on the first and second floors, and twin lights of cusped lancets with quatrefoils above. Battlements and a stair turret were added.

Sir James Pennethorne's Public Record Office in Chancery Lane was sufficiently advanced by April 1858 to receive for storage the manuscripts and presses that had formerly been kept in the Wakefield and White Towers, where they had been at considerable hazard from possible fire and explosion, as the vaults of the latter were used as an ammunition store. Salvin had first been consulted about the Council Chamber in the White Tower in 1856, when it was proposed that it should be used as a small arms store.[10] Work does not seem to have begun until 1861, when he reported that the Council Chamber roof was weak, although the timbers themselves were sound, and that it was supported by numerous posts that would interfere with the stands for arms. It was also rather dark, and this would get worse when the windows were "reduced to their original form and size." He decided to strengthen the beams with iron girders bolted to them, thus doing away with the posts; the floor was to be reinforced to take the added weight, and the windows restored, a number of new ones being inserted in the west and north walls to take care of the light problem. St. John's Chapel was not taken in hand until 1864, when Myers again won the contract; the work here seems to have been limited to restoring the windows, those on the ground floor being given a plain molding on the inside with nook shafts and cushion capitals outside.

10. PRO Works 31/494.

In June 1862 part of the stonework of the round tower on the east side of St. Thomas's Tower collapsed. The whole fabric was in a poor and dilapidated condition and had been cased in stone a hundred years previously by way of repair. This, however, had not been well tied in with the original walls and furthermore had been much shaken by the firing of a gun from the roof of the tower. The cause of the present collapse, Salvin reported, was the vibration of a hydraulic engine used for driving cranes, which with its boiler, pumps, and accumulators was housed to the east of Traitor's Gate. The Engine Keeper lived on the ground floor on the west side, and an officer in the Buffs had rooms on the first floor above him. The tower was shored up and the engine removed to a new engine house, a plain brick building with a tall freestanding chimney that was built just to the west of the site of the Barbican. The east part of the tower was then restored, the masonry refaced, new windows put in, and the battlements rebuilt. The restoration of the west part involved the clearing away of some brick buildings that abutted the tower on the north and making good the damaged parts with Kentish rag and Bath stone. But when this was begun, the builders came across wooden timbering with cob and brick infilling and two doors that led into a circular stair on the ground and first floors, one above the other. Salvin asked for an additional sum of £150 to preserve all this, though confessing: "Probably the doors can never be made use of again, still I think they should be restored as a piece of history."[11] The upper door, which had led to a bridge of some sort over the road to the Wakefield Tower, was in fact put to use when Salvin built just such a bridge later. The north facade was carefully repaired, retaining its half timbering, herringbone brick nogging, windows with leaded lights, and two oriels of triangular plan.

By September 1866 it was settled that the new Jewel Office should be in the Wakefield Tower. Salvin had already, in 1857, prepared a set of designs for the conversion of the Martin Tower into a proper museum, with the keeper's quarters attached, but this was for some reason not proceeded with. Work was begun in 1867 and involved the restoration of the Wakefield Tower, the provision of a secure display area and a private apartment for the keeper in St. Thomas' Tower that would be reached by the new stone bridge, the conversion of the Martin Tower into warders' quarters, and the building of a new house for the engineer. Messrs. Brawn & Downing, iron founders of Birmingham, whom Salvin used extensively for metalwork, provided an iron cage, glass case, barriers, gate, and railings, within which the Crown Jewels were again put on display in January 1870.

The more general process of restoration continued with the demolition in November 1866 of four old houses that adjoined the Bloody Tower and the building of three new sets of quarters, along with the repair of the walls thus exposed and the rebuilding of the parapet of the curtain wall at this spot. The tower had lost its battlements and acquired sash windows and drainpipes, which were removed and replaced by lancets. The Cradle Tower was also cleared of later accretions, during the course of which the old watergate to the Royal Apartments was discovered. This tower was largely rebuilt. Salvin also prepared a scheme for the Byward Tower, but for some reason this was left untouched, and it retains to this day its brick parapets and sashes protected by gratings, a useful reminder of the state of

11. PRO Works 14/2/2.

most of the towers before Salvin was called in. A proposal for adding another story to the Waterloo Barracks, to be lit by bargeboarded and tile-hung dormers, was also not proceeded with.

The last building with which Salvin was involved at the Tower of London was the Chapel of St. Peter ad Vincula. The rector had written to the Office of Works about the damp and the dilapidations in March 1865, and Salvin was asked to advise two years later. His proposals included removing the gallery and box-pews and putting in open benches, repairing the stone parapets, and general restoration. When the estimates were submitted to be included in the vote for the financial year 1868/1869, the Office of Works was obliged to reject them, owing to the state of the country's finances following the "extraordinary demands for the Abyssinian Expedition."[12] And there matters rested until 1876, when Salvin, now a very old man, was asked to comment on some plans drawn up by the Royal Engineers. He was unable to come up from Fernhurst to visit London himself, and Anthony, Junior, inspected the chapel and conveyed his father's suggestions to the Office of Works. It was the last time Salvin was consulted about the Tower.

On February 8, 1856, Colonel Charles Phipps, Prince Albert's equerry, wrote to Sir Benjamin Hall, who was then the First Commissioner of Works: "With regard to the improvements on the north side of Windsor Castle, what H. R. H. said to Turnbull was this: that the general idea for the plan of alterations in that locality having been considered by the Prince and yourself, neither H. R. H. nor Turnbull had sufficient practical or professional knowledge to be able to work out the plan properly and that their mode of executing what was contemplated would probably be full of faults and unnecessary expense. H. R. H. therefore thought that the principle being decided upon, it would be very desirable that a clever architect should be called in, and being thoroughly informed of the object contemplated, should be asked to propose his plan of execution. The only man whose name occurred to the Prince as being likely to do this well was the architect who planned the works in the Tower, Mr. Salvin."[13]

Sir Jeffry Wyatville had died in 1840 after completing a major rebuilding program in the Upper Ward at Windsor Castle, which he had undertaken for George IV, but the buildings in the Lower Ward remained in a sorry state. The only restoration work here had been the rebuilding of the Salisbury Tower by Edward Blore in 1842; the tower next to this, the Garter Tower, was left a roofless and floorless ruin, and the walls and towers from there around to the Norman Gateway were patched and dilapidated and pierced with numerous windows of every shape and period.[14] Prince Albert may well have become more conscious of the castle's poor condition during the state visit in 1855 of the Emperor Napoleon and the Empress Eugénie, during the course of which they stayed at Windsor. The Emperor took an enlightened interest in ancient monuments and had involved himself in the reconstruction of the fortified medieval town of Carcassonne, which was begun by E. E. Viollet-le-Duc in 1852 and only completed in 1879; in 1857 he was to start the same architect on the splendid rebuilding of the Château of

12. PRO Works 14/1/13.

13. Royal Library, Windsor Castle. Add. MSS Q Office of Works 1855–1867 No. 267. Quoted by gracious permission of Her Majesty the Queen.

14. W. H. St. John Hope, *Windsor Castle* (London: Country Life, 1913).

Pierrefonds, the ruins of which stood near his favorite residence at Compiégne. Once Salvin had received the commission for the works at Windsor, he seems to have taken his instructions directly from Prince Albert, up to the time of the Prince's death in 1862. His letters refer to a conference with the Prince at Buckingham Palace in April 1857, and in November the following year "a long and pleasant interview with the Prince." In April 1860 he wrote: "I have received a mess. per Telegraph that the Prince wishes to see me at Windsor at 12 o/c"; later in the year: "the Prince Consort presses for the completion of the Lodge at the foot of the Hundred Steps."[15]

The Hundred Steps was where they began. These lie on the north of the castle and lead from the Canons' Residences down to the town. Their rebuilding was obviously part of the improvements mentioned in Colonel Phipps's letter. Drawings made during the last part of the eighteenth century show that they were then of brick, with a wooden guardrail terminating below in the muddy lane, which was then the Datchet Road, and at the top in a small terrace and some brick buildings that concealed the entrance to the Residences and to the Canons' Cloister.[16] Salvin produced two models of his proposed new stone steps, which he estimated would cost £12,500 or £13,500, respectively. This was in November 1856, but nothing was done for two years, after which £1,500 was voted to begin the work by demolishing the old brickwork and ordering a supply of granite in preparation for the start. There was then trouble with the builders, a local firm that had been given the contract before Salvin was consulted. He wrote to the Office of Works in January 1860: "In order that the proposed works at the 100 Steps Windsor Castle may be carried on with vigour, some efficient builder must be employed." The job was then put out to tender and was won by George Smith, and the steps, the postern door and passage to the Canons' Cloister, and the steps up to the North Terrace were complete by the end of 1862.[17]

By this time the improvements at Windsor were the subject of widespread comment, not always favorable. The lawyer Henry Vincent wrote to Ralph Sneyd at Keele Hall in conservationist alarm during November 1858: "What in the world is Salvin doing at Windsor? I believe something to be necessary,—where the old Hill houses have been pulled down; but the less he does the better, I even wish (don't smite me) that they wouldn't meddle with your old Wooden Clocktower on top of the big stone one;—of course they will & I suppose must.—I have no opinion of P. Albert's taste;—I must go and see after him."[18] What Vincent was referring to was the Curfew or Clewer Tower.

Before this was taken in hand Salvin restored the part of the outer wall that adjoined the Canons' Residences. An elevation of a section of this drawn before he started shows tiled roofs and chimney stacks with pots rising above the wall; there was not a surviving medieval window, and the wall was pierced at random with casements and sashes (Fig. III). All of the outer wall was in a similar condition. Salvin tidied away the roofs and built a gable, medievalized the chimneys, which are rebuilt in stone, and replaced the windows with cusped lancets and mullioned

15. Alnwick Castle MSS; Salvin to Ralph Sneyd, Sneyd Papers, Keele University Library.
16. A. P. Oppé, *Sandby Drawings at Windsor Castle* (London: Phaidon Press, 1947).
17. PRO Works 19/40/12.
18. No. 236, Sneyd Papers, Keele University Library.

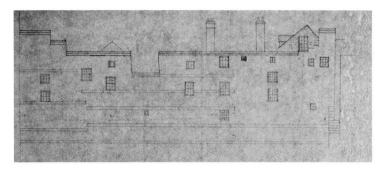

111. Windsor Castle, elevation of outer wall before restoration.

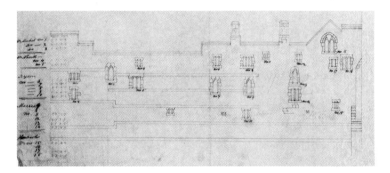

112. Windsor Castle, design for the restoration of the outer wall.

windows in various sizes and groupings (Fig. 112). Then the Garter Tower was repaired as a residence for the Master of the Queen's Household, and Crane's Buildings, an old lodging for five poor knights, was pulled down to make way for a new guardhouse, built against the curtain wall and occupying the entire area between the Salisbury and Garter Towers. This is a two-story range that rose to the height of the outer wall and housed both officers and men, with a loggia of twelve pointed arches opening into the Outer Ward. The wall behind this was restored and appropriately medieval windows put in to light both the guardhouse and those houses in the Horseshoe Cloister that stood against the wall. A plan for rebuilding the Horseshoe Cloister itself was not carried out; this was done by Scott in 1871.

The Curfew Tower, whose improvement Vincent regretted, was restored in 1862. It is the largest of the towers on this particular stretch of wall and dominates the town. Not only does it act as a belfry for St. George's Chapel, but it also contains the clock made by John Davis of Windsor in the seventeenth century. The bells were hung in a wooden belfry, which stood well above the battlements and rested on a staging of massive timbers that rose from the ground floor of the tower. This was weatherboarded and had an ogival lead roof, all of which was stripped off and replaced by the present part-gabled part-conical roof, which is a copy of that designed by Viollet-le-Duc for the Tour du Trésor at Carcassonne (Fig. 113). Viollet-le-Duc's designs for the restoration of this town were exhibited at the Exposition Universelle in Paris in 1855, and Salvin saw them there, but it is inconceivable that

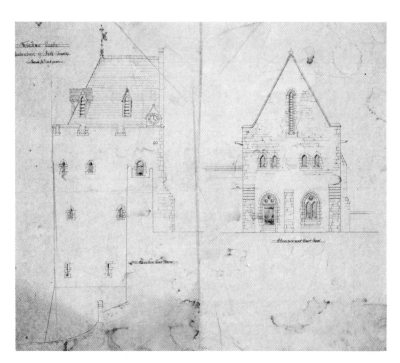

113. Windsor Castle, elevations of the Clewer Tower.

he himself would have contemplated making a direct borrowing from the work of the French architect; it can only be assumed that this was done at the insistence of Prince Albert. Even so, and supposing that it was intended as a compliment to the Emperor, it is a very curious thing to do, and it is surprising that the building of such an obviously French tower in the premier castle in the land did not excite comment and criticism, as the source of the design must have been known to many. As it is, the borrowing seems to have passed unnoticed. The clock was placed in a dormer on the gable facing the town, and three other small dormers acted as louvres to the bell chamber. Old houses built against the base of the tower were removed and the masonry repaired. Work was completed by July 1863 but was complained about by one of the canons, who wrote to the Office of Works to say that the chimes of the clock had not been reconnected, that the rainwater pipes from the tower flooded neighboring houses, and that the bell-ringers were deafened, as the new roof retained the noise of the bells, which could not escape through the small dormers as it had through the louvres of the old timber belfry. After some experiments, all these matters were successfully dealt with.

Salvin also worked for the dean and canons, restoring the next section of the wall, which was their responsibility, adding an oriel window to the north end of the chapter library and restoring the Aerary, which houses the chapter archives. This was completed with the installation of new bookshelves and presses in September 1863. His last work in the Outer Ward was the building of an attic floor and a three-story addition onto the Norman Gateway, which was to become the Deputy Governor's house, all carried out in 1866–1867.

He was, however, also employed on some important alterations in the State Apartments, beginning with Henry VII's Library. This had been created by Wyatville, who knocked a couple of small rooms together, and Salvin's improvements seem chiefly to have been redecorating in accordance with designs approved by Prince Albert shortly before his death. The ceiling was raised and divided into deep coffered compartments; a large chimneypiece and overmantel carved with the royal arms was placed on the south side; and the walls of the library and Queen Anne's Closet, which opens off it, were lined with bookshelves similar in design to those at Alnwick. He also rebuilt the Grand Staircase, replacing that which James Wyat had put in with what had been Brick Court, which by this time was regarded as too dark and insufficiently grand for the main entrance to the castle, something that would have been apparent when Queen Victoria welcomed the emperor. Salvin's new staircase is approached from the State Entrance on the south and from an anteroom on the north, from both of which stairs rise to a half landing, from which a single flight rises east through an arch up to the King's Eating Room. Salvin's stairs are bright, lit from above by an octagonal wooden lantern with cusped lancets and quatrefoils, resting on four deep arches. On the north and south three light windows allow light through into the service stairs.

There was one final project that was initiated in 1867 when Queen Victoria asked for plans to be prepared with the intention of increasing the room for the library by the insertion of an additional floor in the range between the Norman Gateway and the State Apartments. This was not done, but Salvin prepared plans for the part of the building that adjoined Henry VII's Library, taking some of the space as an extension for this and arranging the rest as additional rooms for pages. This completed his work at the castle itself, but he was to continue to work at Windsor, building stables for the canons at the bottom of the Hundred Steps and doing a good deal in the Great Park, making additions to the Royal Lodge and Cumberland Lodge and building the Chapel Royal, the Fishing Pavilion, and estate cottages.

Salvin's restoration and other work on these important public buildings was very well thought of at the time. A generation that has never seen Durham Keep a roofless shell, the Tower encumbered with army storehouses and barracks, the masonry patched with brick, and the walls of the Outer Ward at Windsor punctuated by sash windows must find it difficult to believe how much was done. It is a measure of the care with which he proceeded and the authenticity of the models that he chose that the visitor who can clearly identify as nineteenth-century work the meretricious Gothic of Wyatville at Windsor and the Waterloo Barracks at the Tower finds Salvin's work nearly invisible.

IO

Conclusion

On April 20, 1863, the fellows and associates of the Royal Institute of British Architects were informed by their president that he had some important facts to communicate to them. One was "the 'entire satisfaction'—for that was the language—of Her Majesty with regard to the recommendation that the Royal Gold Medal should be presented to Mr. Anthony Salvin, which recommendation, he was happy to find had met with Her Majesty's entire approbation." The medal was duly presented a month later, and Salvin responded with "his most cordial thanks" and spoke briefly of his gratitude for the unexpected and deeply felt honor.[1] On June 19, at the invitation of the governor, three hundred members of the institute with their ladies met at the Tower of London; Salvin and Lord de Ros conducted the party on a tour of inspection and were congratulated by Beresford Hope on the success of the restoration work. Beresford Hope spoke again at a soirée held that evening, referring to "Mr. Salvin's interesting restoration, in a proper conservative spirit, of the White Tower, including its Royal Chapel, and of other portions."[2]

These occasions marked the apogee of Salvin's architectural career; he was highly regarded by his Queen, the Establishment, the leaders of the Anglican Church, his clients, and by the members of his own profession. Twenty years later his death, and those of Decimus Burton and David Mocatta, were marked by a bare two sentences in a later president's address to the institute, with the comment, "None of them has been much known of late, in the professional world."[3] There is no memoir of Salvin in either the *Journal* or the *Transactions* of the institute, and it was left to *The Builder* and *The Building News* to publish obituaries and to list his works. And yet, as may be seen from the Catalogue, Salvin had continued to practice up until 1879, when ill health obliged him to hand over his last commission, the town house for Lord Leconfield, to his lifelong friend Thomas Henry Wyatt for completion. Even after this, he undertook the restoration of his own parish church, St. Margaret's Fernhurst.

The stroke that he had suffered at Warwick Castle left him partially paralyzed, and recovery proved a slow business. "My father was much more hopeful during the first part of his illness, his slow recovery disappointed him; he felt the powerlessness of his left arm and side in a greater degree and to rouse his spirits and to give him greater strength it was settled we should take a house at Dover."[4]

1. *The Royal Institute of British Architects: Papers Session, 1862–1863* (London: Royal Institute of British Architects, 1863), p. 225.

2. *The Ecclesiologist* (June 1863): 332.

3. *The Royal Institute of British Architects: Transactions Session, 1882–1883* (London: Royal Institute of British Architects, 1883), p. 2.

4. Eliza Anne Salvin, *Reminiscences and Notes of Bye-gone Years.* London Borough of Barnet Library Services. MSS. Acc. 6787/7.

And there they stayed until March 1858, while his principal clerk, William Har-roway, and the young men, Anthony, Willie, and Shaw, ran the practice. But it had become clear to Salvin that he must take things more quietly. "Mr. Wyatt came down to see Papa and it was to him that Papa first spoke of leaving Finchley. He would have to be careful of himself in future, he thought the journeys backwards and forwards in the omnibus were tiring. The irregularity of food was bad and he could never be sure of luncheon. It would be better, he thought, to live in London and in this idea Mr. Wyatt strengthened him promising to keep an eye on houses to let in such situations as he though would please Papa."

Salvin then changed his mind. As he felt better, he recalled the twenty-five happy years they had had at Finchley, where he had built the Holy Trinity Church and become Vicar's Warden, the whole family being much involved with parish affairs. His doctor, however, persisted in advising him to move, warning him that he must avoid all unnecessary fatigue and going all day without eating. "For a long time my father refused to listen to the advice given. He fancied we had previously spoken to Mr. Squibb [the doctor] which had not been the case." Eventually he gave in and began viewing houses, which he found entertaining, and finally took a lease at 11 Hanover Terrace, Regent's Park, which brought him within easy calling distance of W. A. Nesfield, who had moved into a house in York Terrace a few years earlier. Having taken the first step, the family resolved against further delay: "we did not wish to put off our removal as the Season was coming on, a time when Papa could see more of his Clients." And later: "My father left home on business and was to return to the London home, which we hastened to get in readiness for him. . . . By getting into the house we drove the workmen out. . . . Anthony made himself into upholsterer for the occasion."

Salvin's daughters Eliza Anne and Emmeline never married and lived with him, as did Anthony until he married in 1865 and Osbert when he was in England. Osbert had shown a great interest in natural history as a boy, but had studied mathematics at Cambridge. After he came down he joined the Reverend H. B. Tristram on an ornithological expedition to north Africa, where he remained for six months, returning by way of Marseilles and Paris: "Osbert returned from Algeria at 12 o/c last night. We were all in bed but got up and ran downstairs in various costumes to meet him." Three months later he left for Guatemala, with the orchid collector George Ure Skinner, intending to settle there: "My father said little but felt this parting very much." Osbert returned, however, the following year, not having enjoyed life on a cochineal plantation; thereafter he spent twenty years collecting in Central America with Frederick du Cane Godman, recording the results of this in the immense publication *Biologia Centrali-Americana.*[5] He later became a fellow of the Royal Society and Strickland Curator of Ornithology at the University of Cambridge. It was through Osbert and his friends that Anthony, Junior, obtained the commission to build, among much else, the Lion House at the London Zoo.

On June 5, 1860, Anne Salvin died after a long and painful illness. Salvin was stricken and two years later sought some comfort by returning to a recreation that he had enjoyed at Finchley, by purchasing a mixed farm of 145 acres at Fernhurst in Sussex. It consisted of a farmhouse and yard, with barns, stables, cartsheds, and

5. *Proceedings of the Royal Society* 64: xiii.

114. Hawksfold, watercolor by Viola Salvin.

rickyard, set well back up a cart track from the road that ran from Lynchmere to Fernhurst Cross. He built himself a new house, which he called Hawksfold, completed in 1865 and built in the local vernacular style: rubble stone, red brick, half timbering and tile hanging, and much the same sort of thing that Shaw was building at this very time at Willesley near Cranbrook in Kent, but with some recollection of medieval buildings, such as the polygonal stone tower containing the stairs (Fig. 114). The angle of the porch rests on a timber post, each face of which is carved with monograms of his children's initials (Fig. 115). Salvin only attempted the vernacular on one other occasion, at Oeborne House on the other side of the village, which he designed for his friend C. S. Roundell. From now on he divided his time between Fernhurst, Hanover Terrace, and his office, spending more and more time at Hawksfold as he grew older.

Throughout his seventies, when most men might have hoped to retire, and he had no financial reasons for staying at work, as his estate was worth just over £70,000 net when he died, Salvin was engaged in major projects, such as the rebuilding of parts of Petworth House and Warwick Castle after bad fires. His son was actively concerned with Warwick but was the victim of increasing ill health and retired before his father in 1879. The same year, as we have seen, Salvin abandoned his formal practice and restricted his efforts to completing the restoration of St. Margaret's, in some anxiety that his gift of a peal of bells should be hung in time to be rung for his own funeral. Indeed, he must have felt that time was running out. William Andrews Nesfield died on March 2, 1881, and this loss was followed by the deaths of a number of old friends: the contractor George Smith, who had worked with him at Thoresby and Windsor Castle and whose country house he designed; George Edmund Street, William Burges, and Decimus Burton, his exact contemporary, who must like himself have seemed a last survivor of a bygone age. The worst blow of all must have been the death of his son Anthony at

115. Hawksfold, the porch.

the age of fifty-four. Salvin himself died on December 17, 1881, and they are buried side by side in the new graveyard at Fernhurst. Eliza Anne gave the statutory notification to the Registrar of Births, Deaths and Marriages. She gave the cause of death as "old age."

When he took the younger Anthony into his office, Salvin must have hoped, indeed expected, that his son would carry on the business, as had happened in the practices of the Pugins, the Barrys, the Scotts, and with Burn and his nephew MacVicar Anderson. But his son's dismal talent and chronic ill health must have indicated at an early stage that he would be unable to continue on his own. Given this situation, Salvin might have been expected to take other young men into his office with a view to providing a succession, but he seems to have made no attempt to do so. Considering the amount of important work that he had in hand at any given time, experience in his practice would seem to have offered great opportunities for promising assistants, and he must have had a large staff, as he was on one occasion to complain that four of them had left at much the same time, leaving him somewhat shorthanded.[6] Their names are known, and none seem to have gone on to more important things. No architect of great repute received his entire training with Salvin. We know of James Deason, a competent perspectivist, helpful assistant, and the builder of two small churches and restorer of Eton College Chapel; J. L. Pearson, who spent his few months with Salvin busily improving the very rudimentary knowledge of Gothic that he had acquired with Ignatius Bonomi and then moved on; Willie Nesfield and Shaw, who spent about two years with

6. Alnwick Castle MSS.

him, and who like Pearson made important contributions of their own to the architecture of the period, but neither owed anything stylistically to Salvin, although they would have learned a great deal about planning, good workmanship, and the conduct of a busy office.

Salvin therefore lacked a successor, and his practice died with him. It was in any event restricted in scope and would probably have diminshed once he had gone. His business was to a great extent based upon the patronage of the landed gentry and aristocracy. He worked for new money in very few cases: for the flax-spinning Marshalls, the banking Gurneys and Birkbecks, and the haberdasher George Moore. Viscount Boyne had a fortune from coal, Lord Middleton a windfall from the Midland Railway, and Lord Radnor enjoyed the rents of a good part of Folkestone; but the majority of Salvin's clients drew their income from the land, and this was at intervals unreliable. Post-repeal depression afflicted the 1850s, and of the six years beginning with 1873, only two produced average crops of wheat, and four well below average; that of 1879 was the worst since 1816. The consequent shortness of supply was not compensated for by a rise in price, as had previously been the case; the shortfall was made up by wheat from the prairies, and farmers now had to compete with bacon and eggs from Denmark and beef from Argentina, brought in refrigerated steamships. Land was no longer the best investment, and the major country house commissions were tending to come from newly established families migrating from the cities to the countryside, where they spent the profits of trade and industry. This was not the class from which Salvin's clients had ever come.

Finally, since the 1840s he must himself have have seemed increasingly old-fashioned in his approach to architecture, and it is clear that the younger Salvin did not have an original thought in his head. Thoresby Hall or Hodnet Hall could have been built as they were at any time during the preceding fifty years, and that they were built in the 1870s in the same careful mixture of the Elizabethan and Jacobean styles that Salvin had worked out in the 1840s is striking testimony to the conservatism of both the architect and the clients for whom he worked. He stood increasingly outside the architectural trends of his day. After the early years he eschewed publicity, did not submit work to the Royal Academy, and did not enter competitions. Indeed, he had no need to do so. His reputation had been established for careful, archaeologically correct work on old houses and churches, and there was enough of this to provide him with a very comfortable living. He was the man to turn to if one required a comfortable country house and was not out to upstage the local gentry. Even buildings like Peckforton and Thoresby Hall are reticent when compared with Scott's Kelham Hall or E. M. Barry's Wykehurst.

He got on well with these clients and formed friendships that continued over many years. He wrote to George Luttrell when Dunster Castle was finished: "I do not mean to make any further appearance from a professional point of view but hope to do so as an amateur."[7] Thirty years after the chapel at Arley Hall was completed, R. E. Egerton Warburton sent him a copy of his didactic poem *A Looking Glass for Landlords,* with a letter in which he complains that it has been a long time since he heard from Salvin, and asking him to visit him. Sir Robert

7. Dunster Castle MSS.

Shafto Adair of Flixton Hall stayed with the family at Finchley. There were many such cases, but the relationships were not allowed to lead to unseemly familiarity. Salvin kept his place. On the visit to Mamhead, the four horses required to drag the carriage through the mud from Sidmouth were considered too ostentatious to be kept until they arrived at the house. Years later, in 1860, Eliza Anne and the rest of the family visited Sion House on the occasion of a school treat: "The Duke asked us into the house but this we were not to accept according to Papa."[8]

Salvin was an agreeable friend, a competent architect who could rebuild Old England for his clients. But it was the class of client, their circumstances and their lack of any desire for the full-blown Gothic Revival or Victorian classicism as it manifested itself in the mid-nineteenth century, that was to inhibit and finally destroy any originality that Salvin might have developed in his later work. So much was restoration and additions the repetition of well-tried formulas; it is greatly to be lamented that he was not allowed more opportunities to build a Harlaxton or a Peckforton Castle.

But we should remember and be grateful for what we have. What was built adds immeasurably to our present appreciation of Victorian architecture. The traveler leaving London and driving west toward Wales will see Windsor Castle on his left hand. Two features dominate the embattled skyline; one is the Round Tower and the other the bulk and pointed roof of Salvin's Curfew Tower standing at the western angle of the walls. The traveler skirting the Peckforton Hills on the way from Nantwich to Chester will be aware at a distance of many miles of the castle keep rising from the woods, which have now grown up and mask the lower part of the walls. Those crossing the Mersey between Runcorn and Widness will find the elegant spire of All Saints almost the only point of interest in the industrial landscape, and it is spectacular. And finally, the visitor to Thoresby Hall will know he is seeing the home of one of the richest noblemen in England, and visitors to Harlaxton, turning off the Grantham Road and approaching the house, will find themselves proceeding along one of the grandest contrived approaches in England toward one of the greatest houses. All this visual excitement we owe to Anthony Salvin.

8. Eliza Anne Salvin, *Reminiscences.*

Catalogue Raisonné

Abbreviations

B	*The Builder*
BN	*Building News*
Calverley	Material and drawings in the possession of Mrs. Sybil Rampen
CCE	Church Commissioners for England; files at Lambeth Palace
CL	*Country Life*
DNB	*The Dictionary of National Biography*
E	Executed
Eccl.	*The Ecclesiologist*
Fiske	Drawings in the possession of R. C. Fiske
H	William Harroway's list of works and their cost
HoN	Howard of Naworth MSS, Department of Palaeography and Diplomatic, University of Durham
ICBS	Incorporated Church Building Society; files at Lambeth Palace
ILN	*Illustrated London News*
JLP	J. L. Pearson's Sketchbooks, vol. 1, in the possession of Mrs. M. Morgan
NE	Not executed
Priors Kitchen	The Prior's Kitchen, The College, Durham
PRO	Public Record Office
RA	The Royal Academy
RIBA Salvin	The British Architectural Library, Drawings Collection. The references given are those in the *Catalogue of the Drawings Collection of the Royal Institute of British Architects,* where they are described, so no note is made here of their subject.
S	Documentary sources
Toronto	Anthony Salvin Papers, Thomas Fisher Rare Book Library, University of Toronto
Willis and Clark	R. Willis and J. W. Clark, *The Architectural History of the University of Cambridge* (Cambridge: At the University Press, 1886)
Wilson	F. R. Wilson, *An Architectural Survey of the Churches of the Archdeaconry of Lindisfarne* (Newcastle: M. Lambert and M. W. Lambert, 1830)

Catalogue by Date

New Exchange, Leeds (Yorks. W. Riding W.
    Yorks.)
Described as a Design for an Exchange, North
    of England.
NE: 1825
S: RA 1825 908.

Mamhead Park, Mamhead (Devon)
New mansion house, stable, and conservatory
    for Sir Robert William Newman Bart.
E: 1825–1838
Built in the Tudor style of Bath stone, the sta-
    bles modeled on Belsay pele and of local
    red sandstone. The builder was Philip
    Nowell & Son, plumbing and glass by
    Thomas Willement, statues of Tudor per-
    sonages in the gallery carved by Charles
    Raymond Smith (Figs. 8–15).
C: £20,000 H
S: RIBA Salvin/20/1–7; Newman MSS, an
    almost complete set of drawings and
    correspondence; RA 1830 1165; CL
    CXVII 1955, pp. 1336, 1428, 1683;
    Christopher Hussey, *English Country
    Houses, Late Georgian, 1800–1840* (London:
    Country Life, 1958).
South and East Lodges
Remodeling for Sir Robert William Newman
    Bart.
E: c. 1830
Enlarged and picturesque features added (Fig.
    16).
S: Newman MSS, elevations.

Bellasis Cottage, Durham, now part of
    Durham School (Durham)
Alterations for Dr. William Cook.
E: Before 1826
S: H and note by Eliza Anne Salvin; *Durham
    and Northumberland Directory* (Leeds: W.
    White & Co., 1827).

Vicarage, Northallerton, now the Council
    Offices (Yorks. N. Riding N. Yorks.)
New vicarage for the Reverend George
    Townsend.
E: 1826
Tudor style. Rendered brick with stone dress-
    ings (Frontispiece and Fig. 3).
C: £2,521.5.4 1/2d.
S: Calverley: watercolor perspective; Borth-
    wick Institute of Historical Research,
    York: Survey, specification, and working
    drawings; RA 1829 1061.

Picture Gallery, Trafalgar Square (Mddx.
    London, Westminster)
Project for a new gallery for the Old Water-
    colour Society.
NE: 1827
S: J. L. Roget, *A History of the "Old Water-Colour"
    Society* (London: Longmans, 1891).

The Trafford Mausoleum, St. Mary's
    Church, Wroxham (Norfolk)
Mausoleum for Margaret Trafford Southwell.
E: 1827
Burial place for a Roman Catholic family in
    the Parish churchyard (Fig. 7).
S: Norfolk and Norwich Record Office: Nor-
    wich Diocesan Records FCB 6, f.107v:
    RA 1830 1163; *The Gentleman's Magazine*
    (1830) 1: 541.

Kildale Hall, Whitby (Yorks. N. Riding. N.
    Yorks)
Alterations for Robert Bell Livsey.
E: c. 1827–1831
Rearrangement of principal rooms, new cel-
    lars and front porch.
S: Kildale Hall MSS: Specification; Cal-
    verley: perspective sketch.

Magdalen College, Oxford (Oxon.)
Designs for the restoration of the chapel for the president and fellows.
NE: 1828
This was a competition entry, L. N. Cottingham was the winner (Figs. 5 and 6).
S: Toronto: three elevations of reredos and organ screen; Calverley: longitudinal section.

Holy Trinity Church, Ulverston (Lancs. Cumbria)
New church for the Commissioners for Building New Churches and a local building committee.
E: 1828–1832
Early English, nave with north and south aisles, northeast tower and spire, north, south, and west galleries, no chancel. Work contracted out to local masons and tradesman (Fig. 86).
C: £4419
S: CCE 18198; H.

Moreby Hall, Escrick (Yorks. E. Riding N. Yorks.)
New mansion house for Henry Preston.
E: 1828–1833
The second major country house commission, in the Tudor style and built of Park Spring freestone. Thomas Willement carried out painting and plumbing work (Figs. 18 and 19).
C: £40,000 H
S: RIBA Salvin /23/1–3; Calverley: Perspective and design for lamp; RA 1828 1008; C. L. Eastlake, *A History of the Gothic Revival* (London: Longmans, 1872); CL XXI 1907, p. 234.

Somerhill, Tonbridge (Kent)
Alterations for James Alexander.
E: 1828–1838
Greenwood writes: "Its spacious hall and apartments are fitted up in the most costly style having been re-decorated and beautified by Mr. Salvin."
C: £5,000 H
S: C. Greenwood, *Epitome of County History. Vol. I. County of Kent* (London: n.p., 1838).

Brancepeth Castle, Brancepeth (Co. Durham)
Alterations for William Russell.
E: 1829
Some work was carried out in the Great Hall.
S: H.

Village school, Ashcombe (Devon)
New school for Sir Robert William Newman Bart.
E: 1829
Tudor, built of local stone.
S: Newman MSS: elevation.

Westley Manor Farm, Westley (Devon)
Alterations for Sir Robert William Newman Bart.
E: 1829
Additions to old house.
S: Newman MSS: two elevations.

Harpur School, Bedford (Beds.)
Design for new school buildings for the Harpur Trustees.
NE: 1829
This was a competition entry. Edward Blore was the winner. Tudor style (Fig. 4).
S: RIBA Salvin /38/; *Harpur Trust Minute Book* (April 13, 1829); Malcolm Seaborne, *The English School, 1370–1870* (London: Routledge & Kegan Paul, 1971).

St. Paul's Church, North Sunderland (Northumb.)
New church for Lord Crewe's trustees.
E: 1830–1833
Norman style, nave without aisles, apsidal chancel, west door and double bell-cote (Fig. 91).
S: Durham Chapter Office: Crewe Trustees' Minute Books; *The Durham Advertiser,* June 28, 1833; Wilson; John Sykes, *Local Records* (Newcastle: T. Fordyce, 1866), p. 306.

The Cathedral Church of the Holy and Undivided Trinity, Norwich (Norfolk)
Restoration of the south transept, repair and reseating of choir for the dean and chapter.
E: 1830–1834

Rebuilding of south facade of transept and fire-damaged interior, new clock faces, removal of old galleries and seating in the choir, new choir stalls, screens, and pulpitum.

The builder was Watson and the carving by Ollett.

S: Norwich Cathedral Archives: Chapter Act Books, correspondence, some drawings.

Monument to Joseph Turner, dean of Norwich.

Wall tablet for Mrs. Turner.

E: 1830

S: Norwich Cathedral Archives: correspondence.

Methley Hall, Methley (Yorks. W. Riding W. Yorks.)

Alterations and additions for the 3d Earl of Mexborough.

E: 1830–1836

The additions included a library, drawing room, and dining room and rearrangement of the offices around a new kitchen court. Design of elevations based on Heath Old Hall (Fig. 47).

Demolished 1963

C: £17,000 H

S: RIBA Salvin /22/; RA 1831 1015; W. B. Crump, "Methley House and Its Builders," *Thoresby Society Proceedings* 37 (1943).

Parham Park, Pulborough (Sussex, W. Sussex)

Alterations and estate buildings for the 13th Baroness de la Zouche.

E: 1830–1836

Alterations to the house included recasting the exterior in Tudor style, a new main entrance, and improved circulation; on the estate, work on the stables, dairy, gamekeeper's lodge, and gardener's house (Figs. 48–51).

C: £9,700 H

S: RIBA Salvin /26/; Parham MSS: Zouche correspondence, vol. 13; House Notes; three perspectives titled: Alterations at Parham 1830 A.S.; two watercolors s.H.S.H. 1855.

St. Thomas's Church, Mamhead (Devon)

Restoration for Sir Robert William Newman Bart.

E: c. 1831

S: RIBA Salvin /46/.

Vaughan Monument, St. Thomas's Church

Memorial tablet for Sir Robert William Newman Bart.

E: 1831

S: Newman MSS: correspondence.

The Rectory, Barley (Herts.)

Additions for the Reverend W. H. Turner.

E: 1831–1833

The Tudor Rectory was substantially enlarged.

C: £3,500 H

Bamburgh Castle, Bamburgh (Northumb.)

Work for Lord Crewe's trustees.

E: 1831–1833

Repairs to houses at the gateway and a new pump.

S: Calverley: perspective of gateway; Durham Chapter Office: Crewe Trustees' Minute Book.

Harlaxton Manor, Harlaxton (Lincs.)

New mansion house for Gregory Gregory.

E: 1831–1837; William Burn had taken over by 1838.

Salvin's major work in his early career and a much larger house than either Mamhead or Moreby; intended to house Gregory's collections. Style a mixture of Tudor and Jacobean. The Clerk of Works was William Weare, later at Scotney Castle. Ancaster stone, stained glass by Thomas Willement (Figs. 29–39).

C: c. £100,000 including estate buildings.

S: Lincolnshire Archives Committee: PG/2/1/-28/2; RIBA Salvin /12/1–5; *The Lincolnshire Chronicle,* March 4, 1836; *The Gardener's Magazine* (July 1840); ILN, May 7, 1843; *The Civil Engineer & Architects Journal* 1: 392; 2: 5, 39; B, September 10, 1835, p. 569; Mark Girouard, *The Victorian Country House* (New Haven and London: Yale University Press, 1979).

29a Grosvenor Square, Mayfair (Mddx. London, Westminster)
Alterations for Sir Stratford Canning.
E: 1832
It is not known what was done. Demolished 1886.
C: £3,700 H

St. Paul's Vicarage, North Sunderland (Northumb.)
New vicarage for Lord Crewe's trustees.
E: 1832–1833
Built of stone in an eccentric Norman style.
S: Durham Chapter Office: Crewe Trustees' Minute Books.

Holy Trinity Church, South Shields (Durham, Tyne and Wear)
New church for the Reverend James Carr and committee, aided financially by the dean and chapter of Durham.
E: 1832–1834
Early English. Nave, north and south aisles, west tower, and spire. North, south, and west galleries. Altered in 1879 by Austin Johnson & Hicks. Demolished 1980.
C: £3,344.4.9d.
S: ICBS 1460; Durham Chapter Act Books 1838–1847; CCE 17944.

Cowesby Hall, Cowesby (Yorks. N. Riding. N. Yorks.)
New country house for George Lloyd.
E: 1832–1836
Tudor style. Burned down and rebuilt in 1949 (Figs. 20 and 21).
C: £7,500 H
S: Calverley: perspective sketch of first design; RIBA Salvin /6/1–3; *Victoria County History, Yorkshire,* vol. 3.

Skutterskelfe House, Rudby (Yorks. N. Riding N. Yorks.)
New country house for the 10th Viscount Falkland.
E: 1832–1838
Salvin's first attempt at the Italian villa style. Porch added later (Fig. 26).
C: £16,000 H
S: Victoria and Albert Museum E. 482–83. 1980; JLP: 6v, 52r.

Villas at Fortis Green, Muswell Hill (Mddx. London, Barnet)
A pair of semidetached villas in the Italian villa style built by Salvin for himself and W. A. Nesfield.
E: c. 1833
Brick built and stucco rendered, gardens planned by Nesfield. Demolished.
S: *The Gardener's Magazine* (February 1840).

Parsonage, Seaton Carew (Durham)
New parsonage for the Reverend A. Guiness.
E: 1833
Tudor.
C: £700 H
S: JLP: 42r.

Stoke Green House, Conventry (Warks.)
Alterations for Lieutenant-Colonel Rolfe.
E: 1833
This house cannot be identified.
C: £3,300 H

Derwent Sole House, Derwentwater (Cumberland, Cumbria)
Design for a new country house for Henry Marshall.
NE: 1833
It was to have been built in stone in the Tudor style and presumably would have replaced Joseph Pocklington's house (Fig. 22).

St. John's Church, Shildon (Durham)
New church for the Reverend George Fielding and a committee.
E: 1833–1834
Early English. Nave, north vestry, west tower, and spire. Enlarged later by C. Hodgson Fowler (Fig. 88).
C: £1,331.0.11d.
S: ICBS 1436; CCE 16102/
S: Toronto, three elevations; Calverley, two elevations.

Durham Castle (Durham)
Projected additions for the warden and trustees of the University of Durham.
NE: 1833–1835
It was proposed that Bishop Bek's Hall should

be encased in new four-story ranges of buildings providing lecture rooms and students' accommodation.

S: Priors Kitchen 63; C. E. Whiting, *The University of Durham, 1832–1932* (London: Sheldon Press, 1932).

North Runcton Hall, North Runcton (Norfolk)

Additions for Daniel Gurney.

E: 1833–1836

The old house was transformed by the addition of grand new reception rooms and new offices.

Tudor style. Demolished 1965.

C: £4,900 H

S: Gurney MSS: two perspectives of alterations, W. A. Nesfield's plan for laying out the grounds.

Stoke Rochford Hall, Stoke Rochford (Lincs.)

New South Lodge for Christopher Turnor (Fig. 116).

E: 1834

Stone-built Tudor style.

S: Turnor MSS: Christopher Turnor's personal Account of the buildings at Stoke Rochford; JLP: 43r.

The Fitzwilliam Museum, Cambridge (Cambs.)

Project for new museum building for the trustees.

NE: 1834

This was a competition entry. George Basevi was the winner. Salvin's entry was Gothic Revival.

S: JLP: 84r; Willis and Clark.

The Houses of Parliament, Westminster (Mddx. London, Westminster)

Designs for rebuilding the Palace of Westminster, for a select committee.

NE: 1835

Salvin's extraordinary Renaissance design is based on the Palace of Aschaffenburg near Frankfurt. It was singled out for comment when the competition designs were put on public display; Charles Barry was the winner (Figs. 40–43).

S: Toronto: perspective sketches of the proposed buildings from Abingdon Street, Parliament Street, and the Surrey side of Westminster Bridge; Calverley: elevation; *The Architectural Magazine* (1835): 311, 381, 464; (1836): 185, 293, 325, 434.

Grosvenor House, Westminster (Mddx. London Westminster)

Alterations for the 1st Marquis of Westminster.

E: 1835

It is not known what was done. Demolished 1927.

C: £5,900 H

116. Stoke Rochford Hall, the South Lodge.

Gatehouse, Eaton Hall (Cheshire)
Design for a new gatehouse for the 1st Marquis
   of Westminster (Fig. 117).
NE: 1835
S: RIBA Salvin /46/.

Norwich Castle, Norwich (Norfolk)
Restoration for the visiting justices.
E: 1835–1838
Recasing of the whole exterior of the keep,
   rebuilding battlements. The Clerk of
   Works was Elisha Bonner.
C: £4,607.4.2d.
S: Norwich Castle MSS: Visiting Justices'
   Minute Book. "Repair and Restoration
   of the South, West and North Sides as by
   order of Quarter Sessions April 11th
   1834," Correspondence Norfolk and Nor-
   wich Record Office: Correspondence;
   The Norfolk Chronicle, October 25, 1834,
   October 29, 1836.

117. Eaton Hall, design for a gatehouse.

Kimberley Hall, Kimberley (Norfolk)
Additions for the 2d Baron Wodehouse (Fig.
   118)
E: 1835–1838
The quadrant passages were added, and some
   alterations to the facades and rearrang-
   ment of the interiors were carried out.
S: RIBA Salvin /16/1–2; Norwich Cathedral
   MSS: Visiting Justices' Minute Book,
   Visiting Justices' Account Book.

Burwarton House, Burwarton (Salop.)
New country house for the Honorable Gus-
   tavus Frederick Hamilton (later the 7th
   Viscount Boyne).

E: 1835–1839
A large house in the Italian villa style, later
   enlarged but now partly demolished.
C: £11,700 H

Scotney Castle, Lamberhurst (Kent)
New country house for Edward Hussey.
E: 1835–1843
Tudor, built of local ragstone. The builders
   were Philip Nowell & Son; Thomas
   Willement did the painting and plumb-
   ing. William Weare was Clerk of Works
   (Figs. 23–25).
C: £12,928.16.11 1/2d.
S: Scotney Castle MSS: complete set of work-
   ing drawings, the accounts and

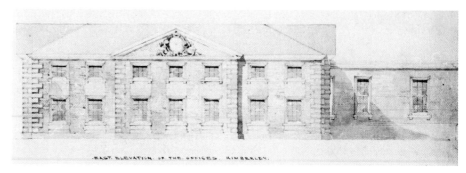

118. Kimberley Hall, elevation of offices.

tradesmens' bills, correspondence, and Edward Hussey's own drawings and diary; RIBA Salvin /32/1–2; RA 1838 1171; CL XI 1902, p. 688, XLVIII 1920, p. 12, CXX 1956, pp. 470, 526, CXLVI 1969, p. 958; Christopher Hussey, *English Country Houses: Late Georgian, 1800–1840* (London: Country Life, 1958).

Chalfont House, Chalfont St. Peter (Bucks)
Alterations for John Nembhard Hibbert.
E: 1836
The exterior was gothicized, details modeled in cement. Interior alterations also.
C: £3,500 H

Pyrgo Park, Romford (Essex)
Alterations for Michael Field.
E: 1836
These included the addition of a Gothic great hall. Demolished 1938.
S: Montague Browne, *Yearly Records of Pyrgo Park from A.D. 946 to A.D. 1888* nl. 1888.

Easton Park, Easton (Lincs.)
Estate buildings for Sir Montague Cholmeley Bart.
E: 1836
Tudor, stone-built.
S: JLP:2r.

Woodlands, Kenn (Devon)
Alterations for William Ley.
E: 1836
A new facade was added to the old house.
C: £3,100 H
S: JLP:1r.

Bishop's Palace, Ripon (Yorks. W. Riding N. Yorks.)
Design for a new episcopal palace.
NE: 1836
Salvin's brother-in-law Robert Nesfield tried to get him this commission, which he lost to William Railton (Fig. 28).
S: Toronto: one perspective; JLP: 53r; University of Durham Library: Salvin MSS, Robert Nesfield to Anne Salvin, October 6, 1836.

Sudbury Hall, Sudbury (Derbys.)
Project for alterations for the 5th Baron Vernon (Fig. 119).
NE: 1836–1837
Extensive alterations were intended, including the remodeling of the exterior in an elaborate Jacobean style and rebuilding the stables and the porter's lodge.
S: Sudbury Estate Office and Sudbury House MSS: Correspondence, thirty-two plans, elevations and perspectives.

119. Sudbury Hall, proposal for alterations to the exterior.

Holy Trinity Church, Darlington (Durham)
New church for the Reverend J. W. D. Merest.
E: 1836–1838
Early English, nave, north and south aisles,
  north tower/porch, west gallery; a
  chancel was added in 1867 (Fig. 87).
C: £3,403.17.3 1/2d.
S: Victoria and Albert Museum E. 484. 1980;
  ICBS 1607; CCE 17795, 17796; *British
  Almanac and Companion* (n.p., 1840), p. 235.

St. John the Evangelist, Keswick (Cum-
  berland. Cumbria)
New church for John Marshall.
E: 1836–1838
Early English. Nave, west tower and spire,
  octagonal vestry. A north aisle was added
  in 1862, the south aisle in 1882, the
  chancel lengthened in 1889 (Fig. 95).
C: £6,197.16.0d.
S: JLP: 119r; lithograph by J. Deason publ.
  Day & Haghe; CCE 15819; *British Almanac
  and Companion,* 1840, p. 235.

Bayons Manor, Tealby (Lincs.)
Additions and recasting for Charles Tennyson
  d'Eyncourt.
E: 1836–1840
Rebuilding of the old house in the castle style,
  including Gothic great hall, in collabora-
  tion with the local architect W. A.
  Nicholson. Demolished 1965 (Fig. 27).
S: Lincolnshire Archives Committee: T d'E
  H/168–169, H/13, H/118-125, H/35; CL
  CXXVII, 1960, p. 430

Danesfield, Medmenham (Bucks.)
Alterations for Charles Robert Scott-Murray
  (Fig. 120).

E: 1836–1841
There appears to have been an extensive
  remodeling of the upper part of the
  facade of an eighteenth-century house in
  the Gothic Revival style. Demolished
  1897.
C: £12,000 H
S: Toronto: elevation; JLP: 51r.

Burtonfields, Stamfordbridge (Yorks. E. Rid-
  ing Humberside)
New house for Charles Darley.
E: 1837
Italian villa style. Darley had married Salvin's
  sister-in-law Marianne Nesfield, and
  their daughter married Anthony Salvin,
  Junior.
C: £3,000 H

Rufford Abbey, Ollerton (Notts.)
Restoration and alterations for the 8th Earl of
  Scarborough.
E: 1837–1841
Considerable refurbishing of the house, new
  grand staircase. Thomas Willement,
  Messrs. Crace, and Armstrong and
  Smith were employed.
C: £13,167. 1. 1 1/2d.
S: Nottinghamshire Record Office: Savile of
  Rufford MSS, DDSR 215/66/1,2,3,4. 215/-
  67/1,6,7,8.; RIBA Salvin /30/; Toronto:
  one detail; Calverley: elevation of library
  side table.

Greystoke Castle, Greystoke (Cumberland.
  Cumbria)
Restoration and major additions for Henry
  Howard.

120. Danesfield, elevation.

E: 1837–1845

A new mansion and great hall were built round a pele tower and other old buildings. The builder was Robinson of Whitbarrow (Fig. 54).

C: £9,000 H

S: Greystoke Castle MSS: complete set of working drawings; RIBA Salvin /II/1–2; Cumbria County Record Office: Salvin's account to December 31, 1941, ref. D/HG/ Acc. 1762.

Heath Hall, Wakefield (Yorks. W. Riding W. Yorks)

Alterations for Colonel John George Smyth.

E: 1837–1845

Addition of fourth story and billiard room.

C: £6,100 H

Parsonage, Keswick (Cumberland. Cumbria)

New parsonage house.

E: 1838

Tudor.

S: JLP: 37r; CCE 15819; Cumbria County Record Office: Specification ref. D/ WM/II/181.

Estate and village improvements, Belton (Lincs.)

Village cross, lower lake boathouse, keeper's house, blacksmith's house, cottages, public house, and hermitage for the 1st Earl Brownlow (Fig. 121).

E: 1838–1839

Mostly in the Tudor style. Salvin began the work but was replaced by the local Clerk of Works.

S: Belton Estate Office: twenty-nine drawings; RIBA Salvin /3/; B, September 10, 1853, p. 569.

Wellow House, Wellow (Notts.)

Alterations for the 8th Earl of Scarborough.

E: 1838–1840

It is not known what was done.

C: £2,346. 4. 1 1/2d.

S: Nottinghamshire Record Office: Savile of Rufford MSS, DDSR 215/67/5.

Rockingham Castle, Corby (Northants.)

Alterations for the Honorable Richard Watson.

E: 1838–1841

General refurbishment and rearrangement of

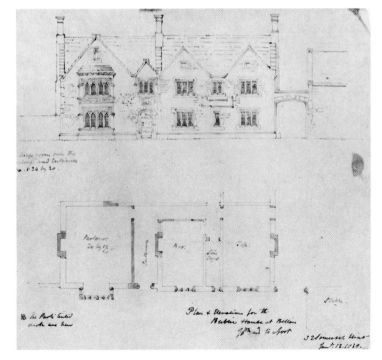

121. Belton, the Public House, plan and elevation.

the house, which had stood empty, rebuilding the battlements and restoring the gateway.

C: £3,969.4.11d.

S: Rockingham Castle MSS: Diaries of Richard Watson; RIBA Salvin /28/1–13.

Durham Castle Keep (Durham)

Restoration for the warden and trustees of Durham University

E: 1839

The keep was converted into sets of students' rooms and linked to the main castle buildings.

C: £5,000 H

S: Prior's Kitchen 66; Calverley: design for building linking keep and castle.

Moor Park, Rickmansworth (Herts.)

Garden terraces for the 1st Marquis of Westminster.

E: 1839

This is probably the layout of the formal gardens to the rear of the house.

C: £3,500 H

Taylor and Randolph Building (Ashmolean Museum and Taylorian Institute) Oxford (Oxon.)

Design for new museum and institute building for the delegates.

NE: 1839

Entry for a competition; a large Palladian building with pantiled roof; C. R. Cockerell was the winner (Fig. 44).

S: Bodleian Library: MS Top.Oxon c. 202; Oxford Univeristy Archives, Delegates of the Taylor Institute Minute Book, November 19, 1839–1840 end TL/M/1/1; lithograph perspective.

Ley Fields, Ollerton (Notts.)

Alterations for the 8th Earl of Scarborough.

E: 1839–1840

New rooms were added.

C: £1,276.14.1d.

S: Nottinghamshire Record Office, Savile of Rufford MSS DDSR 215/67/4.

Sand Hutton Hall, Sand Hutton (Yorks. N. Riding N. Yorks.)

Additions to a country house for James Walker.

E: 1839–1841

It is not known what was done. Demolished.

C: £1,500 H

St. Mary's Church, Sand Hutton (Yorks. N. Riding N. Yorks.)

New church for James Walker.

E: 1839–1841

Early English; greatly enlarged and remodeled by C. Hodgson Fowler in 1885.

S: *The Civil Engineer & Architects Journal* (November 1839): 445.

Christ Church, Kilndown (Kent)

New church for the Reverend W. B. Harrison, Field Marshal Lord Beresford, and Edward Hussey.

E: 1839–1841

Early English. Nave, west tower and spire, no chancel. It was turned into a demonstration of the Ecclesiological point of view by A. J. B. Beresford Hope.

C: £1,600 H

S: Scotney Castle MSS: Salvin to Hussey, August 29, 1840; ICBS 2485; *The Gentleman's Magazine* (1841): 531; Eccl. 4 (February 1842): 91; 31 (May 1844): 127; 2 (March 1845): 91.

Observatory and Obelisk, Durham (Durham)

New observatory for the warden and trustees of Durham University.

E: 1839–1841

A small classical building designed to house the telescope and other instruments (Fig. 106).

C: £1,000 H

S: Durham Chapter Act Books 1838–1847; Durham University Library: Specification Ref. AID-SH-b.10; H. C. E. Whiting, *The University of Durham, 1832–1932.*

Woodchester Park, Woodchester (Glos.)

Proposals for alterations for the 2d Earl Ducie.

NE: 1840

These were chiefly to have been improvements to the offices and bedrooms; the house

was demolished as being beyond repair in 1846; William Cubitt was to have been the contractor.
S: Gloucester County Record Office: Ducie MSS D 340a P14.

St. John the Evangelist, Spittlegate, Grantham (Lincs.)
New church for the Reverend William Potchett.
E: 1840–1841
Early English with rudimentary geometrical windows. Nave, north and south aisles, transept, polygonal chancel with north and south chapels, west tower. The builder was John Collingwood of Grantham. Greatly enlarged in 1882 (Figs. 96 and 97).
C: £4,000 H
S: ICBS 2710; Lincolnshire Archives Committee: Consec. LS 8/1841; Eccl. 4 (July 1845): 186; *British Almanac and Companion* (n.p., 1841), p. 231.

Holy Trinity Church, Sewstern (Leics.)
New church for the Reverend James Lawson.
E: 1840–1842
Norman. Nave and chancel in one, west bell-cote, and west door (Fig. 92).
C: £553
S: ICBS 2807; CCE 16440.

Worden Hall, Chorley (Lancs.)
Alterations and additions for James Nowell ffarington. E: 1840–1845
It is not known exactly what was done. Possibly the chapel and Italian gallery were added; the house was in the Italian villa style. Demolished after a fire in c. 1970.
C: £12,000 H

St. Oswald's Church, Arncliffe (Yorks. W. Riding N. Yorks.)
Restoration and new chancel for the Reverend William Boyd.
E: 1841
One-third of the nave was pulled down and a Perpendicular chancel built. Six new windows in the nave, tracery matching the chancel windows. Buttresses added to nave, new benches put in.

S: W. A. Shuffrey, *The Churches of the Deanery of North Craven* (Leeds: J. Whitehead & Son, 1914).

St. Paul's Church Escholt (Yorks. W. Riding. W. Yorks).
New church for W. R. Crompton-Stansfield.
E: 1841
Early English. Nave and chancel in one, double bellcote (Fig. 101).
C: £800
S: CCE 17237.

The Bishop's Stables, Palace Green, Durham (Durham)
New stables and coach house for the bishop of Durham.
E: 1841
Tudor; now converted into public lavatories.
S: Priors Kitchen 14: Contract drawings.

Savings Bank, Grantham (Lincs.)
New bank building for the trustees.
E: 1841–1842
Jacobean; faced in Ancaster stone. The builder was James Collingwood of Grantham.
C: £1,600 H
S: L. W. Leng, *Grantham Savings Bank, 1818–1968* (n.p., 1968); B, September 10, 1853, p. 569.

Sherborne House, Sherborne (Glos.)
Alterations for the 2d Baron Sherborne.
E: 1841–1842
Lewis Wyatt had rebuilt the house in 1829–1834, but his work was so defective that Salvin was called in to effect repairs and design the interiors.
C: £5,000 H
S: John Martin Robertson, *The Wyatts* (Oxford: Oxford University Press, 1979).

The Rectory, Denton (Lincs.)
New rectory for the Reverend George Thomas Potchett.
E: 1841–1842
Very plain in the Italian villa style.
C: £1,748.12.10d.
S: Lincolnshire Archives Committee: MGA 260.

Helmingham Hall, Helmingham (Suffolk)
Alterations for 1st Baron Tollemache.
E: c. 1841–1842
Alterations to the principal reception rooms
    and staircase.
S: CL CXX (1956): 282, 332, 378, 656, 712, 782,
    843.

The Church of the Holy Sepulchre,
    Cambridge (Cambs.)
Restoration for the Cambridge Camden
    Society.
E: 1841–1844
Rebuilding of the south aisle of the round,
    removal of belfry story, interior stripped
    of wall monuments and box-pews, new
    conical roof, south chancel aisle, bell tur-
    ret. Stone altar installed, which was
    removed after litigation (Fig. 90).
C: £3,921. 16. 5d.
S: John Britton, *Archaeological Antiquities of Great
    Britain* (London: Longman & Co., 1805);
    for a list of the Cambridge Camden Soci-
    ety's ten publications concerning the
    work, see James F. White, *The Cambridge
    Movement* (Cambridge: At the University
    Press, 1962); Cambridgeshire and the Isle
    of Ely Record Office: Citation Mandate
    P21/24/3A, Faculty P21/24/3B; B, August
    10, 1844, p. 391; August 17, 1844, p. 403;
    April 26, 1845, p. 203; December 27, 1845,
    p. 261.

The Rectory, Methley (Yorks. W. Riding. W.
    Yorks.)
New rectory for the Honorable and Reverend
    Philip Savile.
E: 1842
S: JLP:3v.

St. Peter's Church, Cambridge (Cambs.)
Project for rebuilding church for the vicar and
    a committee.
NE: 1842
Early English; it was to have been large, with
    west tower and spire.
S: JLP: III; Eccl. (January 1842): 47; (February
    1842): 63; (March 1842): 77.

The Master's Lodge, Trinity College,
    Cambridge (Cambs.)
Alterations for William Whewell and fellows.
E: 1842–1843
Tudor, new oriel windows and repairs (Fig.
    107).
C: £3,765.19.6d.
S: Trinity College: Whewell MSS a.60; Willis
    and Clark.

The Priest's House, Flixton (Suffolk)
Additions for Sir Robert Shafto Adair, Bart.
    (Fig. 122).
E: 1842–1843
A half-timbered range more than doubled the
    size of the old house.
C: £1,936 H
S: RIBA Salvin /8/.

Garden building, The Castle, Ballymena
    (Co. Antrim)
Design for a shed for a pump for Sir Robert
    Shafto Adair, Bart.
E: c. 1842–1843
S: Calverley: plan and elevation.

Durham School, Durham (Durham)
Alterations for the dean and chapter.

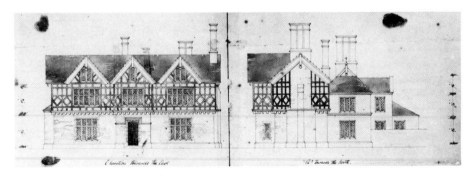

122. The Priest's House, Flixton, elevations.

E: 1842–1844

Bellasis Cottage was converted into the master's house and new schoolrooms built; the school had just been moved from Palace Green.

S: Priors Kitchen 35; Chapter Act Book 1837–1847; B, November 23, 1844, p. 588.

Chapel of St. Mary, Arley Hall, Arley (Cheshire)

Private chapel for Roland Egerton Warburton.

E: 1842–1845

Decorated; nave, chancel with gallery connecting the chapel to the house, octagonal bell turret (Fig. 102).

C: £3,100 H

S: Calverley: south elevation, sections, elevation of chancel arch; Toronto: longitudinal section; Lithograph, "St. Mary's Chapel. Arley. Wherof ye Foundation Stone was laid ye 6 April A.D. 1842. A. Salvin Archt."; Eccl. (June 1842): 136, 141.

The Cathedral Church of St. Cuthbert, Durham (Durham)

Restoration works for the dean and chapter.

E: 1842–1850

Reseating choir, new west door and font, Cosin's choir screen, font and font cover were removed. New choir windows, repairs to clerestorey and cloister, repairs to crypt.

C: The reseating only £1,600 H

S: Priors Kitchen 53,26; Chapter Act Books 1838–1847, 1847–1856; Eccl. (October 1846): 158; (October 1847): 65; ILN, November 14, 1846, p. 316.

Christ Church, Albany Street, St. Pancras (Mddx. London Camden)

Alterations for the Reverend William Dodsworth.

E: 1843

Removal of organ gallery and vestry from the liturgical east end, small chancel built.

C: £1,000 H

S: Henry W. Burns, *The Half Century of Christ Church St. Pancras, Albany Street* (London: n.p., 1887); B. F. L. Clarke, *Parish Churches of London* (London: Batsford, 1966).

New Anglican Church, Alexandria (Egypt)

Designs for the Cambridge Camden Society.

NE: 1843

Early English. The commission was given to J. W. Wild.

S: JLP: ff. 103–7; Eccl. (February 1842): 50; (January 1843): 74; (November 1846): 165; B, June 10, 1843, p. 223.

Afghan War Memorial Church, Bombay (India)

Designs for the Ecclesiastical Society of Oxford

NE: 1843

These have been lost; the church was built to the designs of H. Conybeare.

S: Maharashtra State Archives, Elphinstone College, Bombay. Ecclesiastical Dept. Vol. 3, 1847, No. 92, letter d. September 12, 1847; A. J. Nix-Seaman, *The Afghan War Memorial Church* (Bombay: Thacker & Co., 1938).

The Rectory, Ayott St. Peter (Herts.)

Alterations for the Reverend Edwin Prodgers.

E: 1843

It is not known what was done.

C: £725 H

The Cathedral Church of the Blessed Virgin Mary, Salisbury (Wilts.)

Survey of the chapter house for the dean and chapter.

Carried out in 1843.

This was by way of being a commentary on a report and recommendations put in by T. H. Wyatt, the Diocesan architect.

St. Andrew's Church, Oakington (Cambs.)

Project for restoration for the Reverend G. Whitaker.

NE: 1843

Salvin and Thomas Hollingworth of Cambridge both reported on the church's condition; Hollingworth was employed.

S: Cambridgeshire and the Isle of Ely Record Office: Oakington Parish Records P126/-6/1–2; Oakington Churchwardens' Accounts P126/5/1.

St. Lawrence's Church, Bovingdon (Herts.)
Project for restoration for the Reverend Arthur
Brooking (Fig. 123)
NE: 1843
A number of architects were approached, and
Charles Lee and Talbot Bury got the job.
S: Toronto: west elevation; ICBS 3321.

St. Mary's Church, Hemel Hempstead
(Herts.)
Restoration for the Churchwardens.
E: 1843–1844
Salvin's report and estimate were accepted by
the vestry on September 16, 1842, and the
final accounts passed March 28, 1845. It is
not known what was done.
C: £1,266. 18. 4d.
S: Parish Records: Vestry Minute Book.

Kelham Hall, Kelham (Notts.)
New service wing and project for recasing
house for J. H. Manners Sutton (Fig.
124).
E: 1843–1847
The service wing survived the fire of 1857 and
the subsequent rebuilding by Gilbert
Scott. Salvin produced two alternative
schemes for remodeling the house in Jacobean style. William Weare was the Clerk
of Works.
C: £7,573.13.0d.
S: Nottinghamshire Record Office: Kelham
MSS DDH 161/351; Paul Mellon Collection, Yale Center for British Art, A
67/7/10/10–11. PM 3879–3880.

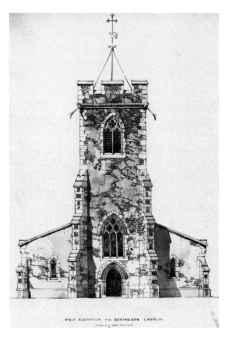

123. St. Lawrence's Church,
Bovingdon, elevation.

St. Mary Magdalene, Torquay (Devon)
New church for the Reverend William Mal-
lock and committee.
E: 1843–1857
Early English, nave, north and south aisles,
polygonal chancel, southeast tower, and
spire. The building period was protracted
due to a chronic shortage of funds (Fig.
98).
C: £7,290.2.1d.
S: Parish Records; Eccl. (June 1843): 166;

124. Kelham Hall, elevation, design for recasting house.

(October 1846): 152; August 1848): 79
(February 1851): 74; D. J. Seymour
Upton—The Heart of Torquay (Exeter: James
Townsend and Sons, 1963).

School, Bangor (Co. Down)
New infant school for Robert Edward Ward.
E: 1844
Demolished.
S: DNB.

Newark Castle, Newark (Notts.)
Restoration for H. M. Commissioners of
Woods and Works.
E: 1844
Clearing out and stabilizing ruins.
C: £649
S: PRO Treasury 1/4966 f. 17131/44, Crest
34/165; University of Nottingham
Library, Manuscripts Dept.: Newcastle
MSS 9011, 8947; *The Stamford Mercury,*
October 18, 1844; December 13, 1844; *The
Nottinghamshire Journal,* November 29,
1844; B, November 16, 1844, p. 568; J. M.
Crook and M. H. Port, *The History of the
King's Works,* vol. 6 (London: Her Maj-
esty's Stationery Office, 1973).

Markham Monument, York Minster, York
(N. Yorks)
Monument to Archbishop William Markham
(1719–1807) for the Markham family.
E: 1844
Carving by C. Raymond Smith, black marble
mensa by Thomas Willement.
S: JLP 30r; The Revd. J. de B. Bateman:
Thomas Willement Ledger 1814–1865 f.20;
Clement Markham, *Markham Memorials*
(London: Spottiswoode & Co., 1913).

Carlton Club, Pall Mall (Mddx. London
Westminster)
Designs for a new clubhouse for a committee.
NE: 1844–1845
Salvin's entry won the competition, but his
elaborate Jacobean designs were put
aside in favor of those by Basevi and
Smirke (Fig. 45).
S: RIBA Salvin /17/1–10; B, May 4, 1844, p.
233; May 11, 1844 p. 245; June 7, 1845, p.
269.

Public Baths, Newark (Notts.)
New bath house for a committee.
E: 1844–1845
Built on the castle grounds and designed to
look like the gatekeeper's lodge.
C: £750. 4. 9d.
S: Newark-on-Trent Museum and Art Gal-
lery: Castle Grounds and Baths
Committee Minute Book; B, January 27,
1844, p. 43.

St. Stephen's Church, South Shields
(Durham, Tyne and Wear)
New church for the Reverend James Carr.
E: 1844–1845
Early English, nave and north aisle, short
chancel, northwest octagonal bell turret.
C: £1,600
S: ICBS 9916; Durham Chapter Act Books
1838–1847, 1847–1856; JLP 119; Eccl.
(November 1845): 284; B, January 18,
1845, p. 29.

St. Paul's Church, Alnwick (Northumb.)
New church for the 3d Duke of
Northumberland.
E: 1844–1846
Decorated, very large nave and chancel with
aisles, west tower. The builder was Sam-
uel Nowell, plaster work by Robert
Robson of Newcastle. East window by
William Dyce, made by Ainmuller of
Munich.
S: Eccl. (October 1846): 153; *The Gentleman's
Magazine* 2 (1846): 637; B, February 3,
1866, p. 74; Wilson.

Blackdown House, Haslemere (Sussex, W.
Sussex)
Alterations and additions for Captain James
Henry.
E: 1844–1846
New principal rooms and offices were added.
C: £2,925 H
S: JLP 47r.

St. John the Evangelist's Church, King's
Lynn (Norfolk)
New church for Daniel Gurney and a
committee.
E: 1844–1846

Early English, nave, north and south aisles, chancel, twin west spirelets. Glass by William Wailes.

C: £4,805. 6. 2d.

S: Building Committee's Minute Book; CCE 15915, 4495; B, November 4, 1843, p. 475; October 3, 1846, p. 477.

St. Andrew's Church, South Otterington (Yorks. N. Riding. N. Yorks.)

New church for William Rutson.

E: 1844–1847

Norman, nave, north and south aisles, chancel, west tower with pyramidal roof (Fig. 93).

C: £2,800 H

Estate buildings, Greystoke (Cumberland. Cumbria)

A bridge, lodge, and village cross for Henry Howard.

E: 1844–1847

S: Greystoke Castle MSS.

Caernarvon Castle, Caernarvon (Caernarvons. Gwynedd.)

Restoration and repairs for H. M. Commissioners of Woods and Forests.

E: 1844–1848

Restoration of the Queen's Gate, windows, loops, and battlements.

C: £1,742

S: RIBA Salvin /46/; PRO Works 14/9, 14/10, Crest 25/53; HoN Salvin to Ramsay, February 12, 1846; *Archaeologia Cambrensis* (1846): 80; (1848): 351; B, February 16, 1850, p. 80; J. M. Crook and M. H. Port, *The History of the King's Works,* vol. 6.

All Saints' Church, Runcorn (Cheshire)

A new church for a committee.

E: 1844–1848

Early English, large, nave with north and south aisles, chancel, southwest tower, and tall spire (Fig. 99).

C: £5,737. 10. 9d.

S: Chester Record Office: Runcorn Parish Records EDP2 34/5, P95/2/1,2/2–19, 2/-77–III, 2/261–92.

Naworth Castle, Brampton (Cumberland. Cubria)

Restoration after the fire of 1844 for the 6th Earl of Carlisle.

E: 1844–1851

Restoration of damaged ranges and of the great hall, addition of Morpeth Tower, rearrangement of offices.

C: £13,000 H

S: HoN: c575/9, c612/224, N122; B, September 7, 1844, p. 462; January 25, 1845, p. 45.

Peckforton Castle, Peckforton (Cheshire)

New castle for 1st Baron Tollemache.

E: 1844–1852

One of Salvin's most important works and an accurate recreation of an Edwardian stronghold (Figs. 79–85).

C: £52,000 H

S: RIBA Salvin /27/1–16; B. Weinreb Architectural Books Ltd., early ground plan; B, January 25, 1845, p. 48; October 29, 1853, p. 670; March 31, 1855, p. 149; Lionel Tollemache, *Old and Odd Memories* (London: Edward Arnold, 1908); E. D. H. Tollemache, *The Tollemaches of Helmingham and Ham* (Ipswich: W. S. Cowell, 1949); CL, July 29, 1965, p. 287; Mark Girouard, *The Victorian Country House* (New Haven and London: Yale University Press, 1979).

Tabley House, Knutsford (Chesire)

Alterations for the 2d Baron Tabley.

Salvin probably transferred the main entrance to the rear of the house, internal alterations.

C: £6,640 H

Carisbrooke Castle, Carisbrooke (Isle of Wight)

Restoration for H. M. Commissioners of Woods and Forests.

E: 1845

Salvin's work has been obscured by later additions.

C: £1,077

S: PRO Works 2/7 pp. 205–6; J. M. Crook and M. H. Port, *The History of the King's Works,* vol. 6 (London: Her Majesty's Stationery Office, 1973).

St. John the Evangelist's Church, High
    Cross (Herts.)
New church for Lady Louisa Giles Puller.
E: 1845–1846
Decorated; nave, chancel, south porch and
    southeast tower. The builder was Samuel
    Nowell.
C: £3,500
S: CCE 15766, 11546; Eccl. (July 1846): 32.

Parsonage, High Cross (Herts.)
New parsonage for Lady Louisa Giles Puller.
E: 1845–1846
Very plain in red brick.
C: £2,000 H

Holy Trinity Church, East Finchley (Mddx.
    London Barnet)
New church for the Reverend Ralph Worsley
    and a committee.
E: 1845–1846
Early English. Nave, chancel, north vestry
    and porch, octagonal bell cote. Aisles and
    clerestorey added later. Salvin was
    Vicar's Warden of this church, and his
    family contributed to the furnishings; his
    wife Anne played the organ, and his
    daughters taught the Sunday School.
C: £2,828. 10. 2d.
S: Vestry Minute Book; ICBS 3548; CCE
    15662.

Jesus College Chapel, Cambridge (Cambs.)
Restoration for the master and fellows.
E: 1845–1846
Salvin's work here was interrupted by his ill-
    ness in 1846, and he was replaced by A.
    W. N. Pugin. He rebuilt the east end fol-
    lowing evidence discovered by Prof. R.
    Willis, and added aisles to the choir and
    north transept.
C: £760
S: Jesus College Muniment Room: Corres-
    pondence and accounts; Eccl. (July 1846):
    36; (December 1848): 146; Willis and
    Clark; A. Gray and F. Brittain, *A History
    of Jesus College Cambridge* (London:
    Heinemann, 1960).

St. Margaret's Church, Stratton St. Margaret
    (Wilts.)

Restoration for the Reverend Charles Nesfield
    and the churchwardens.
E: 1844–1846
Clerestorey rebuilt and roof repaired, tower
    partly rebuilt. A vestry was formed out of
    the Hedges tomb chamber, reflooring
    and reseating.
C: £1,023. 10. 0d.
S: Parish Records: Churchwardens' Accounts;
    ICBS 3642; Wiltshire County Record
    Office: Diocesan Archives, Petition,
    Appointment, Faculty and Exhibits.

St. Lawrence's Church, Castle Rising
    (Norfolk)
Restoration for Colonel the Honorable Fulk
    Greville Howard.
E: 1845–1848
It is not known what Salvin did, due to later
    works by G. E. Street and others in 1860
    and 1883. A complete set of survey draw-
    ings by James Deason exists.
C: £2,300 H
S: RIBA Salvin /46/.

Patterdale Hall, Patterdale (Westmoreland.
    Cumbria)
Substantial additions to old house for William
    Marshall.
E: 1845–1850
The house was recast in the Italian villa style,
    large new stable block, belvedere tower.
C: £11,000 H

St. Michael's Church, Cowesby (Yorks. N.
    Riding. N. Yorks.)
New church for George Lloyd.
E: 1846
Norman. Nave and chancel with central tower
    with pyramidal roof, porch, vestry. Sal-
    vin's best village church in a believable
    Norman manner (Fig. 94).
C: Not known.
S: William Grainge, *The Vale of Mowbray*
    (Ripon: n.p., 1859); B, May 2, 1846, p.
    212.

Hafod, Pont-Rhyd-Y-Groes (Cardigans.
    Dyfed)
Large addition for Sir Henry de Hoghton
    Bart.
E: 1846

Two courts of extra accommodation and
 offices with belvedere tower, Italian villa
 style. Plasterwork by Robert Armstrong
 (Fig. 73).
C: £21,000 H
RIBA Salvin /46/; University of Nottingham
 Library, Manuscripts Dept.: 4th Duke of
 Newcastle MSS: Nec 8 700, 704, 705, 708,
 709, 645a, 645b.; National Library of
 Wales: Auction Particulars of Daniel
 Smith & Co. 1855; Elizabeth Inglis-Jones,
 Peacocks in Paradise (London: Faber &
 Faber, 1950).

St. Mary's Church, Ditchingham (Norfolk)
New fittings for the Reverend W. E.
 Scudamore.
E: 1846
Refloored and reseated, new pulpit and read-
 ing desk.
S: Norfolk and Norwich Record Office: Fac-
 ulty Books FCB7 f.83; ICBS 3240; *The
 Norfolk Chronicle,* September 18, 1847.

St. Mary the Virgin's Church, Lamberhurst
 (Kent)
Proposed restoration of the Scotney Chapel for
 Edward Hussey.
NE: 1846
Hussey was unable to proceed because of a
 difference with the "farmer" of the
 parsonage.
S: Scotney Castle MSS: Designs, estimates,
 correspondence.

St. Mary's Church, Lesbury (Northumb.)
Restoration for the 4th Duke of Northumber-
 land and the 3d Earl Grey.
E: 1846–1847
New north aisle, vestry, and south porch;
 reroofing and repairs.
S: Durham University, Department of Pa-
 laeography and Diplomatic: faculty
 December 23, 1846; Eccl. (October 1847):
 72; Wilson; *History of Northumberland*
 (London: Simpkin, Marshal & Co.,
 1893-1940), vol. 2.

Flixton Hall, Flixton (Suffolk)
Rebuilding for Sir Robert Shafto Adair, Bart.
E: 1846–1847

125. Flixton Hall, elevation
of chimneypiece.

A fire in 1846 destroyed about half the house;
 this was rebuilt, Salvin creating one of his
 most lavish interiors and adding new
 offices, a game larder, a cupola, and
 carved brick chimneys and vanes.
 Demolished (Figs. 52 and 125).
C: £29,100 H
S: RIBA Salvin /10/1–7; ILN, December 19,
 1846, p. 393.

Pennoyre, Brecon (Brecknocks. Powys)
Remodeling and additions for Colonel John
 Lloyd Vaughan Watkins.
E: 1846–1848
Complete recasing of house, addition of
 belvedere entrance tower and conser-
 vatory, all in the Italian villa style.
 Rendered in cement (Fig. 74).
C: £33,000 H
S: William Plomer, ed. *Kilvert's Diary* (London:
 Jonathan Cape, 1938; Theophilus Jones,
 A History of Brecknock, ed. Baron Glanusk
 (Brecknock: Blissett, Davies & Co.,
 1909).

Oxon Hoath, West Peckham (Kent)
Alterations for Sir William Geary, Bart.
E: 1846–1848
The house was remodeled in the French
 Empire style, and a pair of Tudor half-
 timbered lodges were built. Flemish six-

teenth-century paneling reused in both house and lodges (Figs. 75 and 76).
C: £5,200 H
S: RIBA Salvin /25/1–4.

St. George's Chapel, Windsor Castle, Windsor (Berks.)
Work on the west steps for the dean and canons.
E: 1846–1849
Salvin designed new steps and parapets, replaced in 1870.
C: £469.13.od.
S: Aerary Records: XVII-61–11d.

Lanercost Priory, Lanercost (Cumberland. Cumbria)
Restoration for H.M. Commissioners of Woods and Forests.
E: 1846–1849
The choir, transepts, and cloisters were roofless, the nave used as the parish church. When the roof of this fell in, Salvin restored the whole building. The builder was Nowell.
C: £2,780
S: Eccl. (February 1843): 106; B, August 25, 1849; Crook and Port, *King's Works,* vol. 6 (London: Her Majesty's Stationery Office, 1973).

Exeter College Chapel, Oxford (Oxon)
Designs for rebuilding the chapel for a building committee.
NE: 1847
Decorated. Salvin proposed a cruciform structure, much like a parish church but with the benches facing inward (Fig. 103).
S: Exeter College Archives: Plan, elevation and section, correspondence.

Stapeley House, Nantwich (Cheshire)
Alterations and additions for the Reverend James Folliott.
E: 1847–1848
It is not known what was done; now council offices.
C: £6,000 H

National School, Finchley (Mddx. London Barnet)

New school buildings for the Reverend F. S. Green and a committee.
E: 1847–1848
Tudor, red brick.
C: £1,066
S: H. H. Ayscough, *Holy Trinity Church, 1846–1946* (London: n.p., 1946).

Durham Castle, Durham (Durham)
Restoration of Bishop Bek's Hall for the warden and trustees of Durham University.
E: 1847–1848
S: Priors Kitchen 67.

All Saints' Church, Rothbury (Northumb.)
Restoration and rebuilding for the Reverend C. G. Vernon.
E: 1847–1850
Most of the church was rebuilt in Early English and the chancel restored. Salvin added a massive west tower with a saddleback roof.
C: £2,800 H
S: ICBS 4108; Eccl. (October 1847): 78; B, January 11, 1851, p. 53; Wilson, *Churches.*

The Cathedral Church of St. Andrew, Wells (Somerset)
Restoration of the choir for the dean and chapter.
E: 1847–1857
Reseating, new pulpit and organ case, cleaning of stonework. Building work by Nowell, carving by James Forsyth.
C: £7,000 H; organ case £645
S: Wells Cathedral MSS: Chapter Minute Books and correspondence; Toronto: nine drawings of stalls and pulpit; Calverley: two designs for organ case, four for stalls and canopies; Eccl. (November 1842): 36; (April 1851): 153; (February 1853): 42; (April 1853): 95; B, August 9, 1851, p. 49; March 13, 1852, p. 171; L. S. Colchester, "The Victorian Restorations of Wells Cathedral Church" *Tranactions of the Ancient Monument Society,* new series 4 (1956), pp. 79–84.

Wern Eynon, Swansea (Glamorgan. W. Glamorgan)
Work for Henry Vivian.
E: 1848
It is not known what was done.
C: £2,800 H

South Park, Penshurst (Kent)
Alterations and additions for the 1st Viscount
    Hardinge.
E: 1848
The additions included a great hall to house
    Hardinge's Indian trophies. Demolished.
C: £3,000 H

Monument to Grace Darling, Bamburgh
    (Northumb.)
Effigy and tabernacle for Lord Crewe's
    trustees
E: 1848
The canopy has been replaced by another of a
    different design. Effigy carved by C.
    Raymond Smith (Fig. 126).
S: ILN, January 22, 1848, p. 43.

Hatfield Hall, Durham (Durham)
New students' lodgings for the warden and
    trustees of Durham University.
E: 1848–1849
The Red Lion Hotel was purchased by the
    university and converted.
C: £4,000 H
S: Priors Kitchen 4.

126. The Grace Darling Monument,
Bamburgh, from the *Illustrated London News.*

St. Peter's Church, Elford (Staffs.)
Restoration for the Reverend Francis E. Paget
    and the Honorable Mrs. Mary Greville
    Howard.
E: 1848–1849
Salvin's most ambitious restoration; hammer-
    beam roof in chancel supported by angels
    bearing the instruments of the Passion.
    Coronae and other furnishings by
    Hardman.
S: Lichfield Joint Record Office: plans d: Mar
    1848; Hardman Ledger 1849–1854; *The
    Staffordshire Advertiser,* August 25, 1849; B,
    September 15, 1849, p. 439.

St. Andrew's Church, Greystoke (Cum-
    berland. Cumbria)
Restoration of the chancel for Henry Howard.
E: 1848–1849
General repairs to fabric and the sedilia.
C: £800 H

All Saints' Church, Freethorpe (Norfolk)
Restoration for the Reverend T. C. Haddon
    and Richard Henry Vade Walpole.
E: 1848–1850
Addition of north and south aisles. Walpole
    pew built on north of chancel, round
    tower partly rebuilt.
C: £900 H
S: Norfolk and Norwich Record Office: Nor-
    wich Diocesan Records FCB7 p. 148v;
    Faculty d: August 26, 1851; Parish
    Records: Register of Baptisms, Free-
    thorpe, Memorandum d: August 1850.

Langley Park, Loddon (Norfolk)
Alterations for Admiral Sir William Beau-
    champ Proctor, Bart.
E: 1849
It is not known what was done.
C: £520 H

The Rectory, Finchley (Mddx. London
    Barnet)
New rectory for the Reverend T. R. White.
E: 1849
Stock brick and slate roof, very plain.
C: £2,100 H

175
*Catalogue
Raisonné*

St. Stephen's Church, Shepherd's Bush (Mddx. London Hammersmith)
New church for Dr. C. J. Blomfield, the Bishop of London.
E: 1849–1850
Decorated. Nave, north and south aisles, chancel, northwest tower, and spire. The spire was damaged by bombing and removed after the Second World War.
C: £6,100 H
S: Eccl. (August 1849): 62; (January 1850): 62; B, April 27, 1850, p. 199; ILN, April 13, 1850, p. 253.

Rockingham Castle, Corby (Leics.)
Additions for the Honorable Richard Watson.
E: 1849–1851
The Gallery Tower and Keep Tower were built.
C: £3,629.13.0d.
S: Rockingham Castle MSS: Diaries of Richard Watson, accounts and drawings; RIBA Salvin /28/1–13.

Vicar's Island House, Derwentwater (Cumberland. Cumbria)
Alterations for Henry Marshall.
E: 1850
Salvin added Italianate wings to Joseph Pocklington's house.
C: £3,300 H

Farm House, Goring (Sussex. W. Sussex)
New farmhouse for David Lyon.
E: c. 1850
It is not possible to identify this building.
C: £3,400 H

The Parsonage, Lanercost (Cumberland. Cumbria)
Alterations for the 6th Earl of Carlisle.
E: 1850–1851
Repairs and additions.
C: £471. 3. 9d.
S: HoN C575/9.

The National School, Highgate (Mddx. London Haringey)
New school buildings for Harry Chester and a committee.
E: 1850–1852
Very plain, of yellow stock brick. Much altered.
C: £5,043. 14. 1d.
S: J. H. Lloyd, *History of Highgate* (Highgate: Printed by subscription, 1888).

All Saints' Church, North Wootton (Norfolk)
New church for the Honorable Mrs. Mary Greville Howard.
E: 1850–1853
Early English. Nave, chancel, and west tower with octagonal stair turret.
C: £2,200 H
S: B, November 26, 1853, p. 717.

Gurney's Bank, Bank Plain, Norwich (Norfolk)
New bank premises for Messrs. Gurney.
E: 1851
This has been completely rebuilt; Salvin's bank may have been classical with a portico.
C: £8,200 H
S: W. H. Bidwell, *Annals of an East Anglian Bank* (Norwich: A. H. Goose, 1900); Barclay's Bank, *History of Barclay's Bank Ltd.* (London: Blades, East & Blades, 1926).

School, Northbourne (Kent)
New village school for Sir Walter James, Bart.
E: 1851
C: £500
S: Lambeth Palace Library: Sir Walter James' Diary, ref. 1771.

Juniper Hill, Mickleham (Surrey)
Alterations for Cuthbert Ellison.
E: 1851
It is not known what was done.
C: £4,700 H

School, Salisbury (Wilts.)
It is not possible to identify this building, but it may be the school at East Harnham.
E: 1851
C: £800 H

St. Stephen's Parsonage, Shepherd's Bush (Mddx. London Hammersmith)

New parsonage house for Dr. C. J. Blomfield, the Bishop of London.
E: 1851
Tudor, stock brick.
C: £2,300 H

Rose Castle, Carlisle (Cumberland. Cumbria)
Restoration work for the Bishop of Carlisle.
E: 1851–1852
Repairs to the Strickland Tower.
C: £720 H
S: RIBA Salvin /29/1–2.

Sudbury Hall, Sudbury (Derbys.)
Alterations for the 5th Baron Vernon.
E: 1851–1852
Very minor work.
C: £2,200 H
S: Sudbury Estate Office and Sudbury House MSS: Plans and elevations.

The Tower of London
Restoration of the Beauchamp Tower for the H. M. Commissioners of Works.
E: 1851–1853
Houses abutting the tower were removed, the stonework made good, general repairs.
C: £1,500 H
S: RIBA Salvin /18/11–13; PRO Works 14/1/14.

Balliol College, Oxford (Oxon)
Alterations and additions for the master and fellows.
E: 1851–1854
New students' lodgings, alterations to hall and kitchens. The builder was John Kelk.
C: £7,985
S: Balliol College Minute Book; Wells Cathedral MSS: Salvin and Dean Richard Jenkyns correspondence; Eccl. (August 1853): 283; (October 1853): 306; B, May 8, 1852, p. 302.

St. Oswald's Church, Lower Peover (Cheshire)
Restoration for the Reverend John Holme.
E: 1852
Timber church with stone tower; Salvin rebuilt the roof with three pitched gables instead of putting nave and aisle under one roof; sash windows replaced.

C: £1,300. 15. 3d.
S: Cheshire County Record Office: Churchwardens' Account Book P4/12/1 pp.191v-192r; ILN, January 1, 1853, p. 5; Eccl. (October 1856): 377; B, January 1, 1853, p. 6; January 29, 1853, p. 71; Walter Horn and Ernest Born, "Two Timbered Mediaeval Churches of Cheshire: St. James and St. Paul at Marton and St. Oswald at Lower Peover," *The Art Bulletin* (December 196): 263.

Wilderness Park, Seal (Kent)
Alterations for the 2d Marquis of Camden.
E: 1852
The house has been much altered, and it is not known what was done.
C: £600 H

South Grove House, Highgate (Mddx. London Haringey)
Alterations for Harry Chester.
E: 1852
It is not known what was done. Demolished.
C: £1,600 H

The Rectory, Little Stanmore (Mddx. London Harrow)
New rectory for the Reverend B. Tuson.
E: 1852
Demolished.
C: £500 H

Bangor Castle, now the Town Hall, Bangor (Co. Down)
New mansion house for Robert Edward Ward.
E: 1852
This house is something of a problem. Harroway includes it in his list of Salvin's works, but it is attributed to William Burn in the *Transactions of the Royal Institute of British Architects* (1870), p. 126, where the date given is 1847. Mr. David Walker has suggested that Burn began the house, then relinquished the commission, which was then given to Salvin.
C: £9,000 H

St. Mary's Church, Aldridge (Staffs.)
Restoration and additions for the Reverend J. Finch-Smith and a committee.

E: 1852–1853

New north aisle and vestry. The builder was Isaac Highway of Walsall.

C: £1,073. 14. 3d.

S: Toronto: designs for the font d: April 1853; Lichfield Joint Record Office: Citation for Faculty, April 1852; ICBS 4493; Eccl. (October 1853): 374; B, September 18, 1852, p. 595; Jeremiah Finch-Smith, *Notes and Collections relating to the Parish of Aldridge* (Leicester: Printed for private circulation, 1889).

St. Patrick's Church, Patterdale (Westmoreland. Cumbria)

Rebuilding of church for William Marshall and a committee.

E: 1852–1853

Decorated. Nave, chancel, north-east tower with saddleback roof.

C: £1,638 H

S: W. P. Morris, *The Records of Patterdale* (Kendal: T. Wilson, 1903).

Gonville and Caius College, Cambridge (Cambs.)

Alterations and additions for the master and fellows.

E: 1852–1853

New great hall, kitchen, and ancillary accommodation; alterations to the master's lodge, all in the Jacobean style. The contractor was John Kelk.

C: Contract price £10,424, total c. £14,000

S: Gonville and Caius Treasury: plans and elevations, Gesta Book No. 10 1849–1857, Bursar's Ledger No. 12 1839–1859; Eccl. (August 1855): 266; (April 1856): 148; B, October 21, 1854, p. 545; March 31, 1855, p. 149; Willis and Clark.

Stoke Hall, Stoke Holy Cross (Norfolk)

New mansion house for Henry Birkbeck.

E: 1852–1853

East Anglian Tudor: red brick with diapering, polygonal angle shafts, and crow-stepped gables. Demolished c. 1936. The stable block and tower with pyramidal roof survive.C: £8,300

S: Calverley: preliminary designs, perspective and plan; *Eastern Daily Press,* February 26, 1936.

Trinity Hall, Cambridge (Cambs.)

Rebuilding after a fire, and improvements for the master and fellows.

E: 1852–1853

The eastern range of the principal court was rebuilt after the fire of February 1852. The master's lodge was remodeled and the chapel reseated. Classical.

C: £5,200, Lodge £1,800 H

S: Eccl. (August 1853): 266; ILN, February 28, 1852, p. 184; Willis and Clark.

Alnwick Castle, Alnwick (Northumb.)

Extensive remodeling additions and alterations for the 4th Duke of Northumberland.

E: 1852–1861

Interiors rearranged, new porte cochère and staircase, Prudhoe Tower and kitchens. Interior decorated in the Italian seicento style by Italian craftsmen. Estate buildings (Figs. 60–64).

C: c.£100,000, estate improvements c.£12,000

S: RIBA Salvin /2/1–43; Alnwick Castle Muniment Room: correspondence and numerous drawings; Calverley: Contract for building a Tower at Alnwick Castle d: September 19, 1854, perspective of courtyard, section of chapel, two details; B, December 29, 1855, p. 638; February 8, 1862, pp. 89, 97; *RIBA Papers,* 1857, pp. 1–26; Eccl. (February 1860): 56; *The Archaeological Journal* 133 (1976): 148–54.

School, High Legh (Cheshire)

New village school for George Cornwall-Legh.

E: 1853

Tudor, stone-built.

C: £1,000 H

School, Limpsfield (Surrey)

New village school for William Leveson-Gower.

E: 1853

Tudor, ragstone, and red brick.

C: £320 H

Worden Hall, Chorley (Lancs.)

New gate lodge for the Misses ffarington.

E: 1853

Tudor, rustic with half-timbering.

C: £622 H

St. Mary's Church, Wilby (Northants.)
Restoration of the chancel for the Reverend
   Robert Stockdale.
E: 1853
Chancel rebuilt with high-pitched roof rising
   above that of the nave. New vestry and
   organ chamber.
C: £750 H
S: Eccl. (December 1852): 430.

**Warboys Endowed School and Warboys Fen
   School,** Warboys (Cambs.)
New village schools for the Reverend William
   Finch.
E: 1853
Two stock brick buildings, one in the village
   and one on the edge of the Fens for the
   children of the outlying farms.
C: £1,780 H

The Rectory, Warboys (Cambs.)
Alterations for the Reverend William Finch.

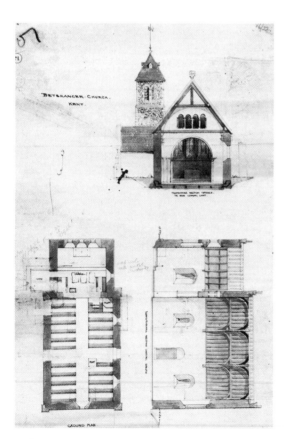

127. St. Mary's Church, Betteshanger, plan and elevations.

E: 1853
It is not known what was done.
C: £306 H

Arley Hall, Arley (Cheshire)
Work on the garden terraces for Roland Eger-
   ton Warburton.
E: 1853
C: £800 H

St. Mary's Church, Betteshanger (Kent)
Restoration for Sir Walter James, Bart.
E: 1853–1854
Addition of tower with pyramidal roof and
   lucarnes, vestry and east window in the
   Norman style (Fig. 127).
C: £1,270
S: RIBA Salvin /5/.

North Runcton Hall, North Runcton
   (Norfolk)
Additions for Daniel Gurney.
E: 1853–1854
The Sheriff's Tower was built. Demolished.
C: £600

St. Mary the Virgin's Church, Headley
   (Surrey)
New church for the Honorable Mrs. Mary
   Greville Howard.
E: 1853–1854
Early English. Nave, north and south aisles,
   chancel. G. E. Street added the tower
   and spire; new east window inserted
   1894.
C: £1,765.5.1d.
S: Parish Records: Press cuttings book; Eccl.
   (April 1858): 133; B, February 14, 1855, p.
   78; February 24, 1855, p. 89.

Keeper's House, Naworth (Cumberland.
   Cumbria)
Alterations for the 6th Earl of Carlisle.
E: 1853–1854
An old building was made habitable and ken-
   nels built.
S: HoN C575/9.

128. St. Mary the Virgin's Church, Weaverham, elevations.

St. Mary the Virgin's Church, Weaverham
  (Cheshire)
Restoration for the Reverend Charles Spencer
  Stanhope and a committee.
E: 1853–1855
Roof largely rebuilt, new pulpit and organ.
  The builder was John Buckley (Fig. 128).
C: £1,412.11.01/2d.
S: Toronto: designs for pulpit and chancel;
  Calverley: south elevation; Parish
  Records: Vestry Minute Books; B, June
  2, 1855, p. 261.

Warkworth Castle, Warkworth (Northumb.)
Restoration for the 4th Duke of
  Northumberland.
E: 1853–1855
Living quarters for the Duke's family and
  rooms for the manorial court were built in
  the great keep.
S: Alnwick Castle MSS; B, May 13, 1854, p.
  253.

St. Paul's Church, Over Tabley (Cheshire)
New church for the Reverend Joseph Horder
  and a committee.
E: 1853–1855, burned down and rebuilt 1856.
Early English, chancel, nave and north aisle,
  bell turret.
C: £1,316

S: Calverley: perspective of interior; ICBS
  4590; CCE 17336.

Holy Trinity Church, Upper Tooting
  (Streatham. London Wandsworth)
New church for a committee.
E: 1853–1855
Early English. Nave, north and south aisles,
  chancel with north and south chapels; a
  tower planned but not built. The contrac-
  tor was Samuel Nowell. Aisles enlarged
  in 1889, and tower built to another
  design.
C: £4,200
S: Parish Records: correspondence between
  Salvin and the committee; ICBS 4791;
  CCE 16302; B, July 14, 1855, p. 333; July
  21, 1855, p. 346.

New museums and lecture rooms,
  Cambridge (Cambs.)
New buildings for the Syndicate.
E: 1853–1869
New museums, lecture rooms, studies, and
  laboratories for the science professors, a
  major planning exercise. Demolished.
C: £22,109.8.8d.
S: Cambridge University Archives:
  CUR.55.1; B, January 11, 1862, p. 31;
  March 14, 1863, p. 187; November 7, 1863,

p. 789; July 2, 1870, p. 530; Willis and Clark.

Gurney's Bank and adjoining house, Great Yarmouth (Norfolk)
Remodeling bank building for Messrs. Gurney.
E: 1854
A good deal of work was done to the bank building, and a house on the south with shaped gables was either built or altered at the same time.
C: £9,000 H
S: C. J. Palmer, *The Perlustration of Great Yarmouth* (Great Yarmouth: n.p., 1872). ·

Church, Hermitage (Newfoundland, Canada)
New church for Thomas Newman Hunt.
E: 1854
Early English, nave and chancel, bellcote. Demolished 1944.
C: £1,050 H
S: Philip Tocque, *Newfoundland: As it was and as it is in 1877* (Toronto: Sampson, Low & Co, 1878); D. W. Prowse, *A History of Newfoundland* (London: Macmillan & Co, 1896).

Betteshanger Lodge, Betteshanger (Kent)
New lodge for Sir Walter James, Bart.
E: 1854
Not identified.
C: £660 H
S: Northbourne MSS.

The Rectory, Holdenby (Northants.)
New rectory for the Church Commissioners.
E: 1854
Red brick in simple Italian villa style.
S: Northamptonshire Record Office: Specification, plans and elevations.

Royal Cork Yacht Club's Clubhouse, Queenstown (Cobh, Co. Cork)
A new clubhouse for James Hugh Smith Barry.
E: 1854
Two-story classical building on the seafront.
C: £1,800 H

S: Fiske: plans and elevations; B, June 21, 1851, p. 393; November 13, 1851, p. 720; May 14, 1853, p. 315; July 2, 1853, p. 424.

Holy Trinity Church, Bollington (Cheshire)
New church for a committee.
E: 1854
Early English. Nave, chancel, and single bellcote; half-timbered porch in Cheshire black and white. South aisle intended but not built, and three-bay arcade blocked up.
S: H. S. Goodhart Rendel's index of nineteenth-century churches and their architects, British Architectural Library & National Monuments Record.

Thornbury Castle, Thornbury (Glos. Avon)
Restoration for Henry Howard.
E: 1854–1855
Extensive repairs, made habitable and used as a hunting box.
S: Greystoke Castle MSS: east elevation, details of chimneypieces, windows, and bookcases; Calverley: elevation and details of newel.

All Saints' Church, Scotby (Cumberland. Cumbria)
New church for George Head Head.
E: 1854–1855
Early English, nave, chancel, and south tower.
C: £1,000 H
S: CCE 25584; B, November 18, 1854, p. 598.

Keele Hall, Keele (Staffords.) Now the University of Keele.
New mansion house for Ralph Sneyd.
E: 1854–1860
Jacobean. The work started as alterations to the old house, which proved so derelict that it had to be demolished. Admired at the time for its convenient plan. The builders were the Paton Brothers of Ayre. The Clerk of Works was Thomas Lewis (Figs. 65-67).
C: £34,635.6.8d.
S: University of Keele Library: Sneyd, and Sneyd and Vincent MSS; RIBA Salvin /15/1–6; Toronto: section and three details; Calverley: Contract d: March 21, 1857, designs for rainwater head and royal

arms, section through great hall, details ceiling and gatepier; J. M. Kolbert, *Keele Hall: A Victorian Country House* (Keele: University of Keele, 1986).

Trinity College, Cambridge (Cambs.)
First Master's or the Whewell Court for the Reverend William Whewell.
Designed 1854, E: 1859–1860.
Additional students' accommodation in twenty-five sets of rooms arranged around a courtyard. Tudor. The builder was George Smith (Fig. 109).
C: £9,900
S: Trinity College Library: contract drawings; Willis and Clark.

Grantham Lodge, Belvoir Castle (Leics.)
Designs for a new lodge for the 7th Duke of Rutland.
NE: 1855
Almost certainly the work of W. E. Nesfield, adapted from French town gates such as the Port de Croux, Nevers (Fig. 129).
S: RIBA Salvin /4/1–9

Monument to Sir Robert Lydston Newman, Bart., St. Thomas's Church, Mamhead (Devon).
Memorial portrait tablet for the Newman family.
E: 1855
S: Newman MSS.

St. Leonard's Hospital, Alnwick (Northumb.)
Restoration for the 4th Duke of Northumberland.
E: 1855
The foundations were stabilized.
S: *Archaeologia Aeliana* N.S. 1: 48.

Lindisfarne Abbey, Holy Island (Northumb.)
Restoration for H. M. Commissioners of Works.
E: 1855–1856
The abbey ruins were cleared and stabilized.
C: £550 H
S: B, November 17, 1855, p. 553; *The Archaeological Journal* (1856): 283, 394, 411; (1857): 281.

The Tower of London
Restoration of the Salt Tower for H. M. Commissioners of Works.
E: 1855–1857
General repairs. The contractor was George Myers.
C: £1,290
S: PRO Works 14/2/3, 31/488, 31/528, 31/487, 31/490.

Marbury Hall, Marbury (Cheshire)
Alterations for James Hugh Smith Barry.

129. Design for the Grantham Lodge, Belvoir Castle.

E: 1855–1858

Extensive remodeling changed the eighteenth-century house into a French Second Empire Château. Demolished 1969 (Figs. 77 and 78).

C: £7,700 H

The Church of St. Philip and St. James, Rock (Northumb.)

Restoration for the Reverend R. W. Bosanquet.

E: 1855–1858

Repairs, addition of apsidal chancel and double bellcote. The builder was Armstrong & Co.

C: £632.19.10d.

S: Parish Records: correspondence between Salvin and Bosanquet; Alnwick Castle MSS: correspondence between Salvin and F. R. Wilson; B, February 3, 1866, p. 74.

Christ Church, Caernarvon (Caernarvons. Gwynedd.)

New church for the Reverend Thomas Vincent and a committee.

Designed 1855, E: 1861–1864

Early English. Large, nave, north and south aisles, chancel, southeast tower and spire.

C: £7,610.0.4d.

S: Parish Records: Subscription Book, statements of account, etc.; Alnwick Castle MSS; *Archaeologia Cambrensis* (1864): 178.

Trinity College, Cambridge (Cambs.)

Restoration of the range between the great gate and the chapel for the master and fellows.

E: 1856

Refacing and addition of oriel on the Trinity Street facade (Fig. 108).

C: £700 H

S: Toronto: elevation; Willis and Clark.

Hartford House, Hartford (Hunts.)

Additions to a house for W. H. Desborough.

E: 1856

Salvin added a wing, which was demolished c. 1924.

C: £2,200 H

S: Fiske: ground plan.

Prudhoe Castle, Prudhoe (Northumb.)

Survey for the 4th Duke of Northumberland.

E: 1856

Restoration may have been intended, but probably only minor repairs were carried out.

S: RIBA Salvin /46/.

Abbotts Ripton Hall, Abbotts Ripton (Hunts. Cambs.)

Alterations and additions for the Reverend Plummer Pott Rooper.

E: 1856

The old house was remodeled with Jacobean detail and a large nursery and office wing built.

C: £3,200 H

S: Abbotts Ripton Estate Office: drawings of the house as altered.

The Rectory, Buckworth (Hunts. Cambs.)

Additions for the Reverend J. D. Shafto.

E: 1856

Reception rooms and bedrooms over added to old house.

C: £1,380 H

St. Mary's Church, Flixton (Suffolk)

Restoration for Sir Robert Shafto Adair, Bart.

E: 1856

Major rebuilding, particularly of the chancel. The west tower was entirely demolished and rebuilt with a helm roof similar to that at Sompting, Sussex.

S: Eccl. (July 1842): 166; *The Archaeological Journal* 14 (1857): 360.

The Royal Yacht Squadron's Clubhouse, West Cowes Castle, Cowes (Isle of Wight)

Conversion for the commodore of the Royal Yacht Squadron.

E: 1856–1857

One of Henry VIII's Solent Castles was rebuilt in the French château style and turned into a clubhouse.

C: £5,000 H

S: Alnwick Castle MSS.

The Tower of London

Restoration of the White Tower for the War Office.

Designed 1856–1857 E: 1861–1862

Conversion of the council chamber into a
    museum and armory.
C: £9,947
S: PRO Works 14/2/5, 31/494; RIBA Salvin
    /18/17; B, April 5, 1862, p. 252; April 19,
    1862, p. 175.

St. Mark's Church, Torquay (Devon)
New church for Lawrence Palk and a
    committee.
E: 1856–1857
Nave, north and south aisles, central tower,
    transepts, and chancel. One of Salvin's
    most ambitious and strange designs, the
    transepts rose well above the nave roof.
    Problems of stability were not overcome,
    and the tower collapsed and was never
    completed.
C: £3,700 H
S: Eccl. (December 1856): 455; B, September
    30, 1854, p. 513; November 18, 1854, title
    page. Toronto: elevation; Fiske:
    lithographic perspective.

St. Mary's Church, Shouldham Thorpe
    (Norfolk)
Restoration for Sir Thomas Hare, Bart.
E: 1856–1857
Rebuilding of south and west walls, new ves-
    try and double bellcote.
C: £1,000 H
S: RIBA Salvin /34/; Norfolk and Norwich
    Record Office: Norwich Diocesan
    Records FCB7. p. 224v. Faculty d: April
    28, 1856.

All Saints' Church, Sherburn-in-Elmet
    (Yorks. W. Riding. N. Yorks.)
Restoration for the Reverend James
    Matthews.
E: 1856–1857
A Perpendicular clerestory was removed from
    the nave, and new windows inserted
    throughout (Fig. 104).
C: £2,276.17.6d.
S: RIBA Salvin/33/1–8; ICBS 5084; Toronto:
    elevation of porch; Parish Records:
    Churchwardens' Account Book; *The York-
    shire Archaeological Journal* 13 (1895): 395; 21
    (1911): 195.

St. Mary's Church, Great Budworth
    (Chesire)
Restoration of the church and the Dutton
    Chapel for the 2d Baron Tabley and

James Hugh Smith Barry, and a
    committee.
E: 1856–1857
Chancel restored, a massive stone screen built
    between the chapel and the nave.
C: £300, Chapel £900 H
S: Eccl. (October 1856): 377.

Officers' Quarters, Dover Castle (Kent)
New mess and accommodation for the War
    Office.
E: 1856–1857
The plan was the work of George Arnold, a
    Clerk of Works in the Royal Engineers
    Department, Salvin designed elevations
    in the Tudor style.
C: £35,800.
S: Department of the Environment, Dover
    Castle: elevations; B, May 22, 1858, p.
    337; October 9, 1858, p. 678.

Warwick Castle, Warwick (Warks.)
Alterations for the 4th Earl of Warwick.
E: 1856–1958
Work was done on the domestic range.
S: Warwick Castle MSS: drawings 313–18;
    Alnwick Castle MSS.

The Parsonage, Farlam (Cumberland.
    Cumbria)
New parsonage for the 6th Earl of Carlisle.
E: 1856–1857
Tudor, stone-built.
S: HoN C80/13.

Carlisle County Hotel, Carlisle (Cum-
    berland. Cumbria)
New railway hotel for George Head Head.
E: 1856–1857
Second Empire style, three stories with a man-
    sard roof, four-story tower with a pavilion
    roof, brick and stucco. Fox and Barrett's
    fireproof floors were used (Fig. 130).
C: £12,200 H
S: *RIBA Papers* Session, 1853–1854, p. 63.

The Tower of London
Designs for a new Jewel House for H. M.
    Commissioners of Works.
NE: 1857
This was to have been on the site of the Martin
    Tower.
S: PRO Works 31/508, 31/507, 14/2/1.

130. Carlisle County Hotel.

Windsor Castle, Windsor (Berks.)
Reconstruction of the Hundred Steps for H.
    M. Commissioners of Works.
E: 1856–1861
Rebuilding terrace, steps and parapets, new
    lodge at the foot. The contractor was
    George Smith.
C: £29,409.12.1d.
S: The Royal Library, Windsor Castle: plans
    and elevations; PRO Works 19/40/12.

Diddington Hall, Diddington (Hunts.
    Cambs.)
Alterations for George Thornhill.
E: 1857
It is not known what was done. Demolished c.
    1955.
C: £1,400 H

Vine Cottage, Trumpington Road,
    Cambridge (Cambs.)
Alterations and additions for Professor
    William Selwyn.
E: 1857
New reception rooms, yellow brick, restrained
    Jacobean.
C: £1,200 H

All Saints' Church, Silkstone (Yorks. W. Rid-
    ing. N. Yorks.)
Restoration for Mrs. Sarah Ann Clarke.
E: 1857–1858
Chancel rebuilt, hammerbeam roof with

heraldic shields and Gothic lettered
    inscriptions at wallplate level.
C: £1,750 H
S: Leeds City Libraries Archives Dept.: RD/
    AF2/3/39, Citation d: May 7, 1857;
    report, plans etc.; Sheffield City Librar-
    ies: Clarke Records 611/2–92.

St. Matthias's Church, Torquay (Devon)
New church for a committee.
Early English. Nave, north aisle, chancel,
    octagonal bell turret. The nave was
    remodeled and the chancel extended by J.
    L. Pearson in 1882–1885.
C: £1,950 H
S: Parish Records: original seating plan.

The University Library, Durham (Durham)
Restoration for the dean and chapter.
E: 1858
The interior remodeled, new doorway with
    oriel above built on palace green facade
    (Fig. 105).
C: £1,600 H
S: Durham Chapter Act Book 1847–1856.

St. Mary the Virgin's Church, Church Fen-
    ton (Yorks. W. Riding. N. Yorks.)
Restoration for a committee.
E: 1858
It is not known what was done.
C: £650 H

Monument to the 1st Viscount Hardinge, St.
John the Baptist's Church, Penshurst
(Kent)
Memorial for the Hardinge family.
E: 1858
Gothic wall monument with portrait roundel
by the Belgian sculptor Theodore
Phyffers.
S: BN, October 1, 1858, p. 980.

St. Mary the Great, Cambridge (Cambs.)
Restoration for the master and fellows of Trin-
ity College.
E: 1858
Chancel reroofed, new east window.
C: £800 H

St. Margaret's Church, Wolstanton (Staffs.)
Restoration for Ralph Sneyd.
E: 1858
The work was confined to the chancel; new
vestry.
S: Keele University Library: Sneyd MSS,
correspondence between Salvin, Sneyd
and Thomas Lewis, the Clerk of Works.

Whitehall, Allhallows (Cumberland.
Cumbria)
New mansion house for George Moore.
E: 1858–1861
Moore bought the Whitehall estate and the
Harbybrow pele tower, which was incor-
porated in a large country house in the
Tudor style. Demolished except for the
pele in c. 1951.
C: £11,100 H
S: Samuel Smiles, *George Moore* (London: n.p.,
1878).

The White Swan Hotel, Alnwick
(Northumb.)
Alterations and additions for the 4th Duke of
Northumberland.
E: c. 1859
S: DNB.

The School, Flixton (Suffolk)
New school house for Sir Robert Shafto Adair,
Bart.
E: 1859–1861
Brick in simple Tudor style.
S: RIBA Salvin /9/.

Congham High House, Congham (Norfolk)
New mansion house for Robert Elwes.
E: 1859
Built of local stone, plan similar to Cowesby
Hall, style Tudor with Jacobean details.
Demolished.
C: £7,000 H

Unidentified farm, Lanercost (Cumberland.
Cumbria)
New farm buildings for the 6th Earl of
Carlisle.
E: 1859
S: HoN C575/9.

Somerford Hall, Somerford (Cheshire)
Alterations for Sir Charles Shakerley, Bart.
E: 1859–1860
It is not known what was done. Demolished
1926.
C: £10,500 H

Mears Ashby Hall, Mears Ashby
(Northants.)
Alterations and additions for Captain H. M.
Stockdale.
E: 1859–1860
A new wing containing large reception rooms
was added, new stair tower and offices
built (Fig. 46).
C: £4,800 H

St. Thomas à Becket's Church, Farlam
(Cumberland. Cumbria)
New church for the Reverend John Lowthian
and a committee.
E: 1859–1860
Early English, chancel, nave and north aisle,
and double bellcote.
C: £1,530 H
S: HoN C575/9; ICBS 5379; CCE 24071,
23404.

St. Mary the Virgin's Church, Whickham
(Durham)
Restoration for the Reverend H. B. Carr and
committee.
E: 1859–1863
Extensive rebuilding, new north aisle and sec-
ond north aisle, vestry, and organ
chamber. Described as "a work tanta-

mount well nigh to the re-building of their Parish Church."
C: £2,891.16.4d.
S: University of Durham, Department of Palaeography and Diplomatic: Durham Diocesan Records XII/3 Faculty d: July 18, 1861; B, January 17, 1863, p. 49.

Abbot's Farm, Stoke Holy Cross (Norfolk)
New farmhouse for Henry Birkbeck.
E: 1860
Large, three stories, red brick.
C: £3,000 H

Windsor Castle, Windsor (Berks.)
Restoration of the Canons' Residences and Cloister for H. M. Commissioners of Works.
E: 1860–1861
North elevation extensively rebuilt and cloister repaired.
S: The Royal Library, Windsor Castle: plans, elevations and details.

Windsor Castle, Windsor (Berks.)
New guard room for H. M. Commissioners of Works.
E: 1860–1862
Two-story building with a pointed arcade, providing living accommodation for the officers and men of the guard. The contractor was George Smith.
S: The Royal Library, Windsor Castle: Plans, elevations and details; B, April 26, 1862, p. 302; June 28, 1862, p. 467; August 30, 1862, p. 627.

Horsley House, Stanhope (Durham)
Alterations for J. R. Hildyard.
E: 1860–1862
It is not known what was done. Partly demolished.
C: £1,800 H

All Saints' Church, Boltongate (Westmoreland. Cumbria)
Restoration for George Moore and a committee.
E: 1860–1862
New roofs, windows, central heating and repairs.

C: £850 H
S: RIBA Salvin /39/1–8; Parish Records: Vestry Minute Book.

Windsor Castle, Windsor (Berks.)
Restoration of the Garter Tower for H. M. Commissioners of Works.
E: 1860–1865
The tower was a roofless shell; it was converted into lodgings for the Master of the Queen's Household. The contractor was George Smith.
C: £1,525. 4.0d.
S: The Royal Library, Windsor Castle: plans and elevations: PRO Works 19/41/1.

St. Ricarius' Church, Aberford (Yorks. W. Riding. N. Riding)
Restoration for the Reverend Charles Page Eden and a committee.
E: 1861–1862
New north and south aisles and clerestory, new north and south chancel aisles. Metalwork by Thomas Peard of London.
C: £3,000
S: Calverley: elevation of communion rail; York Diocesan Registry: Faculty Book 1858–1870, pp. 29–31; *The Yorkshire Archaeological Journal* 13 (1895): 395–97; 21 (1911): 195–201; 24 (1917): 207–8; *The Church Builder* (1862): 106; B, May 17, 1862, p. 356; G. E. Kirk, *The Parish Church of Aberford* (Shipley: Outhwaite Bros., Caxton Press, 1959).

Lupton House, Churston Ferrers (Devon)
Work for the 1st Baron Churston.
E: 1862
It is not known what was done. Demolished.
C: £750 H

School, Churston Ferrers (Devon)
New village school for the 1st Baron Churston.
E: 1862
C: £750 H

Windsor Castle, Windsor (Berks.)
Rebuilding of the Clewer or Curfew Tower for H. M. Commissioners of Works.
E: 1862–1863
The old tower was taken down and rebuilt following a design by Viollet-le-Duc for

Carcassonne. The contractor was George
Smith (Fig. 113).
C: £2,341. 9. 9d.
S: The Royal Library, Windsor Castle: plans,
elevations, etc.; PRO Works 19/41/i.

Windsor Castle, Windsor (Berks.)
Remodeling Henry VII's Library for H. M.
Commissioners of Works.
E: 1862–1863
New bookcases and interior decorations. The
contractor was George Myers, heraldic
embellishments by Thomas Willement;
the Clerk of Works was Turnbull.
C: £2,857
S: The Royal Library, Windsor Castle: plans,
elevations, and details; PRO Works 19/-
41/2; B, March 5, 1864, p. 168.

Windsor Castle, Windsor (Berks.)
Restoration of the Aerary for the dean and
canons of Windsor.
E: 1862–1864
Repairs, windows renewed, new bookcases.
The contractor was George Smith & Co.
C: £672.6.8d.
S: Aerary Records XVII-61-11d, p. xxxi.

St. Michael's Church, Alnwick (Northumb.)
Restoration for the 4th Duke of
Northumberland.
Early scheme 1856 NE; E 1862–1864
Nave arcade rebuilt, new ceiling for chancel.
The contractor was George Smith.
S: RIBA Salvin /1/1–7; Toronto: elevation;
Calverley: longitudinal, east, and porch
elevations; University of Durham,
Department of Palaeography and Diplo-
matic: Durham Diocesan Records XII/3
Faculties d: October 28, 1862; August 22,
1863; B, August 15, 1863, p. 588;
December 26, 1863, p. 918; September 10,
1864, p. 673; February 3, 1866, p. 74.

St. Peter's Church, North Shields
(Northumb.)
New church for the 4th Duke of
Northumberland.
E: 1862–1864
Early English. Chancel, nave, north and
south aisles, tower, and spire. The con-

tractor was George Smith & Co.
Demolished.
C: £8,219
S: B, September 6, 1862, p. 642; September 13,
1862, p. 656; September 10, 1864, p. 667;
The Church Builder (January 1863): 20; (Jan-
uary 1865): 5.

The Tower of London
Restoration of St. Thomas's Tower for H. M.
Commissioners of Works.
E: 1862–1865
Rebuilding after collapse of eastern part. The
contractor was George Myers.
C: £2,790
S: RIBA Salvin /18/14; PRO Works 31/491,
14/2/2.

Muncaster Castle, Ravenglass (Cumberland.
Cumbria)
Alterations and additions for the 4th Baron
Muncaster.
E: 1862–1866
Building of new tower and main entrance,
decoration of drawing room and library
by Italian craftsmen from Alnwick (Fig.
131).
C: £16,000 H
S: RIBA Salvin /24/1–2; Toronto: elevations of
wooden doors.

Hutton-in-the-Forest, Penrith (Cumberland.
Cumbria)
Alterations for Sir Henry Vane, Bart.
E: 1862–1867
Internal alterations, new courtyard and
offices.
C: £3,400 H
S: RIBA Salvin /13/1–5.

Campsey Ash High House, Campsey Ash
(Suffolk)
Rebuilding for George Sheppard.
E: 1863
A large house in the East Anglian Tudor style,
red brick crow-stepped gables, etc. (Fig.
53).
S: B, January 3, 1863, p. 15; E. R. Kelly, *Post
Office Directory for Suffolk* (London: Kelly &
Co., 1875).

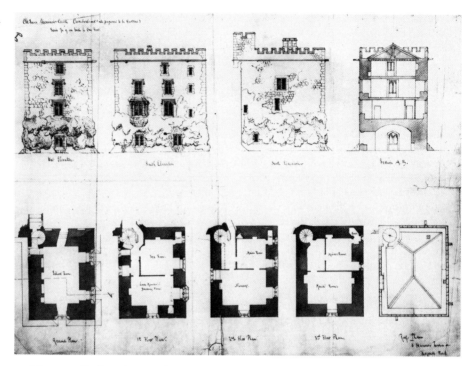

131. Muncaster Castle, pele tower elevations and floor plans.

St. Mary's Church, Flixton (Suffolk)
Restoration for Sir Robert Shafto Adair, Bart.
E: 1863
It is not known what was done at this time.
C: £3,300 H

The Tower of London
New engine house for H. M. Commissioners
  of Works.
E: 1863
Plain brick building with tall chimney
  opposite middle tower.
S: RIBA Salvin /18/18.

St. John the Evangelist's Church, Percy
  Main (Northumb.)
New church for the 4th Duke of
  Northumberland.
E: 1863–1864.
Early English. Chancel, nave, north and
  south aisles, bellcote. The contractor was
  George Smith & Co.
C: £4,565 H
S: B, September 6, 1862, p. 642; September 13,
  1862, p. 656; October 1, 1864, p. 730; *The
  Church Builder* (January 1863): 20; (January
  1865): 5.

Warwick Castle, Warwick (Warks.)
Alterations for the 4th Earl of Warwick.
E: 1863–1864
Further additions to the domestic range.
C: £8,200 H

St. Paul's Church, Whitley Bay (Northumb.)
New church for the 4th Duke of
  Northumberland.
E: 1863–1864
Early English. Chancel, nave, north and
  south aisles, octagonal southeast tower,
  and spire. The contractor was George
  Smith & Co.
C: £5,310 H
S: B, September 6, 1862, p. 642; September 13,
  1862, p. 656; September 10, 1864, p. 667;
  Church Builder (January 1863): 20; (January
  1865): 5.

St. Nicholas's Church, Lazonby (Cum-
  berland. Cumbria)
New church for Mrs. Maclean.
E: 1863–1864
Decorated. Chancel, nave, vestry, and west
  tower with polygonal stair turret.

C: £2,200 H
S: B, September 17, 1864, p. 692.

Windsor Castle, Windsor (Berks.)
Restoration of library gable, wall between the
     Clewer Tower and Canon's Residences
     for H. M. Commissioners of Works.
E: 1863–1864
Masonry repaired, and eighteenth-century
     windows and chimney stacks replaced
     (Figs. 111 and 112).
C: £1,561. 8. 4d.
S: PRO Works 19/41/1.

Hawksfold, Fernhurst (Sussex, W. Sussex)
Salvin's own country house.
E: 1863, the stables 1876
A medium-sized house in the local vernacular
     building style (Figs. 114 and 115).
S: National Maritime Museum, Greenwich:
     Diaries of E. W. Cooke; Pre-registration
     Deeds.

Ryston Hall, Denver (Norfolk)
Alterations for the Reverend Jermyn Pratt.
E: 1864
Addition of bathrooms and sculleries.
S: RIBA Salvin /31/.

St. Brandon's Church, Brancepeth (Durham)
Restoration for the 7th Viscount Boyne.
E: 1864
Conservative repairs, the Cosin furnishings
     were retained.
S: Calverley: "Architectural Tracts" include
     Reverend J. T. Fowler, *A Visit to Brancepeth
     Church in 1863;* B, February 13, 1864, p.
     122.

St. Andrew's Church, Aldborough (Yorks. W.
     Riding. N. Yorks.)
Restoration for the Reverend Richard Walker
     Marriott and a committee.
E: 1864
Old furnishings stripped out and replaced,
     new organ chamber.
S: Leeds Public Libraries Archives Depart-
     ment: RD/AF2/4/21, Faculty,
     specification, and plans.

Crossrigg Hall, Cliburn (Westmoreland.
     Cumbria)
Rebuilding of country house for Colonel Rigg.
E: 1864
The old house was recased and large new
     reception rooms added; Tudor style and
     local stone.
C: £7,500 H
S: Calverley: design for crest.

Perse School, Free School Lane, Cambridge
     (Cambs.)
Additions for the master and fellows of Gon-
     ville and Caius College.
E: 1864
New class room. The contractor was George
     Smith & Co. Demolished.
C: £280
S: Cambridge University Archives: Accounts
     of the Perse Trust 1841–1887, Vouchers to
     Accounts 1864–1879.

Parkhurst House, Haslemere (Sussex, W.
     Sussex)
New country house for Cotsford Burdon.
E: 1864–1866
Plain Italian villa style. Partly demolished.
S: Parkhurst House MSS: Attic and cellar
     plans.

St. Swithun's Church, Nately Scures
     (Hants.)
Restoration for Colonel D. W. Carleton and
     the Reverend Richard Carleton.
E: 1864–1866.
General restoration, large Perpendicular win-
     dows removed and replaced by some in
     the Norman style. New double bellcote
     and fittings in an eccentric Norman
     manner.
C: £300
S: Hampshire Record Office: Draft Faculty,
     Petition and Citation, correspondence.

The Tower of London
Restoration of St. John's Chapel for H. M.
     Commissioners of Works.
E: 1864–1866
Windows renewed. The contractor was
     George Myers and Sons.
C: £1,521
S: PRO Works 31/527.

Brancepeth Castle, Brancepeth (Durham)
Alterations for the 8th Viscount Boyne.
E: 1864–1873
It is not known what was done, but it is possible that Salvin fit up the Westmoreland Tower as a chapel dedicated in memory of Emma Maria Russell.
C: £5,200 H

Thoresby Hall, Thoresby (Notts.)
New mansion house and stables for the 3d Earl of Manvers.
E: 1864–1876
Salvin's last great country house, Jacobean style and by then outdated. The contractor was George Smith & Co., and the Clerk of Works Oldreive (Figs. 68–72).
C: £198,993. 7. 8d.
S: RIBA Salvin /35/; Calverley: elevation of staircase tower and section of great hall; University of Nottingham Library, Manuscripts Department: Thoresby Estate Accounts, plans and elevations; B, September 10, 1864, p. 672.

Naworth Castle, Brampton (Cumberland. Cumbria)
Estate work for the 6th Earl of Carlisle.
E: 1865–1867S: HoN C575/9.

The Tower of London
Proposed restoration of St. Peter ad Vincula for H. M. Commissioners of Works.
NE: 1865–1868
Surveys were made and estimates prepared.
S: PRO Works 14/1/13.

Capesthorne Hall, Macclesfield (Cheshire)
Restoration for Arthur Henry Davenport and William Bromley Davenport.
E: 1865–1869
Rebuilding of the major part of the mansion built by Edward Blore after a fire in 1861, following the original closely so far as the exterior was concerned. The contractor was George Smith & Co., metalwork by Brawn & Downing of Birmingham.
C: £14,000 H
S: The John Rylands Library: Bromley Davenport MSS, correspondence and accounts.

Sudbury Hall, Sudbury (Derbys.)
Proposed reconstruction of the house in the Second Empire style for the 6th Baron Vernon.
NE: 1866
This project was probably sought before E. M. Barry was instructed.
S: Sudbury House MSS: elevation.

Windsor Castle, Windsor (Berks.)
Grand staircase for H. M. Commissioners of Works.
E: 1866
The new stairs with octagonal lantern above replaced the dark ones built by James Wyatt in Brick Court.
S: The Royal Library, Windsor Castle: plans and elevations.

Windsor Castle, Windsor (Berks.)
Proposed rebuilding of the Horseshoe Cloister for H. M. Commissioners of Works.
NE: 1866
Salvin made plans for a total rebuilding with covered walkway and gables with carved bargeboards. The work was carried out by G. G. Scott in 1871.
S: The Royal Library, Windsor Castle: plan, elevations, and details.

The Parsonage, Stanwick (Yorks. N. Riding. N. Yorks.)
New parsonage for Eleanor, Dowager Duchess of Northumberland.
E: 1866
Plain Italian villa style.
C: £1,700 H

Stanwick Park, Stanwick (Yorks. N. Riding. N. Yorks.)
Wrought iron gate for Eleanor, Dowager Duchess of Northumberland.
E: c. 1866
Very elaborate and manufactured by Brawn & Downing of Birmingham.
S: Calverley: elevation; Toronto: three photographs.

Castle Howard, Malton (Yorks. N. Riding N. Yorks)

Restoration work for the 6th Earl of Carlisle.
E: 1866
Salvin seems to have carried out some repairs
to the Robinson Wing.
S: University of Keele Library: Sneyd MSS,
Salvin to Sneyd, April 18, 1866.

Windsor Castle, Windsor (Berks.)
Additions to the Norman Tower for H. M.
Commissioners of Works.
E: 1866–1867
Enlarged as a residence for the deputy
governor.
S: The Royal Library, Windsor Castle: plans
and elevations.

Hampton Court (Mddx. London Richmond)
Reseating of the Chapel Royal for H. M.
Commissioners of Works.
E: 1866–1868
New pews and central heating.
C: £1,272.15.0d.
S: PRO Works 19/13/3.

Second Master's Court, Trinity College,
Cambridge (Cambs.)
New building for William Whewell.
E: 1866–1868
Another seventy sets of rooms arranged
around a courtyard. Tudor. The contrac-
tor was George Smith & Co.
C: £35,000 H
S: Trinity College Library: Contract draw-
ings; Willis and Clark.

Fawsley Hall, Fawsley (Northants.)
Alterations and large additions for Sir Rainald
Knightly, Bart.
E: 1866–1868
New reception rooms and family apartments
were built on the north and south of the
great hall.
C: £13,300 H
S: Keele University Library: Sneyd MSS,
Salvin to Sneyd, April 18, 1866.

The Tower of London
Restoration of the Wakefield Tower for H. M.
Commissioners of Works.
E: 1866–1869

The tower was repaired and converted into the
Jewel House; the contractor was George
Myers & Sons, and the protective cases
and railings were by Brawn & Downing
of Birmingham.
C: £2,200
S: RIBA Salvin /18/19–22; PRO Works 14/2/1.

The Tower of London
New warders' quarters for H. M. Commis-
sioners of Works.
E: 1866–1869
Replacing ruinous houses with new; Tudor,
brickwork and half-timbering. The con-
tractor was George Smith & Co.
C: £1,365
S: RIBA Salvin /18/16; PRO Works 14/1/16.

The Chapel Royal, Windsor Great Park
(Berks.)
Addition for H. M. Commissioners of Woods.
E: 1867
The chapel was designed by S. S. Teulon and
had been completed the previous year.
Salvin enlarged this by the addition of a
south aisle.
C: £3,700 H
S: B, January 23, 1864, p. 69; January 5, 1867,
p. 20.

St. John the Baptist's Church, Stanwick
(Yorks N. Riding N. Yorks.)
Restoration for Eleanor, Dowager Duchess of
Northumberland.
E: 1867
Rebuilding of north nave wall and south nave
arcade, new roofs, etc.
C: £2,500 H
S: Leeds Public Libraries Archives Depart-
ment: RD/AF2/4/19; Citation for Faculty,
Specification and plan.

St. James's Church, Hutton-in-the-Forest
(Cumberland. Cumbria)
Restoration for Sir Henry Ralph Vane, Bart.
E: 1867–1868
Ceiling removed, old tie beams boxed in deal
to conceal worm damage, new west gal-
lery, vestry and double bellcote.
C: £500
S: *Penrith Observer,* March 17, 1868, p. 6.

Royal Fishing Cottage, Windsor Great Park
 (Berks.)
Fishing pavilion for H. M. Commissioners of
 Woods.
E: 1868
Timber framed and hung with red, white, and
 blue ornamental tiles.
C: £1,680 H
S: The Royal Library, Windsor Castle: A. T.
 Draper, "Memorandum Book"
 (unpublished ms.), pp. 7, 8, 97, 137.

St. Mungo's Church, Simonburn
 (Northumb.)
Restoration for Colonel Charteris.
E: 1868
Due to subsequent restoration, it is not known
 what was done.
C: £800 H

St. Nicholas of Myra's Church, Worth
 Matravers (Dorset)
Restoration for the Reverend J. G. Richard-
 son, the 3d Earl of Eldon, and a
 committee.
E: 1868
South wall rebuilt, Norman-style windows
 inserted, roof repairs.
C: £1,000 H
S: RIBA Salvin /44/1; Salisbury Diocesan
 Record Office: Petition for Faculty, Cita-
 tion, Specification and plans.

Stables, Datchett Road, Windsor (Berks.)
New stables for the dean and canons.
E: 1868–1869
Utilitarian, yellow brick and slate roof.
C: £1,905 H
S: Aerary Records: XVII-61–46.

The Tower of London
Restoration of the Bloody Tower for H. M.
 Commissioners of Works.
E: 1868–1869
New windows replaced Georgian sashes, new
 chimneys and battlements.
S: RIBA Salvin /18/10; PRO Works 14/3/2.

The Tower of London
Proposed alterations to the Waterloo Barracks

for H. M. Commissioners of Works.
NE: 1868–1869
An additional story was to be added, with
 bargeboarded, tile-hung dormers.
S: RIBA Salvin /18/15.

The Tower of London
Proposed restoration of the Byward Tower for
 H. M. Commissioners of Works.
NE: C. 1868–1869
A survey was made.
S: RIBA Salvin /18/4–7.

The Tower of London
Restoration of the Cradle Tower for H. M.
 Commissioners of Works.
E: c. 1868–1869
Refaced, upper story rebuilt, stair added.
S: RIBA Salvin /18/8–9.

St. Nicholas's Church, Worth (Sussex, E.
 Sussex)
Restoration for a committee.
E: 1868–1871
Salvin's most controversial work, the movement that was to lead to Anti-scrape was
 getting under way, and the news that he
 was to restore one of the most outstanding Saxon churches caused immediate
 protest. The apse was ruinous and was
 taken down, the belfry replaced by a
 tower and broach spire.
C: £3,000
S: RIBA Salvin /36/1–30 and correspondence;
 B, May 14, 1870, p. 390; August 20, 1870,
 p. 662; October 29, 1870, p. 869.

Dunster Castle, Dunster (Somerset)
Extensive alterations and additions for George
 Fownes Luttrell.
E: 1868–1872
Salvin added the Kitchen Tower, the Drawing
 Room Tower, and made the exterior
 more picturesque. Internal rearrange-
 ments and restoration of the hall. George
 Smith was the contractor (Figs. 55–57).
C: £25,350
S: RIBA Salvin /7/1–11 Somerset Record
 Office: DD/L Estate Office Corres-
 pondence; Dudley Dodd, "Salvin at
 Dunster Castle," *The National Trust Year-*

book 1976–1977 (London: Sotheby, Parke Bernet, 1977).

Knobs Crook Double Cottage, now Nobbs-crook Cottages, Windsor Great Park (Berks.)
New cottages for H. M. Commissioners of Woods.
E: 1869
Red brick. Draper makes a detailed comparison of cottages designed by himself with this pair by Salvin, to the detriment of the latter.
S: The Royal Library, Windsor Castle: A. T. Draper, "Memorandum Book" (unpublished ms.), pp. 126–33.

Cottages at Old Windsor Gate, now Bears Rails Gates, Windsor Great Park (Berks.)
New cottages for H. M. Commissioners of Woods.
E: 1869
Red brick.
S: The Royal Library, Windsor Castle: Draper, "Memorandum Book," pp. 2, 48.

Northumberland House, Park Lane (Mddx. London Westminster)
New ballroom for the 6th Duke of Northumberland.
E: 1869
Nothing is known about this room. Demolished 1874.
C: £13,500 H

Albury Park, Albury (Surrey)
Alterations and additions for the 6th Duke of Northumberland.
E: 1869–1870
New servants' bedrooms in the attics, steward's room, billiard room, and central heating were added to a house that had been Gothicized by A. W. N. Pugin in c. 1849.
C: £34,000 H
S: Albury Park Estate Office: Plans and elevations; B, September 17, 1870, p. 755; BN, May 14, 1869, pp. 432–33.

Paddockhurst, now Worth Priory, Worth (Sussex)
New mansion house for George Smith.
E: 1869–1872
A house of considerable size, stone with red brick chimneys. Stables now demolished to make way for school buildings, the house much altered by Aston Webb.
S: H; Worth Priory MSS: photograph albums.

Hodnet Hall, Hodnet (Salop.)
New mansion house for Algernon Charles Heber Percy.
E: 1870
A large house, Tudor style and old-fashioned for this date; local stone and modeled on the nearby Condover Hall. Mostly demolished in 1967.
S: Hodnet Hall MSS: elevations and plans.

The Parsonage, Flixton (Suffolk)
New parsonage for Sir Robert Alexander Shafto Adair, Bart.
E: 1870
Plain red brick.
C: £1,475.16.7d.
S: Ipswich and East Suffolk Record Office: HA12/A9/2 (B) Specification, contract d: August 1, 1870, draft Affidavit.

Petworth House, Petworth (Sussex, W. Sussex)
Additions and rebuilding after a fire for the 2d Baron Leconfield.
E: 1870–1872
The south part of the house was rebuilt, the porte cochère added, new stables, kennels, laundry, real tennis court, North Street Lodge, and gates. The contractor was George Smith & Co., decorations by Charles Smith.
C: House £20,064.13.0d.; stables, tennis court £16,237; laundry £1,065; kennels £3,714.8.0
S: West Sussex County Record Office: correspondence, estimates, accounts: RIBA Salvin /42/.

Parham Park, Pulborough (Sussex, W. Sussex)

Alterations for the Honorable Robert Curzon.
E: 1870–1873
The ceilings of the great parlour and dining room were raised, new bay windows and water tower.
S: Keele University Library: Sneyd MSS S (Rev WS/HonRC) 467, 469, 470.

Longford Castle, Alderbury (Wilts.)
Alterations and additions for the 4th Earl of Radnor.
E: 1870–1875
Additions by James Wyatt were converted into offices, new dining room, triangular courtyard roofed in, the accommodation rearranged and all made habitable.
C: £54,473
S: RIBA Salvin /19/1–2; Longford Castle MSS: plans; B, February 22, 1973, p. 150.

St. Michael's Church, Haselbech (Northants.)
New chapel for F. J. Foljambe and Selina, Viscountess Milton.
E: 1871–1872
The chapel was built on the north of the chancel.
S: Northamptonshire Record Office: FS 24/58.

Cumberland Lodge, Windsor Great Park (Berks.)
Restoration after a fire in 1869 for H. M. Commissioners of Woods.
E: 1871–1872
It is not known what was done.
C: £9,100 H

Encombe House, Kingston (Dorset)
Alterations and additions for the 3d Earl of Eldon.
E: 1871–1874
The main entrance was moved from the garden or south front to the north, new grand rooms were created and offices built.
C: £40,000 H
S: Encombe House MSS: ground plan.

Birdsall House, Birdsall (Yorks. E. Riding. N. Yorks.)

Alterations and additions for the 8th Baron Middleton.
E: 1871–1875
New north wing, additional story to central block, laundry, offices, and kennels.
The contractor was Bromwich of Rugby.
C: House £43,636.16.0d.; laundry £1,776; gardens £12,000
S: Middleton MSS: Correspondence, estimates.

Melbury House, Melbury Sampford (Dorset)
New library for the 5th Earl of Ilchester.
E: 1872
The original design shows the library on a north/south axis; it was built running east/west. An elaborate Tudor design to agree with the old house.
C: £4,000 H
S: RIBA Salvin /21/.

Rogate Lodge, Rogate (Sussex, W. Sussex)
New country house for George Hugh Wyndham.
E: 1872–1874
Second Empire style, mansards and pavilion roofs. Partly demolished.
C: £7,000 H
S: W. T. Pike, *Sussex in the Twentieth Century* (Brighton: W. T. Pike & Co., 1910), p. 41.

Muncaster Castle, Ravenglass (Cumberland. Cumbria)
Further additions for the 5th Baron Muncaster.
E: 1872–1874
It is not known what was done.
C: £15,000 H

The Parsonage, Muncaster, Ravenglass (Cumberland, Cumbria)
New parsonage for the 5th Baron Muncaster.
E: 1872–1874
C: £2,900 H

Warwick Castle, Warwick (Warks.)
Repairs and restoration for the 4th Earl of Warwick.
E: 1872–1878
There was a serious fire here in 1872, destroy-

ing much of the domestic range and the roof of the great hall. The contractor was Bromwich of Rugby.

C: £26,423. 7. 1d.

S: Warwick Castle MSS: Restoration Account Book; H. T. Cooke & Son, *An Account of the Fire at Warwick Castle* (Warwick: H. T. Cooke & Son, n.d.); B, December 9, 1871, p. 974; December 16, 1871, pp. 995, 989; December 30, 1871, p. 1023; January 6, 1872, p. 18; March 16, 1872, p. 213; April 6, 1872, p. 178; June 15, 1872, p. 474; January 18, 1873, p. 53; January 24, 1874, p. 80; May 9, 1874, p. 400; September 5, 1874, p. 758, April 3, 1875, p. 296; *The Times* (London), March 30, 1872; January 14, 1873.

St. Michael's Church, Mancaster, Ravenglass (Cumberland. Cumbria)

Restoration for the 5th Baron Muncaster.

E: 1873

It is not known what was done.

C: £2,520 H

Oeborne House, now Verdley Place, Fernhurst (Sussex, W. Sussex)

New house for Charles Savile Roundell.

E: 1873–1875

One of Salvin's two attempts at the vernacular revival; tile-hanging and half-timbering, now much enlarged.

C: £15,129 H

St. Lawrence's Church, Burwarton (Salop.)

New church for the 8th Viscount Boyne.

E: 1874–1876

Decorated. Chancel, nave, north and south aisles, west tower. The contractor was George Smith & Co., carving by Dayman of London.

C: £10,760 H

S: CCE 5114O; B, August 21, 1875, p. 762; September 11, 1875, p. 826; September 2, 1876, p. 865.

St. Peter's Church, North Shields (Northumb.)

New reredos.

E: 1875

Demolished.

S: B, March 27, 1875, p. 290.

St. John's Church, Perlethorpe (Notts.)

New church for the 3d Earl Manvers.

E: 1875–1876

Salvin's best church and the most expensive. Decorated. Chancel, nave, north and south aisles, west tower, and spire. The contractor was George Smith & Co. (Fig. 100).

C: £17,633.17.5 1/2d.

S: University of Nottingham Library, Department of Manuscripts: Thoresby Estate Accounts; B, December 23, 1876, p. 1250.

Greystoke Castle, Greystoke (Cumberland. Cumbria)

Restoration and additions after a fire for Henry Charles Howard.

E: 1875–1878

Repair of the great hall, addition of two stories to the staircase range, rebuilding of west front with copies of the bay windows at Thornbury Castle, which also belonged to Howard.

C: £5,138 H

S: Greystoke Castle MSS: drawings; RIBA Salvin /11/3.

Haughton Castle, Humshaugh (Northumb.)

Alterations for George Crawshay.

E: 1876

Internal rearrangement and new west wing.

S: *A History of Northumberland,* vol. 15, Newcastle-upon-Tyne, 1893–1940; W. Douglas Simpson, "Haughton Castle," *Archaeologia Aeliana* 29 (1951); M. S. Taylor, *The Crawshays of Cyfartha Castle* (London: Robert Hale, 1967).

St. Edmund the Bishop's Church, Sedgefield (Durham)

Restoration for the 8th Viscount Boyne and a committee.

E: 1876

Work was restricted to the south transept.

C: £722 H

St. John the Baptist's Church, Northchapel (Sussex, W. Sussex)

Restoration for the Reverend James Knight and a committee.

E: 1876–1877

New north aisle built to replace old transept.
S: Parish Records: Vestry Minute Book;
    Chichester Diocesan Records: Faculty d:
    March 9, 1877.

Burwarton House, Burwarton (Salop.)
Additions for the 8th Viscount Boyne.
E: 1876–1877
It is not known what was done.
C: £8,645 H

Cumberland Lodge, Windsor Great Park
    (Berks.)
Additions for H. M. Commissioners of
    Woods.
E: 1877
These were new nurseries for the children of
    Prince and Princess Christian of
    Schleswig-Holstein.
C: £1,350

Inverary Castle, Inverary (Argyll)
Restoration of the castle after the fire of 1877
    for the 8th Duke of Argyll.
E: 1877–1879
Salvin produced a series of designs that
    destroyed the symmetry of Roger Mor-
    ris's castle with a keep, dormers, and
    bartizans. Only the restoration and a sin-
    gle-story addition was allowed (Figs. 58
    and 59).
S: Inverary Castle MSS: perspective sketches;
    Calverly: sketch; RIBA Salvin /14/1–7; B,
    October 20, 1877, p. 1065.

Longford Castle, Alderbury (Wilts.)
New stable block for the 4th Earl of Radnor.
E: 1878
Plain, stock brick with stone dressings and
    slate roof.
C: £8,817 H
S: RIBA Salvin /19/1.

The Royal Lodge, Windsor Great Park
    (Berks.)
New stables for H. M. Commissioners of
    Woods.
E: 1878
C: £600 H

9 Chesterfield Gardens, Mayfair (Mddx.
    London Westminster)
New townhouse for the 2d Baron Leconfield.
E: 1878–1879
Demolished. No drawings or photographs of it
    survive. The contractor was George
    Smith & Co.; Salvin became too infirm
    to complete the commission and handed
    it over to T. H. Wyatt.
C: £30,428 up to date of resignation.
S: West Sussex Record Office: Petworth
    House Archives, correspondence.

St. Margaret's Church, Fernhurst (Sussex, W.
    Sussex)
Restoration for the Reverend Christopher
    Watson and a committee.
E: 1881
Tower rebuilt, new north aisle; Salvin gave the
    peal of bells.
S: Chichester Diocesan Records: Faculty d:
    June 15, 1881; Vestry Minute Book.

Book Illustrations

Salvin produced drawings used for the illustra-
tion of two books: James Raine, *Catterick
Church in the County of York* (London: J.
Weale, 1834); Mrs. J. A. E. Roundell,
Cowdray (London: Bickers & Son, 1884).
Osbert Salvin allowed the use of draw-
ings that had been made by his father in
about 1844.

Works by Anthony Salvin, Junior

All Saints' Church, Middleton (Essex)
Restoration for the Reverend O. E. Raymond.
E: 1853
The contractor was Elliston of Sudbury. It is
    not known what was done.

All Saints' Church, Curbar (Derbys.)
New church for the Reverend Jeremiah Stock-
    dale and a committee.

E: 1866–1868
Early English. Chancel, nave, north and
south aisles. Local stone. The builder
was a Mr. Boan.
C: £2,000
S: ICBS 36560, 36167.

The Parsonage, Curbar (Derbys.)
New parsonage for the Reverend T. F. Salt
E: 1869
Tudor, stone-built.
C: £800

School, Curbar (Derbys.)
C: £300

Christ Church, Overstrand (Norfolk)
New church for John Henry Gurney and the
Reverend Paul Johnson.
E: 1867
Early English, built of flint pebbles, stone
dressings. Nave and north aisle, chancel,
vestry, northwest bellcote. Demolished.
S: CCE 34607, 19595; B, October 5, 1867, p.
738.

The Parsonage, Overstand (Norfolk)
New parsonage for the Reverend Paul
Johnson.
E: 1859–1861
C: £1,100
S: CCE 19595.

The London Zoo, Regent's Park (London
Westminster)
Work for the Zoological Society of London.
New dining room.
E: 1869
Demolished.
C: £3,528.18.8d.
S: The *Annual Report* of the Zoological Society,
1872.
Refreshment room.
E: 1872
The contractor was James Simpson & Son.
Demolished.
C: £2,249.13.9d.
S: The *Annual Report* of the Zoological Society,
1872.
The Lion House.
E: 1874–1875
The contractor was James Simpson & Son, the
cages by Hickson. Demolished.
C: £11,727.7.3d.
S: The *Annual Report* of the Zoological Society,
1876; B, April 10, 1875, p. 334; December
4, 1875, p. 1079; December 25, 1875, p.
1159; January 22, 1876, p. 88; ILN January
29, 1876, pp. 99-100; April 1, 1876, p. 325.
The second-class restaurant.
E: 1877–1878.
The contractor was George Smith & Co.
Demolished.
C: £956.9.5d.
S: The *Annual Report* of the Zoological Society,
1877 and 1878.

Bibliography

Anstruther, I. *The Knight and the Umbrella* London: Geoffrey Bles, 1963.

Barry, A. *The Life and Works of Sir Charles Barry, R.A., F.R.S.* 1867. Reprint. New York: Benjamin Blom, 1972.

Beresford Hope, A. J. B. *The English Cathedral of the Nineteenth Century.* London: John Murray, 1861.

Boase, T. S. R. *English Art 1800–1870.* Oxford History of English Art. Oxford: Oxford University Press, 1959.

Brockman, H. A. N. *The Caliph of Fonthill.* London: Werner Laurie, 1956.

Brodrick, G. C. *English Land and English Landlords.* 1881. Reprint. Newton Abbot: David & Charles, 1968.

Chadwick, O. *The Victorian Church.* London: Adam & Charles Black, 1970.

Clark, K. *The Gothic Revival.* Harmondsworth: Penguin Books, 1962.

Clarke, B. F. L. *Church Builders of the Nineteenth Century.* Newton Abbot: David & Charles, 1969.

Cole, D. *The Work of Sir Gilbert Scott.* London: Architectural Press, 1980.

Colvin, H. *A Biographical Dictionary of British Architects, 1600- 1840.* London: John Murray, 1978.

Delheim, C. *The Face of the Past.* Cambridge: At the University Press, 1982.

Dodds, J. W. *The Age of Paradox.* London: Victor Gollanz, 1953.

Eastlake, C. L. *A History of the Gothic Revival.* 1872. Reprint. Leicester: Leicester University Press, 1978.

Faber, G. *Oxford Apostles.* London: Faber & Faber, 1974.

Fawcett, J., ed. *Seven Victorian Architects.* London: Thames & Hudson, 1976.

Fergusson, J. *History of the Modern Styles of Architecture.* London: John Murray, 1891.

Ferrey, B. *Recollections of A. W. N. Pugin and his Father Augustus Pugin.* 1861. Reprint. London: Scolar Press, 1978.

Ferriday, P., ed. *Victorian Architecture.* London: Jonathan Cape, 1963.

Franklin, J. *The Gentleman's Country House and Its Plan, 1835- 1914.* London: Routledge & Kegan Paul, 1981.

Girouard, M. *Sweetness and Light: The 'Queen Anne' Movement, 1860–1900.* Oxford: Clarendon Press, 1977.

———. *Life in the English Country House.* New Haven & London: Yale University Press, 1978.

———. *The Victorian Country House.* New Haven & London: Yale University Press 1979.

———. *The Return to Camelot: Chivalry and the English Gentleman.* New Haven & London: Yale University Press, 1981.

Goodhart-Rendel, H. S. *English Architecture Since the Regency.* London: Constable, 1953.

Hitchcock, H. R. *Early Victorian Architecture.* New Haven: Yale University Press, 1954.

———. *Architecture: Nineteenth and Twentieth Centuries.* Harmondsworth: Penguin Books, 1963.

Hussey, C. *The Picturesque.* London & New York: G. P. Putnam's Sons, 1927.

———. *English Country Houses: Late Georgian, 1800–1840.* London: Country Life, 1958.

Inglis-Jones, E. *Peacocks in Paradise.* London: Faber & Faber, 1950.

Kerr, R. *The Gentleman's House.* 1871. Reprint. New York: Johnson Reprint Co., 1972.

Liscombe, R. W. *William Wilkins, 1778–1839.* Cambridge: At the University Press, 1980.

Macaulay, J. *The Gothic Revival, 1745–1845.* Glasgow: Blackie & Son, 1975.

Muthesius, H. *The English House.* Edited by Dennis Sharp. London: Crosby, Lockwood, Staples, 1979.

Muthesius, S. *The High Victorian Movement in Architecture.* London: Routledge and Kegan Paul, 1972.

Pevsner, N., ed. *The Buildings of England.* Harmondsworth: Penguin Books, 1951-.

————. *An Outline of European Architecture.* Harmondsworth: Penguin Books, 1961.

————. *Ruskin and Viollet-le-Duc.* London: Thames & Hudson, 1969.

————. *Some Architectural Writers of the Nineteenth Century.* Oxford: Clarendon Press, 1972.

————. *Studies in Art, Architecture and Design, Victorian and After.* London: Thames & Hudson, 1982.

Port, M. H. *Six Hundred New Churches.* London: SPCK, 1961.

————. *The Houses of Parliament.* New Haven and London: Yale University Press, 1976.

Quiney, A. *John Loughborough Pearson.* New Haven and London: Yale University Press, 1979.

Rickman, T. *An Attempt to Discriminate the Styles of Architecture in England.* Oxford: Parker 1881.

Robinson, J. M. *The Wyatts.* Oxford: Oxford University Press, 1979.

Royal Institute of British Architects. *Catalogue of the Drawings Collection.* Farnborough: Gregg International, 1969-.

Ruskin, J. *The Seven Lamps of Architecture.* London: Smith Elder & Co., 1849.

Saint, A. *Richard Norman Shaw.* New Haven and London: Yale University Press, 1976.

Scott, G. G. *A Plea for the Faithful Restoration of Our Ancient Churches.* Oxford: Parker, 1850.

————. *Remarks on Secular and Domestic Architecture.* London: John Murray, 1857.

————. *Personal and Professional Recollections.* Oxford: Parker, 1879.

Soloway, R. A. *Prelates and People: Ecclesiastical Social Thought in England, 1783–1852.* London: Routledge & Kegan Paul, 1969.

Stamp, G. *The English House, 1860–1914.* London: Faber & Faber, 1986.

Stanton, P. B. *The Gothic Revival and American Church Architecture.* Baltimore, 1968.

————. *Pugin.* London: Thames & Hudson, 1971.

Street, A. E. *Memoir of George Edmund Street.* London: John Murray, 1888.

Summerson, J. *John Nash, Architect to George IV.* London: Allen & Unwin, 1949.

————. *Heavenly Mansions.* London: Cresset Press, 1949.

————. *Victorian Architecture: Four Studies in Evaluation.* New York: Columbia Univerisity Press, 1970.

Summerson, J., ed. *Concerning Architecture: Essays on Architectural Writers and Writings Presented to Nikolaus Pevsner.* London: Allen Lane, Penguin Press, 1968.

Thompson, F. M. L. *English Landed Society in the Nineteenth Century.* London: Routledge & Kegan Paul, 1963.

Thompson, P. *William Butterfield.* London: Routledge & Kegan Paul, 1971.

Trappes-Lomax, M. *Pugin, a Mediaeval Victorian.* London: Sheed & Ward, 1932.

Watkin, D. *The Life and Work of C. R. Cockerell.* London: A. Zwemmer, 1974.

Wedgwood, A. *A. W. N. Pugin and the Pugin Family.* London: Victoria and Albert Museum, 1985.

White, J. F. *The Cambridge Movement.* Cambridge: At the University Press, 1962.

The principal deposits of material used in the compilation of this biography are:
The Salvin Collection: eleven diaries, memoirs, and sketch books acquired by the London Borough of Barnet Public Libraries in 1955, Reference Nos. 6787/1-11.
The Salvin Papers: University of Durham, Department of Palaeography and Diplomatic.
Salvin and Nesfield Correspondence: University of Durham, University Library.
The largest number of drawings by Salvin and his family are in the Drawings Collection of the British Architectural Library and are listed in their catalogue. There is a small collection of nineteen drawings in the Department of Prints and Drawings and Paintings at the Victoria and Albert Museum, South Kensington. About a hundred drawings are in Canada, of which half are in the Thomas Fisher Rare Book Library of the University of Toronto, and the rest in private hands. Many other drawings are to be found in public and private collections in Great Britain, and they are listed here in the catalogue.

Index

Photographic Acknowledgments

Airviews (M/cr) Ltd.: 1

Borthwick Institute of Historical Research: 3

British Architectural Library Drawings Collection: 4, 9, 10, 12, 13, 14, 15, 18, 19, 20, 23, 25, 30, 31, 36, 45, 49, 55, 56, 57, 63, 75, 76, 79, 80, 85, 110, 117, 118, 119, 122, 125, 127, 129, 131

Copyright holder unknown: 130

Country Life: 8, 37, 61

David Durant: 68, 69, 70, 71, 72

Durham County archivist and the Brancepeth Estate: 2

Exeter College Oxford: 103

St. John the Evangelist's Church, Grantham, Parish Records: 97

Stafford Howard: 54

Keele University Library: 66, 67

Lincoln Archives Office: 27

Bildarchiv Foto Marburg: 41

Paul Mellon Collection: 124

Lady Anne Newman: 11, 17

Parham Park Ltd. and the trustees of the Parham Estate: 48, 50, 51

Mrs. Sybil Rampen: frontispiece, 21, 58, 64, 121

Russell Read: 29, 38, 39

Royal Commission on Historic Monuments of England and the Victoria County history: 46, 61, 77, 78, 84

Suffolk Record Office, Ipswich: 53

Anthony Salvin Papers, Thomas Fisher Rare Book Library, University of Toronto: 5, 6, 22, 28, 40, 42, 43, 67, 104, 120, 123, 128

St. Mary Magdalene's Church, Torquay, Parish Records: 98

Board of Trustees of the Victoria and Albert Museum: 26, 87, 88

National Library of Wales: 73

B. Weinreb Architectural Books Ltd.: 81

Sir Bruno Welby, Bart.: 32, 33, 34, 35

The Royal Library, Windsor Castle; copyright reserved. Reproduced by gracious permission of Her Majesty the Queen: 111, 112, 113

Yale Center for British Art, Paul Mellon Collection: 124